T0295773

Uncertainty

Uncertainty

Individual Problems and Public Solutions

Patrik Aspers

OXFORD
UNIVERSITY PRESS

Oxford University Press is a department of the University of Oxford. It furthers
the University's objective of excellence in research, scholarship, and education
by publishing worldwide. Oxford is a registered trade mark of Oxford University
Press in the UK and certain other countries.

Published in the United States of America by Oxford University Press
198 Madison Avenue, New York, NY 10016, United States of America.

Library of Congress Cataloging-in-Publication Data
Names: Aspers, Patrik, 1970– author.
Title: Uncertainty : individual problems and public solutions / Patrik Aspers.
Description: New York, NY : Oxford University Press, [2024] |
Includes bibliographical references and index.
Identifiers: LCCN 2024009122 (print) | LCCN 2024009123 (ebook) |
ISBN 9780197752753 (hardback) | ISBN 9780197752777 (epub) |
ISBN 9780197752784
Subjects: LCSH: Uncertainty—Social aspects. | Risk—Social aspects. |
Decision making.
Classification: LCC HM1101 .A87 2024 (print) | LCC HM1101 (ebook) |
DDC 302/.12—dc23/eng/20240307
LC record available at https://lccn.loc.gov/2024009122
LC ebook record available at https://lccn.loc.gov/2024009123

DOI: 10.1093/oso/9780197752753.001.0001

Printed by Integrated Books International, United States of America

CONTENTS

Preface   *vii*
Acknowledgements   *ix*

1. How Much Can We Know?   *1*
   Decision-Making Under Uncertainty, Risk, and Ambiguity   *4*
   Attempts to Turn Uncertainty into Risk   *7*
   Knowledge as a Remedy for Uncertainty   *9*
   The Hermeneutics of Knowledge   *16*
   Private Ways of Reducing Uncertainty   *17*
   Public Ways of Reducing Uncertainty   *21*
   Outline   *22*

PART I: Principles of States of the World
2. Informal Institutions   *27*
   Informal and Formal Institutions   *28*
   From Struggle to Informal Institutions   *31*
   The Lifeworld of Informal Institutions   *35*
   Institutionalization   *37*
   How Informal Institutions Show Up   *38*
   How Do Institutions Reduce Uncertainty?   *40*
   Conclusion   *43*

3. Formal Institutions   *46*
   Decisions for Others in Public   *47*
   Setting Laws   *52*
   Standards   *57*
   Conclusion   *65*

4. Evaluation   *68*
   Evaluations and Their Prevalence   *69*
   Evaluation Against Objective Scales   *73*
   Evaluation as a Discourse—Towards Decisions for Others   *79*
   Conclusion   *79*

PART II: Forms Producing States of the World

5. Convaluation   87
    Convaluations as Forms   88
    Value Uncertainty   89
    Mutual Adjustment   91
    Grown and Decided Forms of Convaluations   92
    Producer Markets as Grown Economic Convaluations   100
    Convaluations as Result of Decisions—Organization   103
    Elections as Decided Convaluations   104
    Exchange Markets as Decided Convaluations   106
    Conclusion   109

6. Deciding for Others   113
    Valuation Arising from Decisions for Others   115
    Valuation as an Evaluation Discourse   116
    Reviews   120
    Ratings   122
    Prizes as Indirect Competition   124
    Rankings   127
    Predictions   129
    Conclusion   131

7. Contest   134
    Concepts of Contest   135
    From Violence to Peaceful Contests   139
    Indirect Contests and Competition   141
    The Culture of Contest   144
    The Making of Forms of Contest   146
    Conclusion   147

8. Making and Reducing Uncertainty   151
    The Making of Means of Uncertainty Reduction   152
    Addressing Uncertainty   154
    The Opportunity of Uncertainty   155
    Existential Uncertainty Reduction   158
    Private Truth Claims and the Public   159

Appendix. A Typology of Convaluations   163
Notes   167
References   191
Index   213

PREFACE

The economist Frank Knight writes in *Risk, Uncertainty and Profit*: 'We live only by knowing *something* about the future; while the problem of life, or of conduct at least, arises from the fact that we know so little. This is as true of business as of other spheres of activity' (1921: 199). It is thus not the probabilities of outcomes, in the literature characterized by risk, but uncertainty that is the condition of decision-making. But to seek complete certainty would be naïve, given what we know today about knowledge production. My aim with this book is both more modest and more realistic: to analyse ways in which actors can reduce uncertainty. Research has clearly focused on private means, which suggests that existing research should be complemented by focusing on publicly available means of uncertainty reduction. Furthermore, the relevance of publicly available knowledge is central for building a society that enables communication based on shared ideas and understanding, instead of falling into bubbles, echo chambers, or private truths.

The wider context in which this research sits is the ongoing debate about what human beings can do to reduce uncertainty. This sociology of knowledge treatise connects to works such as John Dewey's *Quest for Certainty*, and Berger and Luckmann's *The Social Construction of Reality: A Treatise in the Sociology of Knowledge*, with a clear focus on the issue of uncertainty and its reduction.

This book analyses means of uncertainty reduction based on one key idea: to analyse the making of order as a result of either mutual adjustment or decisions made for others. Mutual adjustment leads to order unintentionally, out of a process in which actors adjust their behaviour to one another over time. Decisions made for others refers to the essence of what organizations are and do.

In addition to the sociological analysis, the book opens up to a discussion relevant to business scholars and businessmen. How can public means of uncertainty reduction be created, and how can they be used? The analysis should not just assume that businesspeople and their organizations are passive and constantly adjusting to an already existing world of norms and values, which is the perspective of, for example, new institutional organizational theory. On the contrary, organizations may, individually or jointly with others, actively change the environment to reduce its uncertainties instead of only adjusting to it. The book points at strategic decision-making as partly a collective enterprise, to be conducted in the public and in some senses *for* the public. This, in the end, opens the avenue of public–private partnerships and of corporate citizenship.

The first chapter of this book is quite dense, and for a reader who focuses slightly less on the existing body of research on uncertainty, and wants to get to the results, it is possible to read the first pages of the first chapter, and then move to the section "Public Ways of Reducing Uncertainty," and continue the reading from there.

This book is part of my long-term project 'Being and Order' (2005–2035), and though this book focuses on order, it points to the centrality of being and its relation to uncertainty.

ACKNOWLEDGEMENTS

The first idea of this book was developed while I ran an European Research Council Starting Grant project (2010–2016). An important part of the book was written during my sabbatical year 2017–2018, which was spent at the Center for Interdisciplinary Research (*ZiF: Zentrum für interdisziplinäre Forschung*) at Bielefeld. At the ZiF I was member of the research group 'In Search for the Global Labor Market', headed by Ursula Mense Petermann, Thomas Welskopp, and Anna Zaharieva. Ursula has also commented on chapters of the book. During my stay, the project also benefitted from conversations with Elena Esposito, Sven Kesselring, and Tobias Werron. Seminars were held at Bielefeld, in research groups of sociologists organized by Tobias Werron, and in economics, organized by Frank Riedel. Comments at other seminars have helped to improve the text. At the Max Planck Institute for the Study of Societies in Cologne (summer 2018), a draft was commented on by Jens Beckert, Marcin Serafin, Sebastian Kohl, Akos Rona-Tas, and Mathias Dewey. Another seminar was given at University of Mainz, a result of an invitation by Herbert Kalthoff.

Drafts and ideas for this book have been discussed in the research group The Uppsala Laboratory of Economic Sociology, and I received valuable comments by Reza Azarian, Jonas Bååth, Alexander Dobeson, Dominik Döllinger, Henrik Furst, Greti-Iulia Ivana, and Clara Iversen. Valuable comments have also been given by Nils Brunsson and Richard Swedberg. The ideas have also been discussed at seminars at St Gallen, where I received useful comments from Matias Dewey, Men Hao, Sabine Hoidn, Judith Nyfeler, Felix Keller, Helen Yu Tang, Paula Bialski, Simon Grand, and Nicklaus Reichle. Many others have also contributed in different ways to this book: Achim Brosziewski, Stephan Egger, Stefanie Hiss, Helga Nowotny, Andre Maeyer, and Bernt Teufel. Henrik Dosdall has been assisting me with the content of Chapters 3 and 4 and has made many valuable comments on drafts of the book.

By the kind invitation of Pierre Michel Menger to the College de France in November 2018, I had the opportunity to lecture and discuss the matter of uncertainty reduction. In the fall of 2018 I gave a research seminar at Uppsala University, in which chapters of the book were discussed with students. The students at the University of St. Gallen who took my courses on uncertainty reduction discussed drafts and wrote essays and made comments that contributed to my work with problems and the text. In falls 2022 and 2023 I co-taught a course on uncertainty with Roger Moser, and his perspective and knowledge added valuable elements to this book. I have also held seminars in Bern (2021), with comments by many, including Ben Jann, Christopher Joppke, and Achim Edelmann; and at the University of Zürich (2022), where comments that improved the text were given by, among others, Henrich Nax and Jörg Rössel.

Henrik Fürst did a close reading of the manuscript that resulted in many improvements, and Caroline Aspers Dahlberg has substantially contributed to this book in numerous conversations. The anonymous reviewers have made substantial contributions to this book by offering valuable suggestions and comments. Finally, I am most grateful for the comments and support by my editor, James Cook.

This book has been written with the support from several sources. Initial financial support was received from the European Research Council (Grant CEV 263699). Uppsala University, Center for Interdisciplinary Research in Bielefeld, and University of St Gallen have been main sources of financial support while I was writing this book. The Swiss National Science Foundation has provided funds to make it an open-access publication. Chapter 5 draws on research conducted by Edvind Sandström.

My greatest debt is nonetheless to my family: my wife Caroline, and our children Eyvind and Vidar, who also spent the academic year in Bielefeld at the ZiF; and Eija, who was born when we returned to Sweden.

CHAPTER 1

How Much Can We Know?

Uncertainty is inherent in human existence and can be an opportunity or a fundamental problem for individuals and organizations. The environment of actors, individuals, and organizations alike is uncertain (Ahrne 1994), which means that we cannot predict the outcomes of actions. This is to say that uncertainty is a largely future-oriented problem. Uncertainty is always perceived, ultimately, by persons, and different structural positions, knowledge, confidence, and emotions may affect the way different people perceive uncertainties (Schutz and Luckmann 1989: 48). The problem of uncertainty is epistemic, caused by lack of knowledge. But though uncertainty is, on one hand, a problem, it is also, on the other hand, an opportunity for profit and for a dynamic life.

This introductory chapter presents central themes and terms of the book, and outlines where it sits in the research field. Over time, human society has produced much knowledge, and what used to be 'unknown unknowns' (what we do not know that we do not know), have gradually become 'known unknowns' (what we know that we do not know), to known knowns (what we know). This means that what used to be uncontrollable negative effects, that is, dangers, have gradually become issues that still are uncertain but that can be controlled, or at least addressed (Bonss 1995: 53–59). Major societal changes bring about more uncertainty, partly because what one used to know no longer applies, partly because one lacks knowledge about how to act. Some of these changes are sudden, like the outbreak of wars, pandemics, terrorism, or revolutions. To take an example, uncertainty increased in a direct and existential way for people when the former communist states in Eastern Europe fell apart (Reiter 2010). How

Uncertainty. Patrik Aspers, Oxford University Press. © Oxford University Press 2024.
DOI: 10.1093/oso/9780197752753.003.0001

does one cope with a new world in which the old states of the world no longer apply?

Regardless of the level of complexity agents face, they must make decisions. Decisions have to be made in all spheres of life based on what we know or can know. What shall our party do to convince voters to support our proposal in the upcoming referendum? How do we choose which artist should make the opening performance at our art festival? Because 'everyone knows that motion pictures are uncertain products' (De Vany and Walls 1999: 285), how does one know what film will make it? How do I know which novels are good? Foreign policy and intelligence assessments are additional fields in which questions of uncertainty and the ambition to reduce it apply. This may, for example, involve 'predicting the behaviour of terrorist groups, determining the security of Pakistan's nuclear arsenal' (Friedman and Zeckhauser 2012: 824). Many examples of decision-making under uncertainty are economic: will the demand for cell phones increase sufficiently to make investment in a new plant worthwhile? What will be the outcome of investment in time and money in developing a new line of an existing fashion brand? These examples reflect the types of decisions and knowledge problems that economic actors deal with (Priddat 1996). The problem of uncertainty is not restricted to capitalism, or capitalistic societies (Hayek 1976), but is a more general problem about how actors can cope with uncertainty (Fiddle 1980), including their own existential uncertainty.

What means can be used to reduce uncertainty? There is a great variety of approaches to making strategic decisions based on more knowledge, including drawing on one's personal knowledge, knowledge of one's network, and research and development. The literature is full of examples of how managers should act and deal with uncertainty. The key idea with this book is to complement, above all, the existing business study literature that focuses on individual actors' strategies and decision-making to reduce uncertainty by private means. It does this by zooming in on the ways in which means of uncertainty reduction are made—intentionally and unintentionally—in the public domain.

It is in the public sphere that we should seek answers to many of the private problems actors face. The public represents a common reservoir, available to all and created by us. Laws and standards are examples of public means of uncertainty reduction, but there are also forms that produce outcomes that reduce uncertainty, for example, ranking lists and markets. The specific set of informal institutions that make up the culture and virtues of people is the most profound means of uncertainty reduction. When these informal institutions are present, the knowledge and order they bring about facilitate decision-making.

The notion that accounts for reduced uncertainty is 'state of the world'. A **state of the world** is defined as public knowledge about facts, relations between things, and what will happen to these, given certain conditions. States of the world are often codified in language. When this knowledge is used, it tends to lead to expected results. It is knowledge that people refer to as valid and what Schütz calls 'recipes' (1975: 95). Examples may be almost anything—for example, a relationship between age and alcohol consumption, or status level for products and their prices. 'State of the world' demarcates knowledge from other claims about 'knowledge', such as myths and witchcraft that do not lead actors to achieve their ends more effectively—which points at the relevance of a more sociological notion of knowledge analysed by Foucault 1989) that reveals the relation between power and knowledge (Rouse 2003).[1] Facts such as 'Winston Churchill was Prime Minister of the United Kingdom during most of the Second World War', as well as laws such as employment laws, are examples of states of the world. Also, practiced ways of doing business, cultural norms, industry standards, technologies, and clear-cut ways of evaluating product quality are examples of states of the world that reduce actors' uncertainty when they make decisions.

States of the world are publicly known, socially manufactured, consensual, because they can be used by many to make decisions with less uncertain outcomes. However, these states must not be 'true', if they can be used to reduce uncertainty. Commonly held social values and other informal institutions may order social life and increase predictability and thus reduce uncertainty, but they are neither true nor false. The fact that knowledge is public does not necessarily mean that it is free—merely that there is neither discrimination nor restriction against gaining access to it, except perhaps minor monetary costs.[2]

To focus on public means of uncertainty reduction is to address what is, in our time, the acute issue of public knowledge in contrast to 'private truths'. It is also to address the central role of publics and public arenas (Arendt 1988), which are characterised by being open, also to scrutiny, by anyone. Public arenas produce some of the conditions for 'rational communication' (Habermas 1998: 310–317), which is a basis for an open society. Although any real decision-maker will use any means available, private and public, to increase the chance of achieving their ends, the approach presented here emphasizes communal 'truths'. This approach rejects ideas of perfect information, private truths, and absolute truth, but without turning into the dead-end of postmodernity and its correlated offspring, nor an analysis of individual character (Sennet 1977).[3] The public is here seen as a condition for reflexivity, awareness, and debate about states of the world, but also as a way to fashion states of the world, be it online or in real life.

DECISION-MAKING UNDER UNCERTAINTY, RISK, AND AMBIGUITY

It is one thing to know much, but still another thing to make decisions. Though we daily make a very large number of decisions, such as selecting from the lunch menu, the focus of this book is on more 'strategic' and operational decision-making. Strategy is typically concerning the long-term ends of an organization, such as achieving success in the competitive market or launching a political campaign. The term may also include a wider range of decisions, such as major reorganisations, new product development, opening of a new department or unit, and the like. Operational decisions refer to the implementation at a more concrete level and with a shorter time horizon. These types of decision-making mean that there is often a large investment of time and resources before making the decision. Consequently, different ways to reduce uncertainty can be considered.

Even though decisions and decision-making are central to how states of the world are used, the exact meaning of decisions is not thematised in this work (Abend 2018), and the practice of decision-making is a topic largely beyond the scope of this study. What is assumed is some general idea that human beings are oriented towards 'ends' and that those ends are reasonably coherent (Davidson 2004: 35), so that ideas of uncertainty reduction make sense.[4] The idea of decision-making includes the presumption that individual actions are emotionally constituted, that confidence and hope (Miyazaki and Swedberg 2017) are components for actors in relation to uncertainty, and that these dimensions are socially produced (Barbalet 2001). There is, in sum, a large literature on how actors try to cope with and to reduce uncertainty. The existing literature also pays much attention to how decisions are made under uncertainty, and how to reduce it (Kampourakis and McCain 2020).

Uncertainty in a broad sense is a problem that plagues people, and some have called it fear—'uncertainty under a different name' (Bauman 2006: 99–101). Historically and anthropologically, there are of course large variations in the concrete ways in which uncertainty has been manifested (Douglas 1992). Uncertainty, in short, is a human condition (Bonss 1996: 169), or put differently, 'enmeshed with human existence' (Nowotny 2016: vi), relevant to identity and the existentiality of human beings (Wohlmb-Sahr

1993). It is, to quote Parsons, a 'built-in feature' (1980: 145) of living organisms, which makes it also a basic social science concept (Brosziewski 2014) to be used in many disciplines and for questions spanning a large number of cases across time and space (Reddy 1996).[5]

This notion of uncertainty is, a bit unfortunately, frequently called risk, especially in some sociological literature. There is a large discussion of risk (Zinn 2008) related to uncertainty, which focuses on the potential consequences at the societal level of events and processes that often result from human activity. Global risk (Beck 1999) is often the sociological term for the uncertainty that complex societies (Luhmann 1987: 422) face. This notion refers to such phenomena as nuclear weapons, pandemics, and global heating—phenomena that have created uncertainties at the systemic level that single actors cannot reduce.[6]

Uncertainty is a central term in economics (Bylund 2021; Keynes 1973; Knight 1921; Williamson 1985: 30), management (Alpers 2019; Simon 2016) and sociology (cf. Beckert 1996: 3–4; 2016; Azarian 2016; Dequech 2003; Godart and Mears 2009; Karpik 2010; Podolny and Hsu 2003; White 2002), and also in anthropology (Douglas 1992; Douglas and Wildawsky 1982). The importance of the research conducted by business scholars has been shown in several reviews (Leung et al. 2015; Sniazhko 2019). This literature, to be discussed in detail below, offers many different usages of the notion of uncertainty, but to clarify what it is, I draw on the works of Frank Knight (1921). Similar ideas exist in the Austrian and in the performativity schools (Callon 1998; Boettke 2002), whose notion is sometimes called 'radical uncertainty' to avoid confusion above all with economists who speak of uncertainty as something calculable using the notion of risk. Knight has a broad and profound understanding of uncertainty, and said that 'Life is made up of uncertainties' (1921: 234), although he concentrated on the economy. It is increasingly the case that business studies, too, has identified uncertainty rather than risk as the main scientific problem (Boeckelmann and Mildner 2011).

Uncertainty here means that we cannot know the 'future consequences of present action' (Arrow 1974: 33–34; March 1994: 5, cf. 178). Uncertainty is caused by lack of knowledge. If there are no states of the world, we cannot know whether our actions will lead to the ends we aim at. The underlying criterion of the state of uncertainty is epistemic, which means that we do not know which of these states is, or will be, the correct one. We cannot predict or foresee what will happen when acting or not acting, nor what others' actions will lead to, because we cannot assign probabilities to actions (March and Simon 1958: 133–134). Consequently, we 'cannot arrive at a way of insuring against an occurrence' (North 1991a: 106). Uncertainty is primarily not an objective condition that exists independently of actors; uncertainty must be connected to an actor's horizon of relevance (Schütz 1971, cf. Eberle 1984), such as when a bachelor student and an experienced researcher stand in front of a problem, and view and address it differently.

It we could present probabilities of 'uncertainties', we could clearly speak of risk. Risk requires objective probabilities of outcomes. If we can assign probabilities to the categorised thing and calculate the likelihood of various outcomes of the decision alternatives—that is, by putting numbers on different means and ends so that there are probabilities of the different outcomes—we speak of **risk**, as Frank Knight (1921) argued (cf. Guseva and Rona-Tas 2001: 626; North 1991a). Hence, when we can assign probabilities of outcomes of different actions, we can refer to rational actions grounded on empirical and objective evidence (cf. Pareto 1935). Originally, risk referred to the only marginally calculable and largely speculative trade of ships and their cargo in early mediaeval Italy (Bonss 1995: 49–50). This early idea of risk resembles what we today call uncertainty.

Put in concrete terms: risk is about probabilities, so that if there are five red and five black balls in a box, the likelihood of drawing a black one is 50 percent. Uncertainty can be described as a situation in which there are balls in the box, but one does not know the distribution between black and red balls (nor knows the colour nor the number of balls). Hence, under such conditions one cannot ascribe probabilities to different scenarios, although in this case one can find out by opening the box. This means that uncertainty in principle is an epistemic problem. In the case of **ambiguity** there is interpretative openness, and it is unclear what is in the box, and even if we open it, it is not clear what is in it; it has to be 'determined' 'framed' or 'invented' (Goffman 1974). Even the box itself may be open to debate. It is thus no longer an epistemic issue, and neither can we then 'just' find out what it is. This means that the conditions for a decision between alternatives cannot be met; one has first to determine what the alternatives 'are about'.[7] Concrete decisions under risk may then be embedded in conditions of uncertainty, and uncertainty may be embedded in ambiguity (Nowotny 2016). These three concepts are here defined in a clear way, to avoid the somewhat confusing terminology used in economics.[8] Thus, to summarize, the three terms 'risk', 'uncertainty', and 'ambiguity' are related in a hierarchical order, with ambiguity as the most profound. Scientific work has clearly moved from being ambiguous, to being uncertain, and in some cases, we have an achieved knowledge enough to speak of risk.

ATTEMPTS TO TURN UNCERTAINTY INTO RISK

The distinction between uncertainty and risk is theoretically clear, although many economists have questioned it and have reduced uncertainty to risk (Arrow 1984: 8–22). A necessary condition to move from uncertainty to risk is knowledge sufficient to make calculations possible. Calculations require numbers, which often means that commensuration—'the transformation of different qualities into a common metric' (Espeland and Stevens 1998: 314)—has to occur.[9] If it were possible to make all decisions based on probabilities, strategic decision-making would be easy. This, however, is rarely possible. Still, many actors may have an interest to present the world and the different alternatives with numbers to make it appear as if it is possible to make calculations and decisions based on probabilities. In other words, the transformation of uncertainties into probabilities means that the decision logic of risk can be employed. It is clear that our advancement in terms of science and technology in some cases enables a transformation of uncertainties into risks (Nowotny 2016: ix–x).

There are many concrete procedures that 'transform' uncertainty into risk, some of which are reasonable, others less so. Insurance and reinsurance of climate change is one case in point (Lehtonen 2017). Insurance is an example of how uncertainty about possible outcomes is very high at the individual level, but organizationally manageable at an aggregated level. Probabilities can sometimes be calculated based on a population of actors from which the average risk factors can be identified (O'Malley 2008: 57), as is the case in the welfare sector and in the health sector (cf. Hadziabdic and Kohl 2022; O'Malley 2004). This transition was furthered by the shift of 'scientific epistemologies from the deterministic to the probabilistic' (O'Malley 2004: 17), which enables calculations (Collier et al. 2021). In other situations, however, it has been observed that 'insurance work . . . is calculated by "uncertain" experience-based techniques, and sometimes just plain hunches' (O'Malley 2008: 75). Obviously, when this transformation is justified, uncertainty is reduced.

We can sometimes identify performative acts by which numbers are assigned to create the sense of calculable risk, although the assignment is quite arbitrary. Such assignment suggests in theory a reduction of complexity, which may transform part of reality into a quantifiable and economic world. It has been shown (e.g., Kay and King 2020) how the financial and economic crisis of 2007–2008, seen from the perspective of risk, was improbable but makes perfect sense from the perspective of uncertainty. Michael Power (1997) has described and analysed how, in particular, organizations manage uncertainty and risks, and above all how uncertainty is turned into risk (Power 2007) as a form of economisation of reality. Lethonen and Van Hoywegen add that 'when uncertainty is standardized, homogenized and made calculable, it can be given a price and it can be bought and sold' (2014: 332), which clearly is an economic good. They claim that this process has been made 'an essential commodity of current capitalism' (p. 332), as diverse technologies have been developed with the purpose of predicting and controlling harm, or, in other words, 'taming' uncertainty. With regard to the financial sector, by managing the probabilities of an uncertain future, chances are taken in a controlled manner (Lehtonen and Van Hoyweghen 2014: 333). Betting is a good example of how uncertainty is turned into a discourse of risk; and as such it is an example of the manufacturing of risk. Transformation of uncertainty into risk may thus be done also when the conditions that Knight outlined are not present. These are examples of how uncertainty is hidden by putting a coat of risk discourse on the analysis of uncertainty, which suggests that the real, as well as the scientific focus should be on uncertainty rather than on risk. Though there is a general societal trend towards quantification (Mennicken and Espeland 2019), it is neither relevant nor possible to put numbers on most alternatives, which means that uncertainty prevails in these cases.

Despite both sociological insights and Knight's awareness of the relatively limited role that risk plays in real life,[10] economics is still largely a discipline about risk, although uncertainty has been given more attention in the past decade. For some time, uncertainty has also been discussed in leading journals of the discipline (Zeckhauser 2014: xx). Alvarez (2005: 777) points out that there is 'widespread agreement that most business decision-making does not take place under conditions of certainty'; it is rather uncertainty, or what the economist calls radical uncertainty, that businessmen face. Increasingly, economists not only view risk as 'much less important than uncertainty', but it has become clear that 'many phenomena that were often defined as involving risk—notably those in the financial crisis before 2008—actually involve uncertainty' (Zeckhauser 2014: xvii). The increased attention to uncertainty was reflected in the 2018 call by the Academy of Management on 'The implications of uncertainty for management and organization theories' (Alvarez, Afuah, and Gibson 2018). When these articles were published in 2020, they argued that more attention should be given to uncertainty. Kay and King (2020) make a similar point, saying that uncertainty is the central issue to be addressed by practical decisions makers.

Thus, uncertainty, rather than risk, ought to be the main field of research (Zinn 2008: 209). The issue of risk and the correlation of probabilities, and decisions with calculable probabilities, are well covered in economics, mathematically oriented economics, and statistics, and has its place in decision-making, not the least when used in a pragmatic fashion. Less is known about the topic of this book, uncertainty, and even less about public means of reducing uncertainty that can be used by actors making strategic decisions.

KNOWLEDGE AS A REMEDY FOR UNCERTAINTY

To deal with uncertainty, people are ready to go far. Dewey says, 'in the absence of actual certainty in the midst of a precarious and hazardous world, men cultivated all sorts of things that would give them the feeling of certainty' (1929: 33). Dewey (1929: 1) points out that one can either actively try to eliminate the sources of uncertainty or peril, or develop means to cope with it. In some cases it is possible to eliminate the source of uncertainty, for example by disarming actors or by closing nuclear plants. This type of solution is not what this book analyses. Although we neither want nor can achieve complete certainty, it is still valid to say that the more knowledge an actor has, the less their uncertainty about the world. However, the main road to reducing uncertainty, also in the business literature (Lipshitz and Strauss 1997), is to cope with the uncertainty one faces. Coping is not easy, and Douglas says that understanding the uncertainties that we face requires '[n]othing short of total knowledge (a mad answer to an impossible question)' (Douglas and Wildawsky 1982: 3). It is, she says, 'mad' to believe that knowledge alone will solve all problems, not least because it is well known that not even science can provide certain knowledge (Husssserl 1989: 82; Kampourakis and McCain 2020; Kuhn 1962; Nowotny 2016). However, given our knowledge, there are typically many possible ways to cope with uncertainty. One of them is that actors can try to reduce the uncertainty they face.

Dewey does not just focus on rational means to address uncertainty. Historically, there are many examples of how people have tried to deal with uncertainties: fortune tellers, shamans, and astrologers are some examples of societal roles attempting to interpret past events and to predict future events using prophecies (Weber 1978b: 444ff) in order to reduce people's fear or uncertainty. Religion is of course the dominant means of coping with uncertainty (Weber 1946: 272–275), including important meteorological predictions relevant for survival. The 'uncertainty of the weather renders dubious the operation of irrigation procedures,' was, for example, in China dealt with by 'sacrifices, public atonement, and various virtuous practices' (Weber 1978b: 449). From an anthropological historical perspective, it appears to be only when the possibility of managing and controlling the world due to our increased knowledge that the 'problem' of uncertainty, and even more so the problem of 'risk', appeared (Bonss 1995).

The interest in making predictions is the reason why firms spend a lot of money to find out about customers and hire consultants, and why the military tries to find out about its enemies. Generally speaking, many activities aim at acquiring more accurate information (i.e., data) and knowledge (i.e., the capacity to conceptualize what there is and what to do). In other words, these activities aim at the conceptualization of information (Amsden 2001) in order to relate these two central concepts. Metrological information requires interpretation, experience, and theoretical tools to turn it into knowledge. Strategies to assess uncertainty, when knowledge is hard to come by, are also relevant options (Friedman and Zeckhauser 2012).

Prospecting for minerals (Olofsson 2020) is a good case in point to understand how firms cope with uncertainty and how they attempt to predict the future by gaining more knowledge. It is difficult to know what is in the ground, and it is also uncertain what the price of the minerals will be once the mine is running, the minerals are extracted, and are to be sold on the market. It is obviously possible to call in experts to make predictions. As a complement to these 'private' means of uncertainty reduction that are unique to every decision-maker, individual, or organization, there may be public means of uncertainty reduction.

What public knowledge, or ways of obtaining knowledge, are available to reduce the uncertainty of prospectors? The existence of a stable state, laws that safeguard property rights, and rules that regulate prospecting are means to reduce uncertainty for all those involved. The stability of the social system—with banks, markets, schools, health care and much more—matters, of course, too. One should, however, underline the norms and values in society that enable stable laws. There is even an index, ranking countries on how easy it is to open and run mines, which captures the institutional framework and the possibility of making profit. The fact that there are markets in which prices are set publicly for labour as well as minerals, enabling actors to make decisions about whether to start prospecting or not, is also important for reducing uncertainty when actors are making decisions. If there is a way of publicly ranking the alternatives, one can find out which of the firms that have been evaluated are the most efficient, and also the historical and current market prices for metals. This type of knowledge can be used when actors make decisions about what firms to contact when prospecting for minerals.

More generally, much knowledge has been generated that, taken together, has reduced the uncertainty that humans face. More knowledge increases the complexity of the world in one way, and gives rise to new questions, but it is hard to make the argument that less knowledge decreases uncertainty. Clearly uncertainty will remain, but it is argued here that it can be reduced, for example, by knowledge production. Obviously, latent threats to our knowledge and certainty always exist, and some of these are not just natural disasters but are also the result of human making and design. Pandemics, climate change, development of nuclear power, and much more also result in uncertainties, but it is only partially less reasonable to speak of entire societies as oriented to risk (or uncertainty), as Beck does (O'Malley 2004: 178–181).

Available knowledge, also public knowledge, can be expressed in the form 'if x, y . . . then, z . . .' (Mantzavinos 2001: 24). States of the world are typically based on evidence, logic, or empirically supported facts, and actors have to relate to this knowledge, such as knowledge about prenatal screening (Burton-Jeangros et al. 2013). Knowledge has been built into machines, technologies, algorithms, and the like (Baird 2004),[11] and there are states of the world based on practical knowledge (Aspers 2006), or implicit or tacit knowledge. What is knowledge must not have been intentionally produced. Knowledge can also be an unintended outcome of social processes involving actors and even machines. The knowledge can, for example, be 'know-what', such as a fact, or 'know-how' in the sense of practice. Garfinkel speaks of what he calls institutionalized knowledge as 'facts of social life for the members of society', and this leads to the enforceable character of 'actions in compliance with the expectancies of everyday life' (Garfinkel 1967. 53).

Scientific Knowledge

Over time our knowledge about the world has increased, largely due to scientific work. Originally, many occurrences like famine, illnesses, draught, fire, and the like were uncontrollable, and though religious inventions provided both means of interpretation and comfort, and as such may contribute to the reduction of at least the subjective uncertainty, the objective uncertainty remained. In contrast to religion, the increase of scientific knowledge has made life more predictable, both seen from a subjective and objective point of view. But without denying the centrality and importance of science, it will be shown how it rests on a social bed of norms and values, as well as laws—means of uncertainty reduction that are of a profound character. Nowotny (2016: 152–153) has in detail studied how scientists thrive on uncertainty, that is, on not knowing.

Scientific knowledge is the primary example of states of the world, and it is often seen as the golden form of knowledge because it is 'the sort of knowledge that is as close to certainty as we can get' (Kampourakis and McCain 2020: x). Nowotny summarizes the relation between science and uncertainty as follows: 'Science has developed highly efficient modes of transforming uncertainties into certainties. . . . But . . . the tacit assumption holds that all certainties in science remain provisional.' (2016: 152–153).

Scientific knowledge is normally presented as either logical states of the world, or as supported by empirical evidence (Pareto 1935: 76–78).[12] It is only when 'knowledge is certain and consent complete' that we know things in such a way that 'a program can be written to produce the best solution' (Douglas and Wildawsky 1982: 5).[13] It is based on such knowledge that decisions about the future can be made (Habermas 1973: 263–268).[14] States of the world presuppose that 'the world is made up of things, which, under certain circumstances, always behave in the same way' (Knight 1921: 204). But we live in this world, and we relate to and act upon meaning in such a way that we affect knowledge, making it unlikely that this assumption holds true. This implies that our knowledge, at most, is 'partial', changing over time, suggesting that we have to act based on imperfect knowledge (Knight 1921: 198–199).[15]

Seen in a historical light, the growth of scientific knowledge in all areas—from medicine, technology, natural sciences, and social sciences, including their corresponding domains of practical applicability, such as health care, optics, and organizational leadership—has contributed to the reduction of uncertainty. Our knowledge about life, death, and the objectification of knowledge that depersonalises what is to be known, has had enormous consequences for economic prosperity and social life (Sombart 1927, I: 111–117). Many diseases can be cured; we have invented technology to produce heat, machines for agriculture, standardize production of tools, and much more; we have found ways to generate energy, produce chemical products, gained knowledge about social interaction, to take few more examples. This means that the uncertainty about one's life and well-being is less acute than it was when witchcraft was the means of uncertainty reduction. The Covid pandemic of 2020 was, of course, an issue of concern, and it was initially surrounded by much uncertainty. However, in contrast to previous pandemics, the scientific community could draw on existing states of the world not only to develop vaccines, but also to make decisions on how people should behave in society to diminish the chances that the virus could be spread.

Our increased awareness and use of scientific knowledge, but also of its practical application in the form of technologies, machines, and many more devices, can be used to reduce uncertainty. The development of technological devices to measure time, together with the decision to standardize how to measure time, has reduced uncertainty. For example, before there were clocks, one could make a certain prediction that 'I will come and visit you tomorrow', meaning that I will appear any time between dawn and dusk. But if I today say, 'I will come and visit you tomorrow at 13:45:44' this is uncertain too, because the time is so exact—something made possible by much knowledge production that enables us to have one time, and to have watches that are synchronized and exact (Luhmann 1995: 308). Hence, the subjective uncertainty perception may be the same, but the objective uncertainty has decreased. This subjectively perceived uncertainty nonetheless must be interpreted as embedded in a space of increased certainty due the production of states of the world, above all by scientific work. At the same time as some objective uncertainties have diminished, the correlated complexity of society and the increased body of knowledge may lead to other uncertainties.

A sociological analysis must consider both the production of knowledge and states of the world, and the subjectively expressed uncertainty. It is in this light also possible to see that, despite increased volume and impact of states of the world, there are many who work against hegemonic scientific knowledge—beyond the point of organized scepticism, such as those who are questioning the usefulness of vaccination without having any real arguments—that is built into the scientific community. This question is of great importance, and I will return to it in the final chapter.

Contingency and the Limitation of Knowledge

We can be uncertain about past or future events. States of the world that have already occurred, but whose details are not known, can be investigated and determined. This kind of state includes the answers to questions such as what the inflation rate in Switzerland was in 2000. The answer—a state of the world—can be established using accepted means and is often made up of simple facts. Much knowledge about correlations, such as between religious denominations and suicide rates, represents empirically verified states of the world for a given time. We can find out about the past or use technological devices to find out about facts, such as how much weight this steel bar can take before it bends 1 per cent. My uncertainty about how much money a certain company made last year, or what percentage of the trees in the forest to be harvested are Norwegian spruce, can be eliminated. To put it differently, I know how I can reduce this uncertainty with the help of knowledge. Moreover, this knowledge is not directly contingent on others' behaviour, and is not about the uncertainty of future states.

Some decisions are contingent on many factors that will only unfold in the future, in which the act itself is a largely an undefined ongoing entity (Arendt 1988: 233). A historical example of a real situation of uncertainty is given by Peter Bang, who explains the condition traders faced in the Roman empire: 'the premodern merchant had to act in a highly uncertain market situation, governed by the rhythm of the seasons, where it was difficult to predict or estimate the amount of goods brought to the individual market-place and the number and buying capacity of his competitors' (2008: 138). This uncertainty, to a large extent due to lack of information about prices and much more (i.e., the absence of any states of the world) led to high price volatility because of actors' decisions. Furthermore, the question of whether to plant Norwegian spruce on newly harvested land is still uncertain. This decision is based on the soil, where to plant, the latitude, and many other states of the world, including what the price will be and what type of timber will be in demand when the trees are to be harvested, say, in 100 years. What is known is the current and past prices of timber that can be used when deciding. Thus, facts and correlations of facts—that is, states of the world and other past events—are extrapolated into the future, and they often give us reasons to make predictions about the future. But these predictions are always uncertain, and there are many contingencies.

Despite scientific development, neither future-oriented activities nor states of the world are inherently certain. Many states of the world are uncertain because they are directly contingent on human activity. The predictability of the social world is necessarily limited because our knowledge is contingent on assumptions about the world, including the life-world (Husserl 1970). Put more philosophically, uncertainty is an inherent part of our life; we are not outside a world that can be described objectively. We are characterized by 'being in the world' (Heidegger 2001), meaning that we and the world are co-constitutive. Consequently, uncertainty about facts, rules, and other statements may exist, but as soon as other human beings are involved, individually or in organized form, uncertainty emerges not only about the rule, but also about compliance with the rule. Various states of the world, including established knowledge of human behaviour, can be transcended by actors, also in unpredictable ways.[16] This problem implies that we are co-constructors of the world, meaning that uncertainty is an essential part of life (Esposito 2013).

Ego–alter interaction is the most typical example of contingency. When ego tries to anticipate alter's behaviour, which of course means that alter does the same, uncertainty is created. This situation leads to the so-called double contingency problem (Beckert 1996: 826; Luhmann 1995; Parson and Shils 1951: 15–17), which is also central in game theory—in economics as well as in sociology (e.g., Goffman 1969). The consideration of this type of contingency must be made by businessmen, whose investment decisions are based on their anticipations of what they expect others will think and do, a theme famously discussed in the beauty contest example by Keynes (1973: 154–156).[17] Contingency approaches were 'in vogue' (Tosi et al. 1973: 27) in the business literature in the early 1970s. Contingency causes problems for approaches that deal with probabilities and suggests that, at its root, cases of risk also are essentially problems of uncertainty. It is, consequently, rare that probabilities can be computed, and almost all decisions are contingent because no 'single case is absolutely isolated' (Knight 1921: 234). The outcomes of political decision processes, or negotiation processes, are uncertain and have consequences that must be dealt with, for example in the economy. However, 'some contingencies have relatively stable probability distributions. Mortality rates, health care costs'. But for others, 'the bankruptcy risk of an individual firm ranked "BB" to give a current example, the probabilities are unknown and rather difficult to estimate' (Dana and Riedel 2013: 1385). More generally, the economic problem of uncertainty is always embedded in other uncertainties; it is just a matter of the degree of embeddedness. This is because contingency is inherently tied to social life; and uncertainty, according to Parsons, refers to 'the contingency of unpredictable changes in the situation of action' (1980: 145).

A corollary of us being in the world, and of the contingency that is a constitutive element of our lives, is that complete certainty is utopian. Complete certainty for everyone—if it could be achieved—would mean predictable actions and a situation in which little creativity or innovation could come about (Menger 2014). We can even say that in many situations,

> uncertainty is seen as a resource, as the engine and stimulus of economic activity, allowing for the development of creativity and the generation of novelties. Uncertainty explains the continuous production of surprises and genuinely new information, not simply additions, and then changes their meaning and relevance. Uncertainty also explains the possibility of profit and business, which always have to do with creativity and inventiveness. (Esposito 2013: 19)

To the central question of how uncertainty is a both a necessary and often a positive force, I will return in the concluding chapter.

Contingency matters for the possibility of us knowing things, but also the actor's social and historically situated position matters for what 'is' knowledge, because it requires interpretation (Gadamer 1990). Knowledge does not come in boxes that, once opened, propose decisions that lead to the ends an actor wants to achieve. Actors and their interpretations are central to what is going on, and uncertainty as well as knowledge to reduce it must be related to the actor's position and relevance (Schütz 1964: 92ff). Douglas speaks of cultural analysis to achieve an understanding of how uncertainty and what are here called 'states of the world' are constructed, to account for the limitations on the publicness of states of the world (Douglas and Wildawsky 1982: 1–15). Hence both the sociology of knowledge tradition and the anthropology of knowledge have shown that scientific knowledge is socially constructed, and the use of knowledge differs between cultures and groups as well as between individuals. For example, not everything that is possible to know is known, nor can all people, due to education and other social aspects, make use of all existing knowledge.

Moreover, due to the social distribution of knowledge (Schütz 1964: 120–134), the fact that some know more than others, and that we may not know what others know about a certain thing, it is difficult to reduce uncertainty for all. Actors behave differently due to their backgrounds in terms of class, education, gender, and ethnicity. White men, for example, typically perceive risks to be less than women and minorities, suggesting their structurally privileged position makes them more secure (Flynn et al. 1994). Peoples' values and emotions matter, too, for what is seen as knowledge and how it can be used (Zinn 2008). Put another way, knowledge is unevenly and 'socially distributed', and people have different skills and know different things (Schütz 1976: 81; 1962: 14). Distribution of knowledge has been a central theme of various Austrian scholars, who argue that knowledge is far from perfect because it is distributed among actors (Hayek 1945), an idea pursued by others in developing economic theories of knowledge (Hardin 2009). This distribution of knowledge may be due to talent or structural reasons, but is often an intricate combination of several components (Menger 2014). Because actors act on their knowledge and their interpretation of it (Schütz 2003: 357), decisions and outcomes will differ between people. Not all knowledge is simply accessible to everyone, and actors must be capable of using it if they are to become seekers of knowledge (Gadamer 1990). This requires some type of judgement on the part of the actors, referring to the use (Kampourakis and McCain 2020: 197) and understanding of knowledge.

PRIVATE WAYS OF REDUCING UNCERTAINTY

Given the centrality of uncertainty and the complexity of knowledge, what can actors do? Attempting to organize the conditions pertaining to one's decision-making, individually or by joining hands, is a typical example of uncertainty reduction. Some ways of reducing uncertainty are private because access to them is restricted. For analytic purposes I separate them from public means of uncertainty reduction, to be discussed next.

Paying for experts—for example, consultants—is one way to address the uncertainty firms may face, even if it is done only to justify certain preferred decisions. The knowledge that a decision-maker gains from these means can be used to make decisions that, compared with the situation of not having this knowledge (Karpik 2010), achieve the ends with less uncertainty. Making use of the ties in one's network is probably the single most distinct means of uncertainty reduction for individuals (Beckert 1996). Networks are essentially built from ties—dyadic relations—that are not publicly available. White (2002) has argued that having ties upstream and downstream in the production chain is a way for producers to reduce their uncertainty, compared with having a free market. Uzzi (1997) showed this in great empirical detail when he analysed the garment industry in New York, informing us how a firm's trading partners are useful for handling problems and for finding solutions. Malinowski's (1922) study of the Argonauts illustrates how those trading in the Kula-ring can be safe also on islands far from home while staying with their trading partners.[18] Ties to others who can help interpret what to do, such as mentors or assessors, are other devices that individuals can use to appraise alternatives, such as what is a 'good' manuscript (Furst 2018; Karpik 2010; Nästesjö 2020).

Obtaining knowledge and developing strategies to make decisions with predictable outcomes are typical of individual actors and organizations. To set up a meta-organization (Ahrne and Brunsson 2008)—that is, an organization that has other organizations as its members, such as an industrial association—is a distinct way of trying to control and change the environment in which organizations operate. The meta-organization, for example, lobbies for new rules of the game that would reduce uncertainty.[19] Calculations, using algorithms to seek out more information and different strategies, are all means that actors can use to reduce their private uncertainty. An actor can purchase information from a firm to gain knowledge that gives them a comparative advantage in the market, gaining knowledge about potential customers to better adjust advertisements and product development. Some of these activities fall under the heading of market research. Industrial espionage, bribes, and the creation of cartels are additional means—today often illegal—that actors can use to reduce their uncertainty. Other strategies of uncertainty reduction that individual firms can use include selecting top students to join the workforce of an organization, or investing in computer power or research and development.

It is, more generally, evident that uncertainty can be reduced. Knight was clear about this: 'In the first place, we can increase our knowledge of the future through scientific research and the accumulation and the study of the necessary data'. One can also, he continues, proceed by 'clubbing the uncertainties through large-scale organizations of various forms'. He lists two other options to reduce uncertainty, namely increasing 'control over the future' and 'slowing up the march of progress' (Knight 1921: 347). These may be used to address uncertainty among the public, so that many can benefit from uncertainty reduction, but they can also be employed as individual strategies.

Arrow (1983) goes much further than Knight, and claims that if 'an economic agent is uncertain as to which states of the world will obtain, he can make contracts contingent on occurrence of possible states' (p. 142). He then speaks of 'insurance policies and common stocks' as real-world examples enabling actors to act, if there is risk, and a competitive equilibrium will 'arise under the same general hypothesis as in the absence of uncertainty' (p. 142). It is indeed true that private insurance companies and meta-insurance systems provide stability in the economic system, and to some extent enable risk-based calculations. Many have followed Arrow, but he assumed perfect information while noting the emerging research that problematized this assumption (Arrow 1983: 143–144). Given the critique of the assumption of perfect information, and the acknowledgement of knowledge—or lack of knowledge—as a problem, means that Arrow's assumptions and the solutions to the problem of uncertainty are less realistic.

Decision theories have also been developed for conditions of uncertainty, following Kahneman and Tversky (Wakker 2010). This reflects the dominant focus on uncertainty in the field of organizational research and management of organizations, and how to deal with uncertainty (Alvarez and Barney 2005; Milliken 1987). A substantial branch of this literature draws on psychology and centres on individual decision-making (Milliken 1987). The main issue is how managers can, and do, cope with uncertainty in the 'environment' (Downey and Slocum 1975). The literature has identified ways of coping with uncertainty, including amplification, acknowledgement, and suppression of uncertainty (Alpers 2019: 4). Some emphasize cognitive tools rooted in the mind. Heuristics are seen as 'a realistic alternative to more classical approaches to decision-making under uncertainty'; search is another cognitive tool, that is, 'permitting people to glean information about the future by learning from the environments they encounter'; and finally, collective intelligence, by which is meant a 'group's ability to sometimes outperform individual decision' (Hertwig et al. 2019: 5–6). Managers can use these strategies to make decisions. Also, this literature refers to states of the world, and some agree that differentiation of types of uncertainties can be done empirically, but its usage makes less sense theoretically (Milliken 1987). There are, in addition, approaches that draw on pragmatism and show how value is actually created out of uncertainty by entrepreneurs who behave like scientists (Zellweger and Zenger 2023).

Social psychologists speak of management and control of uncertainty and may even claim that this is a 'very individual endeavour' (Marris 1996: 1). In particular, management scholars have paid much attention to the question of how to reduce uncertainty to make better decisions (Alpers 2019). It has been shown that firms that face uncertainty use a range of strategies, plans, and use consultants to cope with it (White et al. 2007). Seen in this way, private means of uncertainty reduction are like private goods. But the quality of the information that grounds private means of uncertainty reduction may be uncertain if it is not verified (Blank 2007: 2).

'Uncertainty reduction theory' is concerned with how to reduce uncertainty in communications between two persons (Berger 1986). There are studies of how actors perceive uncertainty, how uncertainty can be attributed to different sources, and how actors react to uncertainty (Kahneman and Tversky 1982). Different rules of thumb, and private experience and knowledge (Tversky and Kahneman 1974), are important to enable individuals to reduce uncertainty to subjective odds, that is, as calculable risk—a process that involves much irrationality. This transformation occurs with what Keynes referred to as conventions (Keynes 1973: 152). Private uncertainty reduction, primarily in cases with relatively few actors, is also a key issue in game theory (Luce and Raiffa 1957) and is relevant in theories of monopoly, monopolistic or monopsonistic competition, and niche-making (White 1981). In the field of business studies, there is also the uncertainty avoidance approach (Hofstede 1983), which refers to how different cultures are willing to accept different levels of uncertainty and how they deal with it (Rapp et al. 2010).

Sociologists, too, have contributed to the large literature on uncertainty and on how actors deal with it (Smith 2011). Jens Beckert (2016) has surveyed much of this literature. He does not frame his study in terms of uncertainty reduction, but rather of what actors do in a capitalist economy characterised by uncertainty. Beckert analyses imaginaries concerning future states that motivate action. In a sense, the capitalist future is co-ordinated by narratives (Beckert and Bronk 2018: 5). The most obvious form of narration is firms' and other organizations' attempts at impression management by advertisement. Beckert describes the ways people come to make decisions, given the state of uncertainty, based on their imaginations or hopes about what the future will bring. Narratives that are created in this context may have a performative character and become self-fulfilling prophecies, albeit with unintended outcomes. Weather forecasting, which ultimately has to end with a decision in the form of a prediction, is a typical example of how actors try to decrease uncertainty, in this case based on different forms of knowledge that the actors have (Daipha 2015). Weather forecasting is thus a good example of something that is uncertain (Fine 2007), not the least in history, as the example above taken from Weber clarifies. Once the modern predictions are publicly presented, many actors—for example, camping owners, ski resorts, and many more—can use them to make better predictions. However, some pay to get weather forecasts privately, such as farmers, beach managers, ice-cream and umbrella sellers, as well as many others selling goods and services. The military tries to reduce its uncertainty by having their own weather forecasting service.

But although much of this research on uncertainty mentions collective solutions, the outlook is still that of the individual actor. There are different takes on how actors—individuals or organizations—cope with uncertainty. March and Simon, and later Luhmann (1997: 837), spoke about uncertainty absorption, which means that 'interferences are drawn from a body of evidence and the interferences instead of the evidence itself are then communicated' (March and Simon 1958: 165). In other words, the information (or the uncertainty) from outside the organization is transformed into an interpretation that is less complex for those within the organization to grasp. Hence, the reduction or absorption of uncertainty by decision and processing of incoming information to something that is already known within the organization (Luhmann 2000, 1988) may reduce some uncertainties, but is likely to create others. An organization that offers contracts until retirement most likely reduces the uncertainty of loyalty, but may create uncertainty about the productivity of its labour force. To behave like other organisations do, and to adopt existing solutions—in other words, a form of isomorphism—is a strategy that has been analysed in new institutional organizational theory (DiMaggio and Powell 1983; Meyer and Rowan 1977). Organizations can also be seen as ways of reducing the uncertainty of the environment because they reduce the transaction costs (Coase 1937).

By using states of the world, actors can achieve their ends with more certainty. In contrast to private knowledge, public ways of reducing uncertainty uses knowledge that 'can be seen and heard by everybody' (Arendt 1988: 50) and which is 'made' together.[20] Publicly available means of reducing uncertainty refers to states of the world that many actors can use (cf. Zeckhauser 2014: xxiv),[21] at least those with specific roles, in a certain domain or in terms of any other kind of demarcation. The point is that such demarcation is not done based on individual traits. The knowledge in question here is, in principle, available to many, today facilitated by various media. Public uncertainty reduction, to present what will be discussed in this book, means that actors orient themselves to one another and share states of the world. That there is a consensual idea of these states of the world not only reduces uncertainty, but also facilitates interaction and coordination in social and economic life.

Markets with information illustrate how states of the world can be established, that is, knowledge in public that actors can use to reduce uncertainty. Jevons is clear about the importance of this publicness of markets, and says, '[o]riginally a market was a public place in a town' (Jevons 1871: 84). Increasingly such marketplaces, many of which do not generate public prices (Geertz 1979), have been accompanied by more abstract and specialized markets, such as 'public exchange, mart or auction rooms, where the traders agree to meet and transact business.' Such as 'the Stock Market, the Corn Market, the Coal Market, the Sugar Market, and many others' (Jevons 1871: 85). All these markets offer information about prices. This information is crucial, at least for businessmen when they make decisions. Prices and other public means of reducing uncertainty represent a public good, available to all, essentially without cost. As a reader of books, you may have your own knowledge about what is good and not good, based on the books you have read. This is private knowledge. But by reading reviews of books—or any other thing reviewed (Blank 2007)—you may also benefit from public knowledge.

Ideas on uncertainty reduction in public are mentioned by Beckert, who speaks of "social devices' encompassing all forms of rules, social norms, conventions, social structures and power relations' (1996: 819–820). Though certainly hinting at public means of uncertainty reduction, he does not elaborate on this. Uncertainty, although central, is not always present and not always noticed. Also, standards, technologies, and rules, as well as objective ways of evaluating alternatives are publicly available means of uncertainty reduction. Laws and money are additional examples of institutions. Institutionalized knowledge can be used to turn our personal or collective uncertainty into certainty.

Clearly, the existing literature has paid much more attention to analysing different private means of uncertainty reduction than analysing public ones. It therefore makes sense to focus here on the publicly available means of uncertainty reduction that, together with the existing literature on private means, enables us to understand better how to reduce uncertainty.[22] The phenomenologically inspired approach of this book stresses the future orientation of actions and inscribes them in a social system of anticipations and institutions, which actors by and large will follow.[23]

OUTLINE

Part I consists of three chapters, all of which deal with principles of states of the world that can be used in many and different contexts. The task of Chapter 2 is to clarify the institutionalization of knowledge. More specifically, this chapter discusses questions of what informal institutions mean, and how they can reduce uncertainty. Chapter 2 is more general and, at the same time, more profound than the other chapters, also because it discusses how uncertainty is reduced unintentionally, by mutual adjustment. This is important because the informal institutions provide the foundation for the other means of uncertainty reduction. Chapter 3 zooms in on the most distinctive way of reducing uncertainty by organizing order, exemplified by laws and standards. Chapter 4 mirrors Chapter 3 by looking at how uncertainty is reduced but focuses on evaluation. Evaluation is defined in relation to measurement of what is evaluated against objectively existing scales. In everyday language, evaluation is used in a whole range of activities, but the definition of evaluation as pertaining to objective scales in Chapter 4 provides clarity.

While Part I studies states of the world that exist, Part II examines the ways in which they come about. The understanding of how states of the world come about becomes the problem when there are no principles of uncertainty reduction. The focus is on forms that produce states of the world, and which particular states of the world, in contrast to the principles that are the focus of Part I.

Each of the chapters of Part II deals with a particular form that produces states of the world. Chapter 5, on what I call 'convaluation', analyses forms that reduce uncertainty via actors who, together and in processes of mutual adjustment, generate ranks and values and, more generally, orderliness. Actors and things are positioned in relation to one another, and this also reduces uncertainty about what they will do. Chapter 6 analyses forms that are partially organized by the attempt to make decisions for others, which reduces uncertainty for actors. In contrast to formal institutions, this form produces outcomes that are based on judgements and not enforced by sanctions. Chapter 7 deals with contests as a form of uncertainty reduction. Contests are characterized by the adversaries'—contestants'—frequent direct interaction and conflicting interests. Over time, social life has become more civilized (Elias 1969b), and direct hostilities—physical struggle, as exemplified by war and duels—have to a large extent been replaced by negotiations and even sport. This largely intended process also points towards the interest of actors to organize uncertainty for others, and some actors whose interest is in exposing themselves to uncertainty. Put differently, with less uncertainty there are also fewer opportunities—and organized uncertainty, for example in the world of sport, is also an attempt to generate 'controlled' uncertainties. The final chapter pulls together the issues covered in the book and puts the role of the public at the centre of the societal analysis of the issue of uncertainty.

PART I
Principles of States of the World

Principles of states of the world refers to generalized public knowledge that actors can use to make decisions with reduced uncertainty. The reduction of uncertainty is thus achieved by way of this knowledge about how to behave and what to do to achieve an end, and the possibility of predicting how others will act and what they will do to achieve their ends. A principle is based on a 'scale' that is general enough to guide actors who are in different positions and have different characteristics and interests, and it applies to many situations or objects. Principles guide behaviour and make it possible for actors to predict how to act, and how others will act. The first part of the book covers the baseline of order by analysing informal institutions that are grown (such as virtues), formal institutions that are decided (e.g., a law), and evaluations based on standards (e.g., the hardness of steel). Part I is mainly about already existing principles of uncertainty reduction.

CHAPTER 2

Informal Institutions

Uncertainty reduction makes sense only against the backdrop of certainty: because we are certain about something, something else may appear to be uncertain. Both informal and formal institutions—to be discussed in Chapter 3—are upheld by sanctions, provide regularity of behaviour, and offer decision-makers predictability concerning actors' behaviour (cf. Greif 2006: 30). Both informal and formal institutions represent principles of states of the world, and are thus public ways of reducing uncertainty that can be used by many.[1] There are many examples of informal institutions, including values, practices, norms, and ideas. There are also many instances of formal institutions, including regulations and laws. These two types of institutions are characterized by their different processes of making, and the different ways they are upheld. To overcome some research problems that do not differentiate between types of institutions, I follow, but also elaborate on, ideas developed by North (cf. Mantzavinos 2001; North 1990: 4), who is explicit about the distinction between what he calls formal institutions, which are created by means of decision, and informal (evolved) institutions, which grow out of mutual adjustment by actors over time. But these two ideas are often conflated in the literature, and both are frequently called institutions. To specify these ideal types, and the conditions under which they can be employed, is of great relevance to anyone who wish to reduce the uncertainty they face.

This chapter addresses the informal institutions that have grown as a result of actors mutually adjusting to one another. These institutions are taken for granted; they are upheld by people because they are internalized and 'embodied'. Norms and established ways of doing things are examples

Uncertainty. Patrik Aspers, Oxford University Press. © Oxford University Press 2024.
DOI: 10.1093/oso/9780197752753.003.0002

of what brings certainty to one's own actions and one's expectations of others' actions. I can orient myself to an institution to predict the outcomes of my actions, and I can predict that others will comply with existing institutions; thus I can also predict their behaviour.

The first section of this chapter concerns the distinction between informal and formal institutions, to be followed by discussion of a concrete situation in which the members of a society are facing much uncertainty. It clearly shows how profoundly important institutions are for any activity, zooming in on economic activities. Then I discuss the notion of 'institution' and the lifeworld of which institutions are part. The issues of institutionalization and how institutions show up or come to our attention are analysed. In addition to giving concrete examples of institutions that diminish economic actors' uncertainty, this chapter, provides the basis for the analyses in the following chapters of Part I, because other public means of reducing uncertainty build on informal institutions that are grown out of mutual adjustment.

INFORMAL AND FORMAL INSTITUTIONS

Institutions are profoundly important for predicting what others will do, and their role in coordinating social life, including the economy, is substantial (Braudel 1992a,b,c). Laws, as instances of formal institutions backed by force, are the paradigmatic example of principles for states of the world. Actors can orient themselves to laws, and they enable actors to predict also how others will act. In both cases these states of the world will reduce the uncertainty actors face. For example, a law that regulates how CEOs must behave when they are trading stocks in their own company, thereby reducing uncertainty for other actors, exemplifies such principles. This means that, as a CEO is likely to know how to handle buying and selling stocks in their own company—as do investors—these other actors can count on other CEOs to relate to and even follow similar rules. These are all states of the world that are publicly known and often taken for granted or accepted. Such states of the world enable actors to make decisions with reduced uncertainty because most people have internalized many institutions and have adjusted to laws. Ideal-typically, these states of the world are clear and do not depend on who is doing something or who is interpreting; principles are independent of any individuals' views. That all are 'equal before the law' is one practical example of a person-independent principle.

In the literature, the distinction is drawn by some between formal institutions and informal institutions, sometimes in relation to concepts such as standards and the unintended emergence of norms (Busch 2011: 3–4). Although the notion of institutions is clearly present in the contemporary literature, the important distinction between informal institutions and formal institutions is not always made. Mark Granovetter (2017), for example, argues that institutions are fundamental, but he sees them essentially as grown, while at the same time seeing them as resources on which actors can draw. Greif, whose discussion of institutions is elaborate and detailed, defines institutions as 'a system of social factors that conjointly generate a regularity of behavior' (cf. Greif 2006: 30). Moreover, he makes no strong distinction between informal and formal institutions. He argues that institutions grow in a historical process. However, he presumes a more or less 'rational' foundation for institutions: 'New institutions emerge or are created in response to new needs, to reinforce existing ones, and to replace ones that no longer function well' (Greif 2014: 57). Thereby, Greif gives institutions an almost functional explanation. Furthermore, 'for an institution to prevail, it has to be self-enforcing in the sense that each agent's expected behavior is the one he would choose to follow when expecting others to follow it as well' (p. 58). This neglects the possibility that institutions may emerge as unintended consequences. Some new institutional scholars even argue that the aim of reducing uncertainty explains institutions (cf. Gudeman 2009: 32). In this chapter on informal institutions, and in the next chapter on formal institutions, I show that, although informal institutions may reduce uncertainty, only formal institutions can intentionally aim to reduce uncertainty.

Despite the centrality of institutions, the sociological literature is not clear about the meaning of the term, and many speak of institutions in a broad way. Economists are in some respects more precise. North, for example, is explicit about what institutions do: 'Institutions reduce uncertainty by providing a structure to everyday life' because they are the 'rules of the game in a society, or more formally, are the humanly devised constraints that shape human interaction' (1990: 3; also Mantzavinos 2001: 96, who elaborates on this matter, but he tends to stress the intentional change of institutions). Seeking a clear-cut definition of the notion of 'institution', encyclopaedias (e.g., Abercrombie et al. 2006; Eisenstadt 1968; Hamilton 1932) and books generally show that the use of the term has varied considerably, which is reflected in the many rather vague definitions.[2]

Texts by Coase, Williamson, and North have been central to modern economics' understanding of institutions, and it is the distinction between informal institutions and formal institutions—discussed above all by North—which serves as starting point of the analysis of these phenomena.[3] Williamson (2000) speaks of four levels of institutions, starting with the most deeply rooted. This level he calls 'embeddedness', comprising institutions and customs (to be studied by social theory, that is, sociology). Then comes 'institutional environment', referring to formal institutions (the object of study of the economics of property and positive political theory). The third level is 'governance', by which he means a proper political system for settling conflicts, including contractual conflicts (transaction costs: economics deals with these issues). The fourth level refers to 'resource allocation and employment', which means price setting and adjustment to production (which is a task analysed by neoclassical economics).

According to Williamson, the first level changes only very slowly. Changes in an informal institution, he argues, take 100–1,000 years. The important point is that change is so slow that people notice it only with great difficulty. Obviously, this stability reduces actors' uncertainty. Change, especially at levels three and four, happens much faster. Williamson openly states that level one is normally assumed by institutional economics—and, it can be added, by many institutional sociologists. This suggests that, from the perspective of economics, the notion of informal institutions is little understood (but see Mantzavinos [2001: 65–130] for a discussion). To speak of levels, however, mystifies the notion of institution because it reifies existing approaches and their different presumptions.

To Douglas North, institutions represent the incentive structure for individuals, which evolves incrementally. He makes a clear distinction between informal constraints—sanctions, taboos, customs, traditions, and codes of conduct—and formal institutions, that is, constitutions, laws, and property rights (North 1991b: 97), which is a distinction also made by others (e.g., Streeck and Thelen 2005). Ahrne and Brunsson (2011: 7) argue that formal rules are to be connected with decisions and organizations, and thus differ from informal institutions.

The discussion of informal institutions that are grown, and the formal institutions that are decided, does not imply a specific theoretical perspective. Action-oriented researchers, including most economists, rational choice sociologists, phenomenologists, and organizational researchers, realize the importance of institutions. In what follows, primarily the phenomenological perspective is used for analysing informal institutions. The ideas presented in phenomenology have many similarities with how evolutionary economics views institutions (Hodgson 1988; Murmann 2003; Nelson and Winter 1982) but are more detailed and more oriented to the level of actors.

To see how fundamental informal institutions are for reducing uncertainty, I turn to classical anthropology. I go into more detail here because of the profound role of informal institutions in analysing uncertainty. It is possible to study the importance of institutions by analysing what can be described as the lack of them. Although we cannot be certain about how life really was, nor how it was perceived in the past, it suffices to look at anthropological studies or the work of historians to acquire a picture of the types of uncertainties that people used to face, bearing in mind the problem of ascribing the meaning of 'uncertainty' to a group of people who did not use this term (Gadamer 1988; Douglas 1992). Moreover, and despite the caveats, we gain an idea of how uncertainties have changed over time.

To see how fundamental the lack of what we today consider basic social institutions can be for the uncertainty actors face, let us look at one pre-modern society, that of the Inuit in Greenland, as it appears in an anthropological text (Mirsky 1937), which synthesizes the then existing research on this society, but clearly in a less positive light.[4] This text draws on fieldwork done at the end of the 19th century, and one should consider this when reading about the conditions. Inuit society lacks written records and is not characterized by a separate economic sphere. It would therefore be wrong to speak of 'economic' decisions, although many decisions have economic consequences. This society exemplifies a socio-economic life with few or hardly any formal institutions, and relatively few informal institutions that can reduce uncertainty.[5] Moreover, it does not meet the main criteria that Elias (1989) sets for a 'civilized' society, namely, that violence is centrally controlled. In this situation all members face uncertainty—not just economic, but also about life and death.

The Ammassalik community on Greenland was characterized by a high degree of individualism with little differentiation, apart from sex and age. All items were owned by individuals, who made them themselves, and their social life was also characterized by a high degree of individuality. The central function of 'economic production' was characterized by a strict division of labour and distinct roles for men and women. Hunting was done by men, often alone, and with a high death rate. While men were hunting, they had to rely on women to prepare food, take care of the children, and make clothes. Hence, every man had to have 'a wife as an economic partner and it is desirable for him to have two such parties' (Mirsky 1937: 60). Each couple constituted a 'completely self-sufficient unit and the struggle for existence is continuous, precarious and dependent on factors outside the individual's control' (Mirsky 1937: 54–55). A couple with small children made up the economic unit of the household. Partnerships could be formed when a child was born, but 'a father may provide for his son, and this is the usual picture, but may also abandon him; a mother may aid her daughter in getting a husband or may compete for her daughter's husband; a son may look out for his mother or . . . be indifferent to her fate' (Mirsky 1937: 63). The society was characterized by a minimal kinship structure and marriage meant little; instead, it was 'deeply rooted in economic necessity' (Mirsky 1937: 66), although women in this male-dominated community also had a role as sex partners. This condition explains the competition for women, primarily as economic partners, because the satisfaction of sexual needs could be met by the game called 'putting out the lamp', or by exchanging women, purchasing a wife from her father, or by an unmarried man trying to steal another man's wife (Mirsky 1937: 62). A man could leave his woman, even during pregnancy, because she was seen as 'a bad housekeeper' or because she 'eats too much' (Mirsky 1937: 67). An Inuit man could treat his woman as he wished, ranging from 'caressing to beating and stabbing, from devotion to desertion' (Mirsky 1937: 62). Women could also leave 'their' men, and marriages are 'as varied as people' (Mirsky 1937: 68), pointing at the lack of both formal and informal institutions and the concomitant uncertainty that people faced.

In some tribes, female babies were frequently killed unless they were already promised to someone at birth. This led to a shortage of women (Smith-Birket 1948: 181). The competition for women often ended in quarrels. This was the case because their social life was largely unregulated. With only one institution—that being, essentially, that there were no rules—no one would directly interfere in the activities of those involved. This condition could lead to 'murder, to revenge by theft, or to a drum match', the latter being not much different from contemporary rap-battles (Lee 2009). These drum-matches can be seen as an institutionalized way of settling conflicts, reducing the uncertainty of the outcome of quarrels. Participants mock one another with music and text in front of onlookers, who then in a sense call the winner. Such 'matches' could go on for years (Mirsky 1937: 68–69), but more frequently the initial conflict, which may have been hostile, was resolved and turned into a social event.

In the Inuit society described, kinship 'does not demand any set patterns of behavior' and every man 'behaves toward other people as he wants to', meaning that social life was characterized by 'suspicion and slander' (Mirsky 1937: 65). Not only were there few institutions, but neither was there organized leadership, although an 'outstanding hunter' or a 'skilful drummer' was usually recognized (Mirsky 1937: 62). But who was considered to be a good hunter might differ between seasons—simply because of luck—and so did the status of individuals in society; past records mattered little. This means that few institutionalized forms of social structure or authority appeared, and uncertainty also about social position prevailed.

Access to food represented a substantial source of uncertainty for the Inuits. Cooperation was limited to certain types of hunting, but without specialization in the tasks of the hunting party. Whatever a man assembled for the winter, he brought to the settlement, which could be 'thought of as a federation of free and sovereign states, composed of members who can join or not at will, and are free to leave at any time . . . retaining a maximum of their individual rights' (Mirsky 1937: 56–57). The division of labour was clear; cooking was done by the women individually, using their individually owned utensils. Only when supply was limited did people collaborate more intensely (Mirsky 1937: 58). Because food could be kept only for a few months, a situation of severe ice conditions could lead to famine. To survive, they first ate the dogs, and then 'the living are forced to eat the dead', including their dead children (Mirsky 1937: 72). Their view of life was also primed by the directness of death and the necessity of being able to contribute. A very sick person who was 'considered moribund will be thrown into the sea to avoid the necessity of handling his dead body', and old people were told that they were 'of no use' and they 'might as well be dead' (Mirsky 1937: 72). Orphans could be killed or abandoned. Moreover, 'no sickly child, or one without a mother, is allowed to live' (Mirsky 1937: 75).

This account, of course, does not give the full picture of Ammassalik life. The most important message, however, is that a person's life, be it a woman, man, or child, depends on the environment and the doings of one or several other individuals. Destiny in this social setting, which 'allows such free uncensored expression to the individual', essentially 'varies from individual to individual, from case to case' (Mirsky 1937: 73). It was a truly individualistic society in which the strong could 'take what he wants without fear . . . without being checked or ostracized' (Mirsky 1937: 73). This was a 'community with a minimum [in relation to other known communities] of social forms, and there are no effective social sanctions to regulate murder, competition for women, or economic activities' (Mirsky 1937: 77).

This long and detailed negative description of a community that is less organized and has fewer institutions than anthropologists have generally observed in traditional societies serves two purposes. The first is to show that life for many people around the world has always been very varied. The stock of knowledge on which we can draw to create a life with, in many respects, fewer uncertainties than those 'natural' to the Ammassalik is enormous. The substantial uncertainty the Ammassalik faced, in terms of both the environment and social life, however, is not radically different from what other classic texts in anthropology have reported, as noted in a recent review text (Alaszewski 2015). It is also clear that lack of knowledge and proper institutions results in much uncertainty, not only about 'economic matters' but ultimately about the essential qualities of life and death. This suggests that social institutions provide a basis also for the development of more elaborated knowledge about the world and our coping with it. The second point is that the cruelty and high degree of uncertainty they faced is far from the everyday life that many of us experience today. The lack of laws and associated law enforcement—that is, formal institutions—is one issue, but more important is the lack of proper informal institutions that can diminish uncertainty: simple things such as the virtues of cooperation, respect for 'property', and even for other peoples' lives.

The Inuit can be discussed within the framework of what Norbert Elias saw as the historical development of institutions, although he focused on Western Europe. Human beings were originally caught in a vicious circle because they 'had little control over natural forces on which they were dependent for their survival. Wholly dependent on phenomena whose course they could neither foresee nor influence to any considerable extent, they lived in extreme insecurity, and being most vulnerable and insecure' (Elias 1956: 231). This insecurity is essentially covered by the notion of uncertainty as it is used here. Only later when men were 'increasing their foresight' could they begin to master nature and control it using 'public standards' that were the same ones that could be used to manipulate nature (Elias 1956: 230–231), and in this way reduce uncertainty. If knowledge, as commonly presented, used to be framed in religious terms and was practice-oriented, contemporary social life is characterized more by scientific knowledge (Alaszewski 2015: 218), which is expressed as states of the world.

But the gradual security gained by formal institutions—that is, laws and a predictable application of these laws, as well as knowledge of nature and social life—also makes humans interact more, and we are becoming increasingly dependent on one another, also globally. Consequently, other forms of uncertainty have emerged that differ from those which were the most pressing in the past (Elias 1956: 232–233). The works of Norbert Elias (1969a,b) on the historical development of civilized society illustrates the general point well, namely that ideas that at first were less 'controversial', such as assaulting or even murdering others, gradually became more or less *taboo*, a development which obviously reduced uncertainty for people. The analysis of processes through which outcomes arise cannot be just a process of rational decisions to reduce uncertainty; if so, we should, across time and space, see a much higher similarity in societal development and outcomes. Path dependency (Djelic and Quack 2007), which is a term that covers how the historically established layers of informal and formal institutions form decisions also about the future, effects future-oriented decisions.

The growth of nation states in their various forms, such as welfare states (Esping-Andersen 1990), as well as the emergence of private insurance companies (Knight 1921: 213, 245), have of course had a profound impact on people and organizations through the possibilities they make available for coping with the world (Lehtonen and Van Hoyweghen 2014). Obviously, some risks and uncertainties have been reduced or even eliminated. Many of the institutions that are taken for granted today, such as social rights, correlate with organizations that maintain these rights. More generally, states of the world, knowledge of both facts and institutions, can reduce uncertainty and increase predictability and ultimately wealth and well-being. Let us now take a closer look at institutions to gain insights into what they are, and thereby understand how they may be used to reduce uncertainty.

THE LIFEWORLD OF INFORMAL INSTITUTIONS

It is at the level of practice that one should look for the uncertainty reduction of informal institutions. Informal institutions are not something that exist outside of human beings. We are partly constituted by informal institutions, and this is one reason why they are so profound, and why they also—with a high degree of predictability—can reduce uncertainty in the public realm. The phenomenological school analyses the notion of informal institutions in relation to the taken-for-granted life-world. Berger and Luckman's (1991) approach to institutions is an early attempt to combine phenomenological ideas about the life-world—a notion taken from Schütz and Husserl (2008, 1992)—and knowledge. This life-world (Husserl 1992: 51, 112–113, 115, 126ff) is pre-given and taken for granted, and refers to human beings' pre-scientific and practice-oriented experience.[6] It may be institutionalized or not, and in it, 'things', including institutions, may be in the foreground or background, reflecting what is, for the time being, relevant. This taken-for-grantedness is central to understanding the conditions of uncertainty reduction.

An **informal institution**, to offer a definition, is taken for granted, the result of mutual adjustment; is maintained by sanctions and offers predictability of behaviour. Informal institutions become taken for granted in public because they grow over time in a process of mutual adjustment by actors. Informal institutions provide regularity of behaviour and thus predictability of actions. Thereby they reduce uncertainty. What is unique about informal institutions is that they gradually become taken for granted and thus internalized. Hence, we simply do things because of what we are and want to be, and this makes our behaviour predictable in a way that reduces uncertainty about what we will do in particular situations. Institutions are upheld by sanctions, which may be either positive or negative.

Informal institutions cover a broad range of social activities. They include behavioural scripts, such as how to do things, practices, rules, values, habits, laws, and the like, as described by Goffman (e.g., 1967, 1972). But also ideas, concepts, and theories, including social sciences, can become institutions, for example, as a result of performativity.[7] Institutions structure situations by prescribing behaviour, such as when one is buying at an auction, acting as a stock trader (Hasselström 2003) or a trader of diamonds (Bernstein 1992), or greeting another person (Weber 1978b: 34). Thus, because there are established ways of doing things, uncertainty of how to do these things is reduced. Other examples include the use of language, or the accepted 'mediators' that an actor can use to do science (Latour 1999: 307). When something becomes a habit, it reduces uncertainty, facilitates action, and becomes a foundation that is 'certain' on which additional actions can be built.

What are here called informal institutions are part of what we know— both explicit and codified, and implicit and non-codified knowledge at a pre-theoretical level. Berger and Luckmann say: 'It is the sum total of "what everybody knows" about a social world, an assemblage of maxims, morals, proverbial nuggets of wisdom, values and beliefs, myths, and so forth . . . [and] every institution has a body of transmitted recipe knowledge, that is, knowledge that supplies the institutionally appropriate rules of conduct' (Berger and Luckmann 1991: 83). Informal institutions are public, a characteristic Berger and Luckmann refer to as 'objectivity' (1991). According to Schütz, what is taken for granted is a form of knowledge that is a 'highly socialized structure', by which he means what is 'taken for granted not only by *me* but by *us*, by "everyone" (meaning "every one who belongs to us")' (Schütz 1962: 75). Thus the 'range' of an informal institution differs in accordance with how many of 'us' there are. The consequence is that different 'opposing' informal institutions may exist at the same time in different groups; clashes between groups can be the reason for or result in conflicts of institutions, such as conflicting moral values. It should be clear by now that informal institutions are public by definition. They are also widespread and relatively stable over time. They are part of the publicly available social infrastructure that can be used by many to reduce uncertainty.

Although 'institution' is a broad concept, it is far from being all-encompassing, because then it would be useless. By definition, anything not taken for granted, anything that is an individualized equivalent of institutions, such as a specific way of saying 'hello', is not an institution. Temporality also puts strong restrictions on institutionalization; things that change rapidly cannot be institutionalized, for example fashion, because something cannot immediately be taken for granted.[8] Informal institutions result from processes in which actors mutually adjust to one another.

Informal institutions are clearly man-made, but not by design, and 'show that some overall pattern of design, which one would have thought had to be produced by an individual's or group's successful attempt to realize the pattern, instead was produced and maintained by a process that in no way had the overall pattern or design in mind' (Nozick 1974: 18). In many cases it is neither necessary nor possible to be aware of, or make explicit, which institutions are used. Institutions operate by virtue of their functioning, in which oneself and others take them for granted in everyday practice, without any prior rational operation or calculation. This also means that informal institutions do not have to be rational, or be answers to specific problems, which is to say that their existence cannot be explained by a functionalist approach.

INSTITUTIONALIZATION

If informal institutions reduce uncertainty because people learn how to behave (Fourcade and Johns 2020: 806), a central issue is to clarify how actors come to use these institutions and how they come about—in other words, institutionalization. Berger and Luckmann say about informal institutions: 'they are built up in the course of a shared history. They cannot be built instantaneously . . . . It is impossible to understand an institution adequately without an understanding of the historical process in which it was produced' (1991: 72).

Institutionalization is the process by which something becomes taken for granted by several actors. Institutions emerge out of social interaction, but if a habit is established between two actors, it only becomes institutionalized when this habit is taken over by a third actor, such as when children take over behaviour from parents, or when newly hired staff adjust their dress code and jargon to the culture of their new workplace. The public dimension is typically a condition for something to become an informal institution in the first sense—by means of the mutual adjustment process of institutionalization (Berger and Luckmann 1991; Gehlen 1986: 97). Once an institution exists, actors may continuously be socialized by a learning process into its practices in situations, so that they internalize it. A result is that they become taken for granted by several people, which means that informal institutions are typically public (Münch 1982). In this process, sanctions are crucial for directing actors and actions. The practice of virtues—which are defined as being rewarding in themselves—is a good example of internalization. As institutionalized, they are not separated from the individual: there is no Man *and* his internalized institutions— Man is constituted by informal institutions (Heidegger 2001). When we trust people, an activity that indeed corresponds to uncertainty reduction, we rely on them, in fact, having internalized some informal institutions. Though both organizations and individuals can be said to act, a difference between persons and organizations is that socialization and internalization are concepts that refer only to persons, not to organizations.

HOW INFORMAL INSTITUTIONS SHOW UP

Informal institutions do not normally come to our attention or 'show up' for us, which is explained by the fact that they are taken for granted 'until further notice' (Schütz 1962: 74). They are practised by actors who maintain them. Because they are taken for granted, essentially followed and thus self-reinforcing, it is by their non-activity that they are called to our attention in a 'negative' way (Heidegger 2001: 72–76; 1979). Informal institutions show up (or stand out as such) when they are used in an incorrect way, when they are not used, or when they are used but do not work (malfunction), as shown in studies (Garfinkel 1967).[9] Consequently, as soon as an institution ceases to work, it leads to uncertainty. A concrete example is the sudden break with the communist conditions when many things that has been taken for granted within this system simply dissolved (Bonss 1995: 23).

Failure to know about the correct behaviour of informal institutions may lead to sanctions. When we are uncertain of an informal institution, or simply unaware of it, it is not possible to predict the outcome at all, because one neither knows how to behave nor how others will behave.[10] There are also cases in which informal institutions show up because they fail to function. Thus, an informal institution may malfunction in some cases (cf. Garfinkel 1967). To these three negative ways of acknowledging informal institutions, one should add the active, or positive, way of showing up, namely in reflection, typically triggered by new experiences—such as being abroad and seeing how things are done 'differently'.[11] Over time, and due to scientific work, we have become aware of many informal institutions, not least to the theory-development of institutions in phenomenology and other traditions.

Given that informal institutions as ideal types are taken for granted, they are not really acknowledged. In reality they are never completely taken for granted, and when informal institutions are acknowledged, it suggests that two different paths are open: they may be reinforced, or they may be questioned. Reinforcement is usually a consequence of actors following sanctions, but if institutions are questioned, they may change. Put differently, a certain behaviour that deviates from what is 'prescribed' by the sanction may either lead to sanctions, or actors may try to cope with a situation in a pragmatic way. Sanctions are the default mode for institutions, although change is possible. These two possible paths are discussed below.

Sanctions

Sanctions preserve informal institutions, either by praising correct behaviour in accordance with the institution or by criticizing behaviour that is not in accordance with it. Sanctions can thus be positive or negative—but in either case they contribute to regularity of behaviour, and in fact to establishing and maintaining an informal institution, such as a certain way of buying properties with expected behaviour of the different actors.[12] Sanctions, and the threat of sanctions, lead to stability of behaviour and the expectation of certain behaviour that reduces uncertainty both for oneself and others. Sanctions may be implemented by a third party, and it may be easier to notice them in the behaviour of others. Children, who are yet not entirely socialized human beings, frequently make us aware of informal institutions; raising children clearly shows how much of social interaction and coordination rest on institutions, as they often have to be reminded about the do's and don'ts. Sanctions can also appear as shame or regret in the user if the informal institution is internalized. Hence, although sanctions due to deviance may be imposed by third parties, self-correction is the efficient way of upholding institutions.[13] Sanctions contribute to certainty because one not only knows what ought to happen when one acts in accordance with an institution, but also what may happen if one does not.

Change

Institutions are reinforced by people using them. The notion of institution, almost regardless of who is using it, is associated with stability, non-change and order, all of which are central to creating certainty. Much of this stability is the result of institutionalization. Above, it was mentioned that clashes between groups may result in changes in an institution. Given that institutions are grown, they are never fixed; instead, they continue to exist, and some ongoing change is already implicit. To account for this, the notion of incremental change of institutions is sometimes used (Streeck and Thelen 2005). If informal institutions are institutionalized by many, and are stable, we would not expect swift changes. But as a consequence of change, uncertainty increases.

In the existing literature there are plenty of attempts to discuss change of institutions, many of which seem to imply that the notion of institution, in effect, is a decided order. Notions such as institutional entrepreneurship (Garud et al. 2007), institutional work (Lawrence et al. 2011), and institutional logic (Thornton and Ocasio 2008: 99) point in the direction of decision-making.[14] Others look more at what strategies actors use that may lead to change within a given field (Möllering and Müller-Seitz 2018).

Heidegger and the convention school (Boltanski and Thévenot 2006; Diaz-Bone 2015) agree that institutions show up primarily in a negative way. If an institution shows up only once, and with limited consequences, the institution in question is not likely to be questioned or to change. But if the consequences are severe and frequent, it may initiate a process of de-institutionalization, by which actors are made aware of the 'institution' and called into question on a variety of grounds—which may lead to its disassociation from sanctions and ultimately to a situation in which the 'institution' is no longer taken for granted. This, *ceteris paribus*, leads to increased uncertainty.

Institutions may also simply fade away, almost without notice if no one implements sanctions. This may mean that we no longer speak of what used to be an institution. To attempt to outline the conditions of institutional change—so far as it is even possible due to its situation-contingent character—is beyond the scope of this study. Here it suffices to say that, although institutions are stable, they are not permanent; old institutions disappear or change, and new ones are established.

HOW DO INSTITUTIONS REDUCE UNCERTAINTY?

Some of the most profound states of the world are informal institutions. There is agreement that informal institutions reduce uncertainty (Emmenegger 2021: 614); here it is argued that they are taken for granted, and they offer certainty because we know how to behave and act in relation to them, and we can also predict how others will act. To many, the role of informal institutions in reducing uncertainty may be self-evident. But let me, before concluding this chapter, give a few empirical examples to show the centrality of institutions in practice—and I start with the most profound aspect that reduces uncertainty, namely trust.

If there is one institution that deserves to be called the 'deepest', trust might be the best candidate. Interpersonal trust is the root of uncertainty reduction, upon which also generalized trust rests. Trust cannot be decided but grows out of human interaction; one cannot decide that people *must* trust one another. Arendt writes: 'The remedy for unpredictability, for the chaotic uncertainty of the future, is contained in the faculty to make and keep promises' (1988: 237). If one cannot keep promises, to behave as one should and to be reliable, there can be no trust, and unpredictability of human action will result in permanent uncertainty. Actors, to recall, are 'always already' in the world, and thus some type of trust is almost always already there.

Trust and many other institutions exist as result of grown process and come to be taken for granted. Many practices, too, become taken for granted. Greeting is a good example: the way people shake hands, cheek kissing, or whatever local practices are used, are taken for granted until further notice. A pandemic, for example, puts such practices into question. States of the world offer certainty, not primarily because they are intrinsically 'true' or because they are 'efficient' (cf. North 1990: 6), but because they are relatively entrenched, or rooted in one another, especially when states of the world are taken-for-granted institutions.

Values are examples of deeply entrenched institutions that may show up only when they come in conflict with other values. Parsons speaks of informal institutions as more or less 'firmly' institutionalized (1977: 307). They are, put differently, part of the bedrock of other institutions (cf. Quine and Ullian 1970:85), and consequently, more difficult to change.

Moreover, the very institution we use to communicate, language (Berger and Luckmann 1991: 83), is not only taken for granted but also the foremost tool for institution-building, a vehicle for storing and expressing other institutions (Heidegger 1997: 187; Schütz 1982; 130), the dominant vehicle (Heidegger 1997: 182) for information and knowledge, and ultimately for what we are and how we behave.[15] John Searle expresses this idea as follows: 'in order to state the fact that the earth is 93 million miles from the sun, we need the institution of language, including the convention of measuring distances in miles' (Searle 2005: 3).[16]

Most interactions are performed in a way that we do not have to think too much about, because one behaves as one does, or should do, and so do others. When actors in their practice resort to the same, or similar, institutions—for example, by valuing the same things, adhering to the same norms—our behaviour, interaction, and coordination are facilitated. A consequence of institutionalization is that our expectations are likely to be satisfied (Luhmann 1991: 122), which increases our certainty (Luhmann 1987: 417–419). If people and organizations behave as expected, interaction runs smoothly, diminishing the uncertainty and the cost of figuring out what one should do and what others will do.

Another way to analyse the role of informal institutions is to see how well they go with the introduction of formal institutions, such as rules or laws that are decided. They to some extent failed implementation of formal Western institutions in former communist states in Europe indicates that the societal bedrock of informal institutions matters. Put differently, there must be a fit between formal institutions and the informal institutions on which these formal institutions depend. Moreover, there is evidence that the degree of ancestral individualism correlates positively with annual earnings across second-generation US immigrants (Hansen 2013). In other words, the institutional values actors hold matter for their incomes, also for second-generation immigrants. This is, of course, even more obvious for first-generation immigrants, whose success in the new country depends, among other things, on the institutions—including values, attitudes, and practices—they bring with them, and how well these 'fit' with their new country.

Institutions are, as such, neither good nor bad, but researchers have found many examples of cases showing the positive role they may have for the economy and society. Firms will grow or not depending on what institutions exist, and above all, on the interaction between informal institutions and formal institutions (Krasniqi and Desai 2016). The interplay is clearly shown in Putnam's (1993) analysis of civic virtues and social capital, as explanations of why the same political (decided) institutions work better in northern than in southern Italy. Thus, many informal institutions such as corruption, but also formal institutions of a bureaucratic nature, may impede economic prosperity, although they may nonetheless increase certainty. It may be certain that one has to resort to bribes to get what is needed, but most likely it is not economically efficient. In some political science and political sociology literature, especially in relation to the debates on the obstacles that characterize democratization processes in developing countries, informal institutions represent problems and obstacles (Lauth 2000; Helmke and Levitsky 2006). In this literature, clientelism, neopatrimonialism, patronage, or even corruption, are examples of informal institutions that, though reducing some uncertainties, also create others. Moreover, these informal institutions typically collide or compete with the formal ones. The point is that a single institution may reduce uncertainty if it increases actors' chances of achieving their ends. In many instances, the overall effect of an institution is less clear; the increased complexity may certainly lead to increased uncertainty, especially if the institutions are in conflict.

CONCLUSION

Informal institutions, as states of the world, bring certainty. This chapter has analysed what informal institutions are and how they come about, and discussed how they reduce uncertainty. Informal institutions are the social bedrock, and as such crucial for enabling uncertainty reduction in public. Because institutions are internalized and taken for granted, they are part of us—or put differently, our existences cannot be understood without them, and we could not understand the world without them. Heidegger is more explicit than any sociologist on how institutions are part of human being, which does not mean that institutions have agency (Douglas 1986: 9–19), or that actors are dupes, or that institutions do not change.

As human beings (Heidegger uses the term *Dasein* ['being there'] because he wants to avoid the misleading subject/object schema) we are 'always already' in the world (2001). Institutions are institutionalized knowledge that is 'publicly' taken for granted. As such, informal institutions reduce our own uncertainty in a direct way, because we know how to behave and act in relation to them, but our uncertainty is also diminished because we can predict that others will also act in line with an institution. This direct uncertainty reduction by informal institutions is profound, so profound that we may not even be aware of it and unable to analyse it in all its dimensions. Institutions are rooted, or 'institutionalized'. This leads us to the following conclusions: 'The more conduct is institutionalized, the more predictable and thus more controlled it becomes' (Berger and Luckmann 1991: 80).

Informal institutions represent a 'grown' order, that is, a state that can be reached only over time and, by definition, presumes that actors are not constantly aware of them, do not cognitively process them, nor do they reflect on them. If they do, they are not institutionalized yet. Institutions are to some extent forgotten, and operate in this sense passively. They are maintained, above all, by practices and sanctions, often at a low cost given the fact they are taken for granted because of internalization. But as we have seen, there are several ways in which institutions show up. That an institution shows up may also lead to changes in the existing, and the development of new, institutions.

The definition of informal institutions, moreover, and the analysis carried out in this chapter have several consequences. Informal institutions, by definition, lead to stability and order. Informal institutions such as trust (Möllering 2006) are profoundly important for formal institutions like contracts. It was shown in the discussion of the Ammassalik community what lack of trust may lead to. Informal institutions also increase the likelihood that actors can act in such a way that they achieve their ends more often than if the institutions did not exist. But although institutions correlate with reduction of certainty, informal institutions are not inherently correlated with security, efficiency, or truth. In other words, the practices of ancient Rome, such as gladiatorial contests and naumachia (staged naval combat), rest on institutionalized values that do not entail security for those involved. Moreover, the institutions of Inuit society lay bare the limited value of human life. An institution such as potlatch cannot, in economic terms, be seen as 'efficient'. Under the practice of potlach 'the most valuable copper objects are broken and thrown into the water, in order to crush and to 'flatten' one's rival. In this way one not only promotes oneself, but also one's family, up the social scale' (Mauss 2002: 47–48). There are, in addition, many examples of institutionalized rules of thumb that people make use of, but which may be incorrect (Kahneman and Tversky 1979; Tversky and Kahneman 1974). Previously, a large majority considered the world to be flat, and many held the view that it rained if they danced. These are examples of older institutions that later were seen as false, in the light of new findings. This underlines that institutions do not have to be 'correct', 'true', efficient, or rational.

Another consequence is that if the notion of institution is taken seriously, it is not possible to speak of an action theory that assumes actors constantly make calculations and deliberations and do a cost-benefit analysis of whether to 'use' an informal institution or not. In other words, the notion of an 'ego' who somehow chooses institutions, and who can freely reflect on all institutions and rationally choose some to follow or support, is a fiction. There are also influential thinkers, such as Mancur Olsen (1971), who operate with quite unrealistic starting assumptions and thereby face the risk of engaging with pseudo-problems: that is, these are problems only insofar as actors are assumed to be egoistic and rational. More fundamentally, the idea that actors develop institutions in a rational fashion to overcome the Hobbesian problem of (dis)order should not be the starting point. In contrast, the observation of the variation of institutional set-ups in different societies suggests that there is one rational foundation of institutions: they emerge in a social process primed by actors who do not just choose institutions, but who are institutions.

Due to the aforementioned inseparability between man and institutions, calculations and deliberation do take place, but never in a 'pre-institutional' context, because man 'is' institutions, and some institutions are always involved when people ponder about other institutions or assess alternative actions. Many agree that more realistic assumptions about informal institutions should be the starting point of any analysis. One central point of this chapter is to say that, although egoism and rationality of course are part and parcel of human interaction, they must also be seen in relation to taken-for-grantedness. Consequently, the abstract problem of double contingency mentioned in the introduction is then, to some extent, a pseudo-problem produced by theories that assume egos.

CHAPTER 3

Formal Institutions

Formal institutions are in many ways similar to informal institutions; both guide actors making decisions, and because of their increased certainty of outcomes, they reduce uncertainty. Informal institutions are the result of a process of mutual adjustment among actors that results in order, and formal institutions follow from decisions for others. While both forms are maintained by sanctions, formal institutions are backed by an organization that has the power to implement sanctions. This chapter analyses attempts to use and to produce rules by means of decisions, or what North (1990) calls formal institutions. North says clearly that, 'throughout history, institutions have been devised by human beings to create order and reduce uncertainty in exchange' (1991a: 97), voicing his somewhat rationalistic view of institutions as the result of decisions. North nurtures the idea that formal contracts backed by enforceable law are crucial for reducing uncertainty and enabling trade, leading to increased wealth (North 1984).

Formal institutions, as informal institutions, provide predictability for actors and can thus reduce uncertainty. In its purest form, a formal institution is clear enough to provide certainty to actors who want to act. A law is a concrete example: it is clear what a given law is about, what to do, and what others can be expected to do. There are also foreseeable sanctions, and there may even be known (that is, calculable) risks attached to alternatives. In ordered societies it means that actors can know how to act, but it also becomes predictable how others will act. The uncertainty is thereby reduced by the existence of these states of the world. Money is another example of a formal institution, which guides actors and can be used to calculate, as a deposit of wealth and, of course, for trading (Dodd 2005). It is

Uncertainty. Patrik Aspers, Oxford University Press. © Oxford University Press 2024.
DOI: 10.1093/oso/9780197752753.003.0003

protected by a set of rules, and when speaking of currencies in particular, formal institutions are even more strongly present (Kirzner 1960) than when one speaks of money.

In this chapter, after presenting the central concept of formal institutions, I develop the idea of decisions on general principles, by analysing how certainty of what is right, wrong, good, or bad is established as a result of decisions for others. Laws and standards are discussed as examples of uncertainty reduction.

DECISIONS FOR OTHERS IN PUBLIC

Formal institutions create states of the world that reduce uncertainty, though this does not have to be the explicit aim of a decision. **Formal institutions** can be defined as the result of decisions for others about principles that are supported by explicitly stated and enforceable sanctions, which leads to predictability of behaviour. Decisions for others can be made with the ambition of affecting 'only' those within an organization or—which is the focus here—for the public. The principles can be about behaviour, such as rules, laws, and standards that inform us what to do or not do, or what is right or wrong, or what quality is high or low. These principles are explicit and made 'public' so that people can follow them. To be implemented, decisions about rules must be made with authority. Attempts to decide on rules, however, do not have to be legitimate; they can be made by a dictator who is not legitimate, or a very legitimate parliament. Weber refers to three forms of legitimate authority (1922: 124–148): rational, traditional, and charismatic. These forms reflect ways in which 'users' voluntarily accept decisions made by an authority that can enforce sanctions.[1]

In contrast to informal institutions, formal setting of rules is a rather straightforward activity based on decisions for others. Many different interests may be behind the attempt to decide for others, an issue largely beyond the scope of this study. But it is clear that these reasons and the history leading up to the decisions may include grown or evolutionary processes (Murmann 2003). A formal institution prescribes what to do, or how something is to be done, and it usually means that it exists for an extended period and is made to be public. A formal institution may be applied to those who voluntarily have agreed to accept it, such as those trading at a marketplace (like a stock exchange). The application may be in a specific domain, determined by the decision-maker. Formal institutions may also be applied to everyone, including those who are against the decision. Hence, it may apply to all citizens and be enforced across several domains, as is the case with national laws.

Second, in contrast to informal institutions, which have evolved historically and are often latent and difficult to change, formal institutions 'may change overnight as the result of political or judicial decision' (North 1990: 6). A third factor seems to separate grown and formal institutions, namely values. Values, being an informal institution, cannot be decided for others. What people think and like cannot be changed with a decision by others, although expressions and behaviour that reflect certain values can be forbidden. These fundamental differences are, in my view, reasons for making a clear distinction and to speak of informal (grown) institutions and of formal (decided) institutions. The issue of values is here key, to which I will return in Part II.

To clarify how we come to have formal institutions I turn to organization theory, because 'organization . . . can create predictability and facilitate interaction among individuals or organizations' (Ahrne and Brunsson 2019: 5). It is primarily in the form of organizations that the authority to make decision for others can be observed, but a clan, 'as an agency of blood revenge and prosecution of feuds' (Weber 1978b: 35) may also have agency to maintain rules. By analysing formal institution-setting within organizations, it is possible to discuss attempts to set rules also in other cases when decisions are made for those outside an organization, or when there is no organization with resources to support its decisions. In these cases, there may be little or no formal hierarchy. An **organization**, such as the state, a company, or an NGO, can be defined as a decision-making identity with a goal, having a structure, collective resources, and a culture, and constituted by five elements: membership, hierarchy, rules, control, and sanctions (cf. Ahrne and Brunsson 2005). The notion of culture refers to informal institutions, whereas rules are decided.

Organizations can reduce uncertainty in two ways. The focus in this book is on decisions for others that generate formal institutions, which reduce the uncertainty for others since it can be used as a means when making decisions. In a second and indirect way, as suggested by Knight (1921: 347) organizations reduce uncertainty essentially by absorbing uncertainty. This is also the message of March and Simon (1958) and Luhmann (2000). For example, uncertainty is managed, according to the Carnegie School, 'through the creation of organizational routines' (Powell and Rerup 2017: 315). There are very many organizations, and to be a member may reduce the uncertainty because one can foresee what will happen if things go bad. Voluntary insurances issued by organizations, which may be owned by its members and holders of the insurances, is one example that shares the risk among many. Such insurances may also be mandatory, such as when everyone who has a car is required to have an insurance that at least covers the costs that the driver causes for others. The welfare state can be seen as one large organization, albeit the outcome of decisions, and it is only in a certain way a means of uncertainty reduction. This is so because once it is implemented, it is a mandatory condition of all actions that it exists, and its complexity makes it hard to install. Though to be a forced member of a state and its welfare system may indeed reduce uncertainty, and though its certainty and safety net may increase the willingness to take some 'risks', the focus here is not on the complex issue of the potential uncertainty reduction of welfare states, since all formal institutions reduce uncertainty. The issue of the advantages and disadvantages with different political economic systems is not only to be decided in relation to which system reduces uncertainty, but also, to the extent they are democratic, which systems allow freedom and make the economy and social life prosperous. The focus here is on organizations, and particularly on the decisions about formal institutions that they make that can be used by others when they make decisions.

The most characteristic trait of organizations is decision-making (Luhmann 2000; March and Simon 1958). A decision may be made by the chief of a tribe, a CEO, a king, a head of department, or by a governing body deemed legitimate to make decisions for a group of 'others'. There is often an expectancy on the part of others that a decision is to be made (Luhmann 1987: 400). Here the focus is on those affected by others' decisions (e.g., Brunsson 2007). All decisions to affect others are attempts to accomplish something chosen (Luhmann 1987: 399). Any decision made implies that there were other alternatives, even if only the option of not making the decision (Luhmann 2000: 184–186). Ahrne and Brunsson, following Luhmann, claim that 'decisions dramatize uncertainty', meaning that decisions for others made by organizations are merely 'attempts at creating certainty, at establishing what the future will look like'. However, they say, decisions also create 'uncertainty by demonstrating that because the future has been chosen, it could be different' (Ahrne and Brunsson 2011: 90). Importantly, they continue, the future is also created for others, and decisions obviously have consequences.[2] A decision is an attempt to determine something to be followed by several others, but there is no guaranteed success (e.g., Brunsson 2007), especially if the decision-maker lacks power to implement sanctions.

Decisions made for others by one actor who has authority to determine good and bad is one obvious way of reducing uncertainty, at least until the next decision is made. Rules are social, and organizations can determine rules for its members, but individuals cannot make decisions on 'private rules' (Wittgenstein 2009). Put differently, organizations cannot enact informal institutions, and persons cannot make decisions about rules for themselves. Most of the points made about the public—that is, for a larger group than just members of a specific organization—also apply to uncertainty reduction within an organization. Decisions by an organization for its members on formal institutions, such as rules that clarify how to behave, how one get promotion, and what one is allowed to do as a member of an organization, bring order within the organisation.[3]

Decisions by organizations that reduce uncertainty in markets is one example of how an organization is always a double-edged sword: decisions reduce uncertainty, but the power to decide is also a source of concern for the market participants subject to the decision, because new decisions can always be made. Dobeson (2016) shows how the digitalization of the marketplace for fish in Iceland means that buyers know much about fishing conditions, as well as about the fishermen, by being able to follow the boats online. By having this knowledge they can cope better with quality uncertainty (pp. 200–203). But the regulation of the Icelandic fishing economy, and market regulations in particular, means that actors face the uncertainty of 'changing rules and regulations' (p. 159).

Decisions can reduce uncertainty, but the point is not that a 'correct' or 'moral' decision has to be made for uncertainty to be reduced; the point is that the decision can be used for guidance by actors trying to diminish their uncertainty because they know what to do, what not to do, what will happen if they do not adjust to the institution, and can assume also that others will comply. However much decisions may diminish uncertainty about the things considered, the same decision may disrupt other things, and consequently—seen in a wider context—increase uncertainty. Frequent and erratic decisions may hence increase uncertainty at a more global level. Leaders with the formal authority to decide, but who are deemed to be irrational or unpredictable, may cause further uncertainty by their behaviour. The uncertainty about decision-making is greater if there are few restrictions on what a decision-maker can make decisions about, and how decisions can be made. A strong constitution in a non-corrupt country is a good example of how even erratic decision-makers may be constrained, and this rests on a bed of informal institutions.

That formal institutions rest on the bedrock of the informal institutions discussed in Chapter 2 (cf. Durkheim [1895] 1984) is a central insight for anyone who tries to reduce uncertainty by making decisions about formal institutions. If a decision mimics, or codifies, an already existing informal institution, it is likely to be legitimate (Boltanski and Thévenot 2006). More concretely, a given formal institution—for example, a law that provides the infrastructure of markets—may be used by those in power to protect or to abuse traders' rights (Greif 2015: 79ff). The extent to which this is accomplished is largely due to the virtues, culture, and norms—the informal institutions—of those enacting the roles of power. It is, to take an example, not enough to install a set of formal institutions to achieve a certain end. The fact that Afghanistan fell apart within weeks after the withdrawal in 2021 of the United States—which had supported the country politically, economically, and militarily for 20 years, and had installed formal democratic institutions—points to the central role of informal institutions for bringing order and reducing uncertainty for people inside and outside a country. Virtues, norms, and values, as informal institutions that are states of the world, are the foundation of social life, and these play a central for the reduction of existential uncertainty. Thus, formal institutions also rest on the assumption that people, both those subject to the rule and those administering it, are trustworthy and behave in such a way that the formal institutions will be enacted.

Given that formal institutions are explicit and maintained by sanctions or the threat of them, they must not be taken for granted. Moreover, even if everyone involved agrees, no formal institution can come into being unless a decision for others is made, and without authority to back it up, we cannot speak of a formal institution. However, the relationship is not always one-directional between informal institutions and formal institutions. A formal institution, such as a law, may overnight make a taken-for-granted practice illegal. Examples of this are plentiful, including the decisions made by 'Islamic State' (ISIS), which for some time controlled territory in, above all, Syria, and those under its sway. By decision many practices, such listening to music were forbidden, and equally fas did ISISestablish new rules, such as forcing all women to wear a hijab. There is thus an intimate relation between formal institutions and informal institutions. However, whereas informal institutions grow slow and only slowly fade away, formal decision may have instant impact. Moreover, a formal institution can, over time, become taken for granted. In such a case the formal aspects—the decision and the sanction—may still be upheld, but if it has become taken for granted, it is maintained more like an informal institution, but one that has not grown out of mutual adjustment.

Formal institutions are enforced with sanctions, and we can speak of laws when coercion is externally guaranteed to make sure that actors comply (Weber 1922: 26–28, 398). The notion of the 'rule of law' combines two central terms of the present chapter and means that the law applies no matter who is in power (Scalia 1989). It is very clear that when actors consider which country to prospect for mineral deposits, uncertainty plays a major role. Countries have been ranked as more or less a 'low risk jurisdiction' (Olofsson 2020: 44) primarily because their rules are relatively easy-going, predictable, and stable. The costs are low, also when minerals are found, meaning that compared to some other countries, it is possible to make more accurate estimates and calculations. There are several types of rules that are applied and that lead to reduced uncertainty. Accounting rules are a clear example (Beckert 2016: 153–154).

SETTING LAWS

Law is perhaps the foremost—and probably the oldest—example of formal institutions. The system of laws is central if states and its citizens are to have order, avoid conflicts, and know how to behave. There is much discussion (Weber 1978b) on the central role law plays in establishing and maintaining order in politics and the economy. Also, sociologists have since the dawn of the discipline paid great attention to law, for example, Durkheim ([1895] 1984) and Weber (1922) (see also Swedberg (2003). The importance of law for reducing uncertainty in social life is the background to the more specific analysis below. Weber expresses this clearly when he says that what is important for 'profit making enterprises is . . . above all . . . the calculability of the tax load' (Weber 1978b: 200).

Laws reduce uncertainty by stating what is allowed, and what is not, by maintaining the expectation that sanctions will be imposed in the case of unlawful behaviour. Laws are examples of formal institutions upheld by authority, typically with legitimacy. They tend to be set in correspondence with customs, or what more generally speaking count as informal institutions. Decision-making is at the heart of the etymologies of words pertaining to law. In the German language, law is *Gesetz*. Etymologically, *Gesetz* is related to *setzen*, to sit or place.[4] In other words, it refers to an active choice, a form of decision.

Law, more specifically natural law, is defined as 'any criteria of right judgment in the matter of practice (conduct, action), any standard for assessing options for human conduct as good or bad, right or wrong, desirable or undesirable, decent or unworthy' (Finnis 2002: 1). This definition encapsulates the core of what is meant by a decision on general principles for others. By setting laws or standards, uncertainty is radically diminished already before adjudications, that is, before judges decide on cases (if it should go that far), because the correct behaviour has been spelled out to be used as guidance by actors. Laws that are set by decisions backed by power generate what I call 'states of the world'. Laws are public and, being general principles of what to do and not to do, apply to all. Given this, actors can orient their own behaviour, and equally importantly be quite certain that others will do the same, thereby reducing the uncertainty of their own decision-making.

Law-setting is much broader than criminal law. Decisions may be taken by national parliaments to establish a particular type of social security net—one that, say, supports people who, due to illness, accidents, old age, unemployment, and a whole range of other reasons, cannot, for a shorter or longer period, support themselves. Such social safety nets differ between countries, but they all reduce people's uncertainty. Thus, someone who invests money to start up a firm—which may turn out badly—can still be certain of some support from society. Private enterprise, too, relies on formal institutions that are profound, and enable people to act. Such systems tend to be tied to citizenship, and opt-outs are not possible, thereby reducing uncertainty (O'Malley 2008: 59–60, 70). Below, one specific law-setting process, the antitrust law in Germany, is analysed in more detail to convey a deeper understanding of what formal institutions are and how they may come about.

German Antitrust Laws

Here I use one law, Germany's Antitrust Law, to see how it reduces uncertainty for actors—ultimately, customers—but also to examine the process of how an economic institution that reduces uncertainty grows. The uncertainty is reduced, first, for firms, but also for customers who previously could not know whether they were subject to cartels—and higher prices—or not.[5]

Antitrust laws aim at preserving competition in markets by regulating activities that impair it to the detriment of actors, most notably consumers. One recent example is whether high-frequency trading takes place in a rigged marketplace (Lewis 2014). Instances of price fixing, mergers that reduce the number of competitors and thereby often competition, the creation of cartels, monopolies, or oligopolies, are yet other examples. It is known that firms do not aim to create perfectly competitive markets, but to make a profit. To achieve this end, creating niches by means of product development, branding, and patents, as well as monopolies and cartels, are different ways of controlling others and maintaining profits by limiting competition (Marshall 1920). Thus, this type of activity that reduces competition from the perspective of sellers, reduces the uncertainty to which they are exposed (Fligstein 1990), but it may increase uncertainty, and costs, for others. The uncertainty may increase, especially if this type of activity is common practice, because neither sellers nor buyers can trust institutions, and do not act on the assumption that others will fall in line.

Some of these activities and non-compliance are illegal, such as when a conglomerate of firms sets a fixed price that tampers with the free forces of supply and demand. Such practices are widely forbidden today, but that was not always the case historically. Quite the contrary, the development of market-organizing is subject to historical developments, often characterized by substantial changes of rules, and consequent changes in states of the world and the uncertainty that actors face. In what follows, one such case of institutional change is described using the example of the historical formation of German antitrust legislation. To this end, this depiction draws on the work of Quack and Djelic (2005), who discuss these processes in great detail. The reason for the detailed presentation is to show, in a concrete way, how the uncertainty actors face changes because of decisions.

Until the First World War, economic thinking in Germany was characterized by the assumption that cartels and other forms of price fixing were natural, or even signs of economic progress (Quack and Djelic 2005: 257).[6] By the end of the war, ideas from the United States converged with a desire to de-industrialize Germany, which, in turn, led to a considerable deconcentration of German industry.[7]

The overall aim of this reorganization was to implement an economic policy aimed at regulating market-manipulating behaviour (Quack and Djelic 2005: 259). To help this process, US officials organized visits by German delegations to the United States where they could familiarize themselves with the US legal framework and consult with antitrust experts (Quack and Djelic 2005: 259). Furthermore, the United States provided help with drafting these new policies.[8]

Despite some differences, the law was clearly modelled on the US Sherman Act (Quack and Djelic 2005: 261). To take one example, the *Bundeskriminalamt*, the German counterpart to the US Federal Bureau of Investigation, was given responsibility for enforcing competition regulations. At the same time, the law also contained features tailored to the German industrial landscape. For example, highly specialized cartels were tolerated that fostered medium- and middle-sized companies—a characteristic structural feature of the German economy—in their competition with much larger counterparts. Moreover, certain industries—such as agriculture, sea, and air transport—were initially excepted from antitrust law regulation (Quack and Djelic 2005: 261). Step by step, however, these exceptions to the general law were abolished under political pressure (Quack and Djelic 2005: 261). This tells us about the political struggle that different institutions may cause, and of which they are the result. However, the struggle per se, and decision-making per se, tend to increase uncertainty. Only when a decision has been made, and actors can rely on it to be enforced and thus have consequences, will it reduce uncertainty.[9]

The German antitrust law is a result of decisions made. In this sense an attempt was made to regulate markets to increase competition, which would, if enforced, shift some uncertainty from customers to sellers. However, uncertainty is ultimately something practical. This means that one must concentrate on how the law was applied to say something more about concrete situations and outcomes. Below follow some examples of the actual application of the laws regulating competition in Germany, zooming in on the legal framework laid down in the Act against Restraints on Competition (as presented by the Federal Ministry of Justice and Consumer Protection, or *Bundesministerium der Justiz und für Verbraucherschutz*). This law formulates the rules to which market actors must orient their actions in order to remain in compliance with antitrust laws. The original German version of the translated legal text can be found in the corresponding footnotes without further comments.

In its first paragraph, the law sets forth in its central statute that 'agreements between corporations, conventions of corporate networks and mutually adjusted behaviour aimed at prohibiting or circumscribing competition are forbidden'.[10] Building upon this basic definition, the law proceeds to give more specific definitions regarding its premises and scope. This includes provisions about market dominance (Chapter 2 of the law), the application of European competition law (Chapter 3), rules of competition (Chapter 4) and special rules for sectors exempted from the purview of the law (Chapter 5).[11] Further provisions concern, for example, compensation regulations (Chapter 6). The analysis here focuses on the linchpin of the law, the definition of market dominance, and subsequently elaborates on how the law is enforced. This is a practical example of how uncertainty is reduced because actors can make use of institutions to act and to predict how others will act; this can be shown by putting the organizational tools into play.

Market Dominance

To regulate the competitive behaviour of market participants, it is essential to state what exactly defines market-dominating behaviour and, more concretely, what behaviour is regulated by the law. In this regard, the law defines a corporation as market-dominating if:

a) there are no competitors;
b) there is no relevant competition;
c) the firm possesses an overwhelmingly strong market position in comparison to its competitors.[12]

In general, a corporation is defined as dominating a specific market if it has a market share more than 40 per cent. To determine a company's market share, usually its sales are measured as a percentage of the respective industry's total revenues. Thus, if a company's the sales account for more than 40 per cent of a sector's overall sales, the company in question is market-dominating. Obviously, when entering a market actors can orient themselves to these decided legal rules and definitions, as well as when merging, and as buyers to know what to expect on the part of the sellers.

Regulatory Bodies

Formal institutions require not only a decision, but also the maintenance of monitoring and sanctions. Article 48 of the law lays down as regulatory authorities responsible for enforcing German antitrust legislation, including ensuring that cartels do not form, primarily the Federal Cartel Office (*Bundeskartellamt*) and the Federal Ministry for Economic Affairs and Energy (*Bundesministerium für Wirtschaft und Energie*).[13] These separate regulatory bodies are meant to work together on infringement cases.[14] The principle of cooperation also holds when violations concern the European level, in which case a close exchange between the relevant authorities is required.[15]

The Federal Cartel Office *monitors* the situation and is obliged to publish a report on developments in its purview every second year.[16] The regulatory authorities are entitled to initiate proceedings—that is, to impose *sanctions* against potential violators of cartel law—of their own accord.[17]

From the perspective of this study, the case of German and European antitrust laws is an example of how, for some actors. certain market uncertainties are successively reduced by means of law, as an instance of formal institutions, at the expense of others. Just as states organize markets by taking decisions about the exact rules on property rights (Campbell und Lindberg 1990), they do so by establishing frameworks that define the legal limits of anti-competitive behaviour. The institutionalization of European antitrust regulation likewise points to the role of law as a driving force of (European) integration (Fligstein und Sweet 2002). At the same time, these regulations show the proximity of standards, laws, and political integration efforts. The closeness is most clearly to be seen in the focal case, standardization (of competition laws), which is the result of legal regulations due to pressure because of political integration (Europeanization). Today, antitrust processes represent one of the mainstays of the organization of the German as well as the European market.

Formal institutions, in the form of law, are perhaps the most distinct form of states of the world that reduce uncertainty. Actors can orient themselves to laws, and failure to follow the laws will be punished to a high degree if there is an organization like the state, or even the Mafia, that can guarantee this. This is to say that outcomes of activities are predictable and even calculable.[18] Next I turn to standards, which in many ways are similar to laws regarding uncertainty reduction, but they do not come with the same degree of enforcement.

STANDARDS

Uncertainty reduction can also be a consequence of standards. Standards meet the requirement of being an 'institution', including being backed by an organization—the 'standardizing organization' (Ahrne and Brunsson 2008). However, there is one difference. Those who do not follow the standards are not subject to direct sanctions. Thus, while standards mainly give rise to illegitimacy costs in cases of non-compliance (Zuckerman 1999), laws sanctioned by power can lead to direct penalties backed by an organization. Moreover, coordination and calculation are facilitated by the introduction of standards, which in some ways resemble formal institutions. **Standards** are objectively accessible ways of doing things resulting from successful attempts to decide for others, but without formal sanctions. A public standard does not require much interpretative work, at least not from experts subject to a given standard, and is therefore 'objectively accessible'. To become successful, standards must, in contrast to formal institutions, be acknowledged 'voluntarily'. Formal institutions, in contrast, can be enforced—also in cases when everyone but the enforcer is opposed to the rule.

Standards in a sector may lead to reduced uncertainty, regardless of whether or not this was the intention. They essentially reduce uncertainty because they inform people about the right thing to do. More practically, standards facilitate the development of new products because they imply simplification of interaction and coordination and are a result of decisions made for others (Grindley 1995). Classification and associated quantification of classes, such as statistics, comprise an example of an economic way of standardizing knowledge of more or less qualitatively different things and dimensions (Thévenot 2016). An often-given example of a standard is the QWERTY (QWERTZ) keyboard. This is an example of how users' and producers' uncertainty is limited; it does not mean, however, that this is the best or most efficient standard today. When QWERTY was developed, it was made to solve a technical problem with mechanical typewriters, namely that they can jam. Digital devices are of course not restricted in this way and could have the letters arranged in a more user-friendly way. The so-called 'Dvorak' keyboard layout was developed for this purpose, making typing much faster. It has failed to break through, however, and the arguably less efficient solution of QWERTY has remained the standard in countries that formerly used it for mechanical typewriters. In terms of uncertainty reduction, it makes no difference which keyboard layout is used, as long as it is dominant.

Time is another example. Initially, perceptions and conventions of time (use) varied according to local conditions, normally based on the position of the sun. Greenwich Mean Time was initially developed as a standard for seafarers and was later used to establish one unified time system for railways. This, for obvious reasons, reduced uncertainty immensely for everyone needing to coordinate their affairs. Only later did time become regulated in law, which meant that the standard was turned into a law. Hence, many institutions support one another, but they can also be used to build new institutions. Different indexes, for example, are built on already existing states of the world (i.e., data).

When industrial-technical standards were introduced, it became possible to relate to standards as facts, and it made business and technical development easier and cheaper (Brunsson et al. 2000; Pentzlin 1959). Standardization is a way of overcoming the uncertainty associated with heterogeneous goods (Karpik 2010) and may be used in markets, to foster homogenous offers of trade (Aspers 2009). It may be used as a form of commensuration of a variety of characteristics to one unified scale of measurement (Espeland and Stevens 1998). Fligstein, in reference to business standards, says that 'product standardization has become increasingly important' (2001: 35). Hence, to adjust to standards may even be seen as more routine than decision-making (Luhmann 1987: 401). A standard can be a scale from good to bad, a spectrum running from accepted to not accepted, or simply a point. Any point, however, must be measurable, and there may be deviance. Standard markets are centred on certain characteristics, or as some would say, 'quality conventions' (Favereau et al. 2002). Such a standard can be used for vertical differentiation of products, thereby indicating quality ratings. The differentiation can be carried out with a continuous quality scale or one with discrete steps. However, both the neoclassical model presented by Knight (1921), and Marshall's (1920:256–258) model of 'organized markets' assume homogenous commodities. Marshall shows that standardization of goods enables future markets to develop (1920: 223). Put differently, from a situation of competition with different products, setting up standards will lead to homogenous products, or at least offers that can be objectively measured against one another using a scale. If this can be done, uncertainty can also be transformed into risk, especially if future markets exist. Thus, these markets are standard markets, which means that the uncertainty of product quality is eliminated, and uncertainty is reduced to a matter of price. The issue of public prices in markets—such as prices in stock exchanges—as a means of uncertainty reduction will be discussed in Chapter 5. Marshall observes that certain products, typically natural resources, are likely to be standardized—but how does a standardized product reduce uncertainty?

Standard Objects and Technology

Technological standards are perhaps the best example of how codified knowledge can be built together to achieve highly complex ends, such as putting man on the moon. The amount of uncertainty that technology can and has reduced over the last 200 years or so is indeed impressive. Standards (Brunsson et al. 2000) are social constructions, which means that they are made explicit by means of decisions, are normally codified, and may be taken for granted. A valid standard can be constituted in material objects (carats of gold, length, weight), such as can be found in technology-driven industries (cf. Schmidt and Werle 1998), or it can be constituted by immaterial values, such as norms. By introducing standards of weight, and quality standards, actors can trade and communicate with prices (See 1968: 27–31) more easily, because uncertainty concerning the objects is reduced. It thus comes as no surprise that standards were crucial for the formation of exchanges, such as the ones in Brügge and Antwerp (Braudel 1992a). At these exchanges, businessmen could trade contracts (i.e., rights) without having the material objects traded, such as metal, in front of them. Marshall, taking the example of England as the leading industrial nation in the 18th century, stresses the role of standardization for coordination and ultimately for economic decision-making and calculation.

For example, he argues that the natural standardization of raw materials for textiles, such as cotton and wool, made it easy to spin it into yarn (also standardized), and spinning wheels and later looms were developed. Already in the early 19th century, 'mechanical standardization spread from one process to another in the same industry, and from one industry to another. And gradually it was found that machines, adjusted to standardized work, helped one another; because the uniformity of the product, when it left one machine, was suited for being operated by the next' (Marshall 1920: 57–58). Machines and standardization later spread to other Western countries, furthering economic development because actors could count on them as states of the world.

The development of screws, for example, shows how standardization may increase certainty. Marshall describes how the development of the lathe and the precision making of screws are intimately tied to one another. In the early days, screws and nuts were produced in pairs, so that they had to be made together, and if a screw broke, its paired nut was no longer usable. This is of course very problematic and complicated for machines when only single parts need to be replaced. The idea arose to develop a 'generating machine' that could produce standardized screws with high precision. This required also that the machine, a lathe, should also be of high precision. It was Maudslay who developed the first precision lathe, but it was Whitworth's screw gauge that came to be adopted as an organized general standard for Britain (Marshall 1920: 208–209).

Standardization refers to the fashioning of institutionalized knowledge that orders behaviour and thereby reduces uncertainty (Busch 2011). The reference point here is general and public standards, attempting to apply to 'everyone' or at least very many, in contrast to 'particular standards' that refer only to the way a particular company produces its goods. Standards are made by decision and are performative in the sense that they shape the world by forming actions. Standards are, in one way, the ideal-typical form of objectively codified knowledge, enabling an almost perfect predictability of human action. A standard can be particular to a specific individual producer, or be general 'to the greater part of an industry or even the whole western world' (Marshall 1920: 201). Technical standards are the paradigmatic examples of standards. In most cases, 'at the back of these there is an implicit standardization by mechanical, chemical, or other tests' (Marshall 1920: 548), which is no surprise, because 'the modern science of industrial technique deliberately standardized some products and many processes' (Marshall 1920: 201). This means that there are objective ways to measure compliance with a standard, or the quality of a product in relation to a standard, implying that one can produce technical machines, or computer programs, based on standards with very low uncertainty.

There are many actors who have an interest in standard-setting. In several fields, economic as well as non-economic, actors join together to create meta-organizations (Ahrne and Brunsson 2008) that organize the field, including standard-setting. Industry organizations are one typical example, in which competing firms nonetheless collaborate to establish some rules of behaviour, not seldom standards. Although standards may be the result of mutual adjustment, they are often promoted or dealt with by organizations that specialise in standardization. The European Committee for Standardization is an example of a meta-organization that accepts national standardization organizations as members, which come together to develop European standards.[19] Safety standards used for the testing of cars are one example. Marshall says that what he calls general standards are decided by governments, or 'a convention of leaders in the industries most directly concerned', and informs us that 'present electrical standards, Watt, Ohm and Ampère' are examples of decisions by international conventions (1920: 201). Today this enables engineers to coordinate work across the world and, in the face of high uncertainty, to do calculations and produce machines to be used with no problems in different parts of the world. This means that product development can be done with some certainty.

Not only sellers and buyers in markets may set standards. There are also many 'others', actors who want to affect what is happening in a field. This can include organisations trying to impose professional standards on an occupation. In many markets, NGOs try to impose ethical standards that actors will have to consider. Standards can even be 'sponsored'. Especially in software technology, standards can give some producers advantages, because their own products are more easily adjusted to it (Garud et al. 2002).

Standards enable economic actors to plan and to reduce uncertainty, and they may even make it possible to frame situations in terms of risk, especially since they enable comparison of alternatives. Standardizations of weight and length are of tremendous importance to facilitate calculations, and so is, of course, money as a generalized medium of exchange (Dodd 2005). By combining product standardization and markets with prices, actors can, at a distance, calculate alternatives. If a set of standardized markets are related, market access can be calculated; and virtually no advertisement is needed for standardized commodities (Marshall 1920: 244–246). Here, a more detailed example of an attempt to standardize cucumbers in the European Union (EU) is analysed.

Standardization of Cucumbers

Standards may reduce uncertainty, and this can also be shown more directly with an example. There are very many examples of standards and standardization, some of which have been less successful than others. The integration of the European market has been achieved to no small extent through the imposition of standards.[20] These standards promote economic integration by reducing trade restrictions. A proposal for introducing a standard can be submitted to the European Committee of Standardization, where standards are developed under the guidance of this committee's principles. The first step is to make a proposal for a new standard, which then is scrutinized and, if deemed worthwhile, a process is instigated that may end with a new standard.

One of the most infamous EU standards—also known as the 'bendy cucumber directive'—concerned the curvature of cucumbers. Published in 1988 by the European Economic Community (EEC), one of the predecessors of the EU, as regulation No. 1677/88, the rule set standards for the quality of cucumbers as of 1 January 1989. The idea was that the standard would lead to the supply of fresh cucumbers to customers. The cucumber standard has been described as a 'partially organized order' (Ahrne and Brunsson 2011).[21]

While some sources trace this standard back to a Danish regulation on vegetables from 1926, the actual origin of the rule was a recommendation of the United Nations Economic Commission for Europe, which prescribed that the cucumber standards regulation No. 1677/88 should be made legally binding. However, it was not the existence of this regulation but the retail sector's desire to standardize the form of cucumbers that was responsible for the adoption of this recommendation by the EEC. For retailers, the legal standard had the advantage that cucumbers could be packaged more easily because of their now standardized size. At the same time, as the standards stipulated the quality level at which vegetables should arrive in shops, consumers were thought to benefit from reliable knowledge about cucumber quality. In essence, it would lead to less uncertainty about what is a cucumber, its handling, and the like. Put differently, it was an attempt to create a homogenous good, which would entail a reduction of uncertainty for many actors in this production chain, sales and logistics included, although perhaps excluding farmers, because in this way they were forced to grow standardized cucumbers. To achieve this standardization, the process proceeded in two steps. First, the standard defined the minimum requirements of cucumbers in the EU. These minimum requirements demanded that a cucumber must be:

- intact;
- sound—this means that it must not be affected by rotting or deterioration, thus making it unfit for consumption;
- fresh in appearance;
- firm;
- clean, practically free of any visible foreign matter;
- practically free from pests;
- practically free from damage caused by pests;
- without a bitter taste (subject to the special provisions for classes II and III under the heading 'Tolerances');
- free of abnormal external moisture;
- free of foreign smell and/or taste.

(Official Journal of the European Communities L150 1988: 23)

On top of these basic requirements that had to be met to sell cucumbers in Europe, four additional quality grades for cucumbers were presented. These grades defined minimum requirements, as well as a tolerance zone for defects. The four classes, in descending quality, are: extra class, class I, class II and class III. The original class characteristics as defined in the regulation are as follows:

(I) 'Extra' class
Cucumbers in this class must be of superior quality. They must first of all meet the requirements above, but they must, in addition:
- be well developed;
- be well shaped and practically straight (maximum height of the arc: 10 mm per 10 cm of length of the cucumber);
- have a typical colouring for the variety;
- be free of defects, including all deformations, and particularly those caused by seed formation.

There are also 'good quality cucumbers of Class I',[22] and the lower level of class II cucumbers. Class II allows, in brief, more defects, including, for example, deformation of surface colouring, damage due to rubbing and handling, and may have bends. Class III is the yet lower standard of cucumbers. (See for descriptions: Official Journal of the European Communities L150 1988: 23f.). Standards of this kind, based on qualities, for example, are also in place for timber and measurements (Aspers 2013).

A standard like this, which was adopted in 1988, automatically defined its 'members' as producers and sellers, that is, people trading cucumbers. In fact, this meant that both producers and sellers for the European market had to abide by the standard as a result of the decision. As the proposed regulation No. 1677/88 was supposed to be legally binding; non-compliance with the standard entailed *sanctions*. The original document states in this regard: 'Those standards [concerning the different quality classes] shall apply at all marketing stages, under the conditions laid down in regulation (EEC) No. 1035/72' (regulation No. 1677/88). This regulation from 1972 sets rules for 'common organization of the market in fruit and vegetables'. It stipulates that 'when quality standards have been established, products to which they apply may not be displayed or offered for sale, sold, delivered, or marketed in any other manner within the Community unless they conform to the standards' (regulation No. 1035/72, p. 3). Thus, the most explicit negative sanction was the exclusion of producers and sellers from the European market in case of repeated infringements. Taken together, the knowledge of what a cucumber 'is' is clear, and many actors in the production chain can orient themselves to this standard, thereby reducing uncertainty for many.

In addition to these formal sanctions, the standard also entailed informal sanctions. These sanctions largely involve mutual adjustment between different parties. For example, sellers and retailers adjusted their packaging sizes to the cucumber standard, thereby effectively ruling out the inclusion of cucumbers that did not fit the designated forms. At the same time, supermarkets imposed sanctions on producers failing to meet quality standards.

Selling food in the EU exposes producers to a variety of *control* measurements. For example, producers from developing countries are subject to three types of checks: documentary checks, identity checks, and physical checks (see CBI Ministry of Foreign Affairs). In addition, importers are obliged to demand traceability documents for wares imported to the EU. To facilitate the import of foods, the EU provides foreign producers with a plethora of support materials to meet the requirements of the European market.[23] The inspectors, in addition to tools, have operationalized the standards and rules, and have developed a useful checklist for cucumbers.[24]

However, this detailed attempt to standardize cucumbers, in effect as a formal institution, was not a success. After the cucumber standard became a magnet for criticism, and because it was ridiculed in a way that gave the EU a bad name and could be exploited for Eurosceptic propaganda, it was abandoned in 2009. However, 15 out of 27 EU member states actually voted to maintain the standard.[25] The reason for this persistence is simple: the cucumber regulation assured that supermarkets would get the quality they ordered. The standard enabled supermarket chains to meet consumers' imputed demand for vegetables in a straight and thus aesthetically pleasing form. In addition, the standardization of cucumbers made

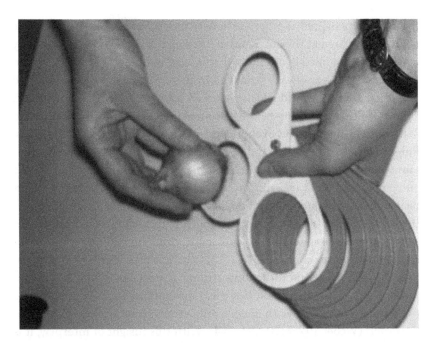

Figure 3.1. Tool for measuring onions. *https://www.laves.niedersachsen.de/lebensmittel/ marktueberwachung/obst_und_gemuese/gueteeigenschaften/obst-und-gemuese---qualitaetskr iterien-73854.html*

packaging and transport easier and cheaper. Consequently, many super-market chains did not give up on what was, for them, an effective device of uncertainty absorption.[76]

Standards, to sum up, are not formal institutions; the main difference is that the sanctions implemented lack direct enforcement. They are close relatives, however. In fact, an attempt to impose a standard will be successful only if it is accepted by others, and the discussion of standards will continue in Chapter 6. But it is clearly the case that successful standards are likely to be taken for granted, that is, to become institutions. Another central but overarching issue is, if standardization is such a useful strategy to reduce uncertainty, why aren't all goods standardized? The short answer, to be discussed in Chapter 5, is that neither producers nor consumers have an interest in such 'complete' certainty.

CONCLUSION

Formal institutions and standards create states of the world, which enable actors to increase the predictability of their own actions. They also increase the possibility to predict others' actions, which obviously also increases the possibility to predict the outcomes of one's own actions. This predictability may not be grounded in anything that is even remotely true, right, or fair. But predictability is always grounded in the norms, values, practices, and other states of the world which are taken for granted by relevant people. Even rules that according to the discourse are person-independent are in reality rarely independent of those performing the roles to enact the rules. Rules must be interpreted, and rest on assumptions that people hold certain virtues. To take an example, who the judge is always matters for the outcome of a court case, and the political circus and the importance attached to the nomination and appointment of Supreme Court judges in the United States clearly shows how much persons and values matter for law. This also illustrates that formal institutions function on a bed of informal institutions. It is thus clear that there is an interplay between informal institutions and formal institutions (Durkheim [1895] 1984), and Weber says, 'Law, convention [informal institutions], and custom belong to the same continuum with imperceptible transitions leading from one to the other' (Weber 1978b: 319, cf. 754). With this insight of interplay, it is possible to explain economic performance (Weber [1904-5] 1968) or political development and democracy (Putnam 1993; Tocqueville [1835] 1969). Each formal institution relies on practices and other informal institutions (White 2008: 173). Moreover, formal institutions operate differently because of the different institutions on which they rest and in which they are nested. This means that laws and rules may be formalizations of already existing institutions. However, the setting of a specific law may, over time, also be institutionalized.

The fact that rules are decided makes it clear that behind each decision stands an intention. Formal institutions represent an active way of shaping human conduct. This should be contrasted with the informal institutions that affect actors, too, but as an unintended consequence of mutual adjustment over time. However, which of these two types has the strongest impact on the reduction of uncertainty cannot be determined theoretically; it is an empirical question. Furthermore, we know that the outcome of actions does not have to be the same as the intention of the decision; the same decision may lead to different outcomes depending on the informal institutions. The attempted implementation of capitalism in the former communist block after the fall of the Berlin wall differed considerably in success. The reasons why formal institutions are introduced in a particular place may be many and varied, including gaining or securing power, increasing efficiency, creating order, or facilitating coordination. However, though a single decision may reduce uncertainty, at least partially, a multitude of decisions for others may create a situation of non-predictability; this issue will be further discussed in the concluding chapter.

When informal institutions are embedded in one another, it is not clear to people how they are related, given the extent to which institutions are taken for granted. With formal institutions it is the opposite. Formal institutions, by definition, are explicit and clear, in principle, though not necessarily in practice. This means that one can use a formal institution as an integrated part of another decision on a rule. This we know from jurisprudence and standardization, as well as patents. The next chapter will deal with evaluations, many of which are based on formal institutions, rules, and standards; others are based on actors' subjective valuations.

CHAPTER 4
Evaluation

Evaluations bring about states of the world in two stages. The first step is that whatever is evaluated is deemed to be either an instance of the category evaluated, or not. This categorization resembles what is done in testing (Marres and Stark 2020b), rating, ranking, or similar phenomena.[1] The second step is that evaluations lead to the ordering of different instances of the category according to the rule, scale, or standard used for the evaluation. It is possible to evaluate the quality of schools, screws, scientific work, higher education, or emissions, to take a few examples. Knowing the quality of different universities, represented in rankings, may be of great importance for families making decisions about colleges for their children. The result of evaluations, in short, can reduce uncertainty about whatever the object of evaluation is, because we know more about what is evaluated. Evaluation is a means to establish the state of the world before a decision is made.[2]

It was shown in the two preceding chapters that both informal institutions and formal institutions are states of the world that can increase predictability and thereby reduce uncertainty for actors. Potentially, both are so clear that they can be used as baselines for evaluations. Informal institutions are taken for granted, are even 'forgotten', and they will most likely show up in a 'negative' way. This means that they are used less frequently as the basis for evaluations. Formal institutions are explicit, which means that they can be the baseline or 'rulers' of evaluations. Rules, standards, and laws—as in the etymologically close connection between rule and ruler—are codified in devices that can be measured objectively. The baseline against which something is evaluated is a ruler, which typically

Uncertainty. Patrik Aspers, Oxford University Press. © Oxford University Press 2024.
DOI: 10.1093/oso/9780197752753.003.0004

resembles formal institutions but without the formal possibility of sanctions. A ruler is an objective device, the use of which generates results that are independent of personal preferences or interests. The ruler of the evaluation is clear, such as a ruler that measures length, or more generally measures something, in an 'objective' way. These socially constructed criteria are normally communicated and expressed in language or based on other scales or rules. A ruler enables states of the world to come about. The everyday usage of evaluation is much broader, but evaluation as a scientific concept is defined, and thus separated from, the 'evaluation' discourse.

This chapter addresses some concrete questions. What is the role of evaluation in uncertainty reduction? What does it do for those being evaluated and those evaluating? Shall we call these activities evaluations?[3] The chapter starts by discussing the origin, as well as the current standing, of the concept of evaluation. This section entails a discussion of how to measure the prevalence of evaluations, and a discussion of the reasons why they have come to be used. The next section deals with evaluation against objective scales, which is a 'pure' form of evaluation. But not all evaluations are 'pure'; in fact, 'evaluations' are often the result of an ordering decided by certain evaluators, to be discussed below as an instance of ratings. Regardless of which type of evaluation is in question, the results of evaluations are states of the world that may reduce uncertainties for many. Evaluations may have other consequences, too, including reactions from those being evaluated. One issue that this chapter will address is how evaluations work, and how people, things, and events are subject to evaluation— with or without the consent of those being evaluated. The question of what happens when uncertainty is evaluated as if it is risk is also discussed.

EVALUATIONS AND THEIR PREVALENCE

Why are evaluations used? I here build on Vedung (2015), who describes potential realms of evaluation. The first is instrumental, meaning that the evaluation is done to make better decisions, such as regarding which of several different medical programmes should be kept or what investment to pursue. A second use refers to conceptual clarity over what is studied or discussed. Third, evaluations can be used to legitimize decisions already made. They can also be used to temporarily block or postpone an activity. Initiating evaluations to obtain results that may guide decision-making can be a way to take some responsibility off the shoulders of those responsible for the decision. A sixth way is to use evaluations mainly as an organisational routine. Finally, evaluations may be used to constitute something that has a special status. All of these are thus reasons for generating knowledge through the means of evaluation, thereby creating states of the world that can reduce uncertainty when decisions are made.

There are several definitions of evaluation. What they have in common, according to Dahler Larsen (2011: 9), are four elements: (1) something is evaluated, an evaluand; (2) an assessment of the evaluand based on existing standards or criteria; (3) a systematic way to observe the 'performance' of the evaluand; (4) an intended use of the evaluation.

An evaluation may be oriented to the ends of an actor, or to more social needs. One example of a highly individualistic use of the term is represented by Parsons. He says, 'The process of deciding among alternatives, of assessing them in the light of their ramified consequences, is called evaluation. Evaluation is the more complex process of selection built upon the discriminations which make up the cognitive-cathectic orientation' (Parson and Shils 1951: 11). Parsons continues and elaborates the details of the actors' role in the 'process of evaluation, which operates unconsciously as well as deliberately, he will very often strike some sort of compromise among his conflicting need-dispositions, both simultaneously and over a period of time' (Parson and Shils 1951: 14). But Parsons talks about evaluation in relation to individual decision-making as if it were some type of internal conversation.

An evaluation can be made by a single actor, or by someone who pays for the service of having an evaluation done, or it can be done in public. There is in principle no difference between a private and public evaluation in terms of how it is done and what it brings to those evaluating—reduced uncertainty. The difference is how available the results are for those who did not perform the evaluation. Public evaluations are available to everyone, at least within a given field. The consequences of the evaluation, however, may differ substantially for those being evaluated and whether it is public or not. Here, the focus is on public evaluations leading to states of the world, though much of what is said applies to public and private evaluations alike.

Evaluations have increasingly become professionalized. At a more general level, evaluation is part of processes such as bureaucratization and rationalization, because it is about measuring and ranking, often in order to increase the quality and predictability of the output. Evaluation is connected to ideas of rational politics, which has to be efficient (Müller 2015: 25). Though this is not a study of the history of evaluations, one trend is the emergence, diffusion, professionalization, and institutionalization of evaluations, indicating how it may reduce uncertainty for actors. Vedung, who has followed this field over time, writes: 'Since around 1990, the evaluation business has completely exploded' (2010: 263).[4] The state

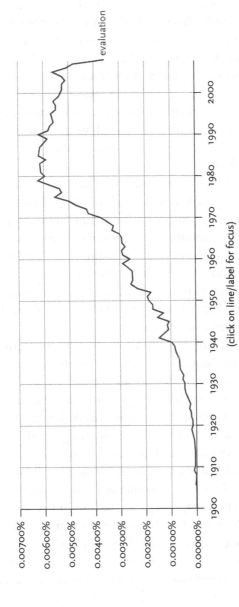

Figure 4.1. Relative frequency of 'evaluation' in English books, 1900–2008. Source: Google Books Ngram Viewer, http:// books.google.com/ngrams

(or state agencies) is often involved in formal evaluations, many of which can be observed or traced in public records. Moreover, it is clear that the formal role of evaluator and the informal institution of evaluation has been established (House 1993), which indeed points at its commonality. There is a literature that covers what is also a rather distinct phenomenon, namely formal evaluations of individuals, activities, and organizations.

Vedung (2010) describes the development of the field in terms of waves of formal evaluations. The first scientific wave came in the late 1950s and early 1960s, stressing rationalism and control by which evaluations were made prior to public-sector decisions. The most recent wave, starting in 1995, stresses the use of experiment, which to some extent was central already in the first wave. The most important thing in his analysis, however, is that the waves have become pronounced, and that more is demanded from those being evaluated.

Correlated with evaluation is auditing. Power (1997) has discussed auditing, and sees many similarities to evaluations. Auditing is oriented to 'compliance as a normative outcome' (Power 1997: 118). This means that auditing is more about controlling whether something is correct according to a decision. When evaluation is about finding out whether a condition is, or is not, present, there is a similarity between auditing and evaluation. Both generate knowledge that can be used to reduce uncertainty for actors when making actions. But outcomes of evaluations result in states of the world that can reduce uncertainty for actors.

The process of evaluation has effects, not least resulting from how the practice and professionalization of evaluation are backed by organizations that channel the evaluators' interests and contribute to the field's professionalization. This means that today there is an institutionalized field of evaluation.[5] The year 2015, for example, was designated by the United Nations the 'International Year of Evaluation'. The general aim was to 'advocate and promote evaluation and evidence-based policy making at international, regional, national, and local levels'. Evaluation, it was argued, 'can enable leaders and civil society to develop and support better policies, implement them more effectively, safeguard the lives of people, and promote well-being for all'.[6] To accomplish this, and much more, there is a need for more knowledge about evaluations and how they are implemented.

The trend towards formal evaluations in many spheres of life is the key factor behind what has been called the 'Evaluation Society' (Dahler-Larsen 2011). The field of evaluation is occupied with its use, and some even define evaluation by its applicability, usefulness, and impact. It is because of the central practice of evaluation, not least in the public sphere, that it can contribute to reducing uncertainty.

EVALUATION AGAINST OBJECTIVE SCALES

Ideal-typically, evaluation refers to the use of objectively existing and pub-licly available scales, rules, or standards against which whatever is at stake can be evaluated. The general idea of evaluation is that the thing or issue that actors are uncertain about can be settled, and it is because actors can make use of these states of the world that uncertainty can be reduced. **Evaluation** is defined as a process by which value is conferred on actors or things, based on a scale that is independent of the evaluands' views or preferences. As an ideal-type (Weber 1985), no one has to make a decision or ask someone whether whatever is at stake is 'good' or 'bad' for an evalu-ation to occur; the standard can be seen as a scale for measuring quality—or whatever is measured—in an 'objective' way (Aspers 2009). Evaluation thus refers to the act of benchmarking of 'things', such as engines, eggs, or people, according to objectively existing scales.

A numerical scale can be used to quantify what is evaluated. If the scale is at least on the ratio scale, the results can be measured directly. If it is a purely technical standard, like the metric scale, it may be obvious that the scale and its associated criteria are objective. Based on scales, or a commensurated scale (Espeland and Stevens 1998), it is possible to evaluate things, human or non-human, directly, according to their proper-ties (e.g., depending on their weight or wealth) or indirectly for their deeds (such as being 'ethical', or running 'fast') or their quality, including their tolerance, such as in screws made for machines. This means that one can rank them as being 'good' or 'bad' or being 'more' or 'less', according to the standard. This information can be used to reduce uncertainty for actors.

As an ideal-type, a standard provides completely objective criteria of evaluation. Standards (Brunsson et al. 2000) are more or less institutional-ized social constructions. This means that they can be used for evaluation. What is valid in the evaluation form can be constituted in material objects (carats of gold, length, weight) such as one can find in technology-driven industries (cf. Schmidt and Werle 1998).

There are plenty of examples of objective standards that are used for evaluations. A large number of them are rooted in technical standards. In the farming sector there are examples of evaluations of products that are not 'naturally' standardized. Eggs represent one example of a product that can be evaluated according to objective rules. US egg standards (Banks 1963; Gaumnitz 1933; Jacob et al. 2002) were developed in the United States in 1923 (Noles and Roush 1962: 21). These standards are based on internal and external characteristics of eggs. Experts were consulted in this process, and it was confirmed that their evaluations of real eggs correspond to the official egg quality standard (Noles and Roush 1962). The egg standard—for example, the Californian standard—is detailed and complicated (Jacob et al. 2002). It is based on observations: for example, whether there are blood or meat spots in the eggs, which makes them of inferior quality.[7] This standard is expressed in words, and it is made to be used by professionals and non-professionals alike. The standard, and the orientation to what an egg is and how to rate it, is supposed to be 'independent' of consumers' and producers' preferences. Producers can thus evaluate the quality of their eggs. By this evaluation they can know the quality and, provided that prices for the different qualities are available, much knowledge is gained for actors who can thus make decisions with less uncertainty than in a situation with no egg standards. The standardised practice is the basis of calculability (Callon 1998) and price formation connected to the different qualities. These are conditions for stock exchanges and futures markets in eggs (Brown 1933). Also in the timber industry, standards are used that can provide the basis for calculating the value of standing timber, that is, the trees still standing in the forest (Aspers 2013).

Theoretically, immaterial values or norms, such as what counts as good meat or a good author (criteria of evaluation), can be used for evaluation. Max Weber (1922: 16–20) argues that the principle of *Recht* can be like a standard (e.g., *ethischer Maßstab* [ethical measure]). This is certainly in line with the argument presented here; as an ideal-type, a scale is unambiguous and completely independent of actors' preferences, wishes, or interests, resulting in evaluations that are clear and 'objective', as discussed in Chapter 2.

Consequently, also in ethical cases it will be possible to reduce uncertainty because actors can consult the standard prior to taking action and thereby predict outcomes such as whether they will meet the criteria of the standard or not. However, by employing technical devices, objective evaluations can be made more easily and more distinctly. In the strictest sense, evaluation implies the elimination of judgement. Evaluation in this sense is independent of who is evaluating and who is evaluated. One can have opinions about how reasonable a standard is, but not about how it is measured. Hence, when people are involved as evaluators it is 'objective', and evaluation is not (supposed to be) based on their 'opinions', 'views', or 'preferences' (Busch 2011: 57–58).

If the scales and criteria are objective, the process of reaching results is normally objective. Given these conditions, there is not much work for those engaged in evaluation to find out what value an object has on the scale of evaluation. In some cases, such as who the tallest girl in the class is, the evaluation can often be done by everyone in the class without even considering the scale in question in detail. In this case the scale is none-theless objective—which is also the case of many indicators that are used to evaluate dimensions of organizations, societies, and nations, and even perhaps as an index measuring the level of corruption in countries.[8]

Because evaluation means orientation to a scale that is clearly defined, it can be carried out across time and space, if the same scale of value is used. Thus, whatever is evaluated can be evaluated independently of other things. It is possible, for example, for all of us to compare our times against the clock when running the 100 metres dash. Thus, everyone who runs 100 metres can in principle be rated in relation to their time, with the world record as the point of reference. This is a stable form for competitions and records, based on speed measured using scales (e.g., the length of the race, wind conditions for setting records, what you may and may not consume to enhance your performance). The results—the times set at this distance—mean that the runners can be ranked or allotted relative positions, which generate identities for them. Those aspiring to become runners can, in short, be evaluated in relation to how close they get to the world record. It means that measuring against the standard is transitive: if A has a higher score than B, and B a higher score than C, then it is clear, by definition, that A also has a higher score than C. Evaluation of the market prices of competitors selling identical products is another example, such as the competition between rivals for a standardized order of oil, who undercut each other's offers. By enabling comparison by price only, it is possible to reduce the uncertainty decision-makers face.

As mentioned above, for a scale of evaluation the first step is binary, and it refers to the assessment of whether the object of evaluation is a member of the category of the evaluation or not. Conditions in some labour markets show this. The scale of length is used to measure the height of potential fashion models, and in most cases only those who are at least 176 centimetres tall will be considered (Frisell Ellburg 2008; Mears 2011). This standard is a state of the world. Anyone who wants to be a model can thus check at home to see if she is tall enough (though some famous models, such as Kate Moss, are 'only' 170 centimetres, one of several exceptions to the rule). The scale is here continuous, but the corresponding criterion—176 centimetres—is dichotomous: a person is either at least 176 centimetres or not. This is objectively clear and does not, in this respect, even require any contact between a potential model and a model agency. But this standard does not imply certainty.

Not everyone who is taller than 176 cm can become a fashion model. To be accepted also requires 'evaluations' made by the bookers at model agencies. This means that the uncertainty that potential candidates face about becoming a model or not is immense. There are no objective scales of 'beauty', 'quality', 'character', or whatever else is judged. For a woman who is at least 176 centimetres tall and who wants to become a fashion model, a direct encounter with model agencies is needed to find out whether they will accept her. Because there is no 'standard of beauty', it is very difficult for potential models to know what the agencies are looking for. There is thus uncertainty due to the lack of objective scales of evaluation of beauty; and 'beauty' is subject to fashion. This is a typical example of different 'evaluations' of length and 'beauty' that are combined, but these two dimensions are not directly commensurable. Length can clearly be measured objectively, whereas beauty cannot. As a matter of fact, these two ways of reducing uncertainty for potential models are so different that strictly speaking, they cannot be included under the same term.[9] The issue of 'beauty' is perhaps captured better by the form of decisions for others (to be further discussed in Chapter 6). A model agency normally divides its models into different categories, such as models who do not meet the regular requirements of size, age, and look.

The selection of models is thus a complex procedure in which several values are commensurated. A single scale for evaluation brings order because it makes it possible to settle uncertainties about things in a direct and unambiguous way. For example, Bugatti and Koenigsegg are two companies that make production cars, though these cars are extremely expensive and are produced only in small series. These companies compete at the high end of the sports car segment, where top speed is an important value for many customers. Though the speed these cars can reach is well above 400 km/h, which may be of little practical use-value, it is nonetheless the central value for companies competing to produce the fastest car. It is, however, somewhat unclear which is the fastest car because neither the notion of production car nor that of speed record is officially defined. Ultimately, such a situation may require a direct competition—face to face—to settle this uncertainty. This issue will be discussed in Chapter 7.

To conclude this section, the availability of clear-cut and objective standards to which actors can orient themselves enables them to predict the outcome of their own actions, as well as the actions of others—for example, competitors—all of which reduces uncertainty. Objective standards do not have to be based on technologies, but it is hard for people to function as 'objectively' as technologies or technological devices such as algorithms. As soon as people enact a role, and are supposed to behave in accordance with an objective scale, the double hermeneutics of those enacting the roles and those who orient themselves to their hermeneutics open up uncertainty.

Only objectivity makes it possible to attach a price system, which means that uncertainty can be turned into something more predictable and be analysed in terms of risk (Knight 1921). However, in many cases activities such as evaluation appear to depend not only on actors' roles, but also on their unique expertise or even identity. In this case, is it still reasonable to speak of evaluations?

Evaluating Uncertainty as Risk

Uncertainty can be turned into risk, given certain circumstances (Knight 1921). However, the notions of risk and uncertainty, as already mentioned, are not always defined and are frequently used interchangeably by some scientists and practitioners. Only if there is an objective scale that can be used to generate numbers, at least on the ratio scale, can uncertainty be turned into risk. To operate with probabilities is key in the credit-rating industry (Carruthers 2005, 2013; Guseva and Rona-Tas 2001), as well as for insurance companies. In the past, much credit evaluation was based on judgements of the character of the person who wanted to borrow money. Today this evaluation is more likely to use an algorithm based on existing 'objective data'.[10] But given the right conditions, risks can be calculated. Guseva and Rona-Tas (2001) have shown that due to the lack of both de-cided and informal institutions in Russia, no calculations can be made of peoples' creditworthiness, and genuine uncertainty prevails about poten-tial consumer credit takers. In the United States, consumers' credit score can be determined by evaluation because there are organizations that pro-vide this information.

Power argues that uncertainty is often 'transformed into risk when it becomes an object of management, regardless of the extent of informa-tion about probability' (2007: 6). In an analysis of credit raters, Besedovsky (2018) has shown how risks are determined. The different conceptualiza-tions of risk are studied using data based on documents and interviews with raters at two major credit-rating agencies, Moody's and Standard & Poor's. These and other agencies rate creditworthiness, normally only for those who pay to be rated. Evaluations carried out to find whether a country is 'healthy' partly concern its political institutions and ability to endure eco-nomic shocks. The analysts interviewed by Besedovsky (2018: 245) indicate that this kind of evaluation can be translated into the term 'vulnerability'.

The term 'risk' used in this context, moreover, does not refer to a nu-meral score on an absolute or relative scale, but to the character of the country, as 'judged' by the agency. High levels of risk mean that a country deviates from what is 'normal' or average. What this deviance represents, more exactly, can be expressed 'in the comments that are published together with rating changes, where they often hint at possible ways for countries to get a better rating' (Besedovsky 2018: 245).

To analyse mortgage-backed securities or collateralized debt obligations the analysts proceed in a slightly different manner than when countries are analysed. For these financial products, credit-rating agencies have been crucial because they developed the means of valuing them. This is to say that the agencies 'not only perform calculations, but are in essence the architects of the security' (Besedovsky 2018: 246).

The ratings done by the sovereign analysts result in a 'relative judgement and an ordinal ranking of how safe and stable countries are with regard to paying their debts' (Besedovsky 2018: 244). One problem that appears in almost all ratings is that a set of different variables must be brought together into one scale. This is the problem of commensuration (Espeland and Stevens 1998). Besedovsky concludes:

> Based on the analysis of the rating practices of two different groups of analysts within their respective agencies—the sovereign (country) rating and structured finance rating groups—this chapter identifies two different conceptions of risk that co-exist within CRAs: the diagnostic conception of sovereign rating and the technical conception of structured finance rating. Due to their different methods and epistemological assumptions, they differ crucially in their attitudes towards Knightean uncertainty. (2018: 238)

What Besedovsky describes is not a mechanical translation of uncertainties into risks; it is much more a process of interpretations in a classic hermeneutic sense (Gadamer 1988) of 'data' that result in 'risks'. The outcome of this social process is not given, and there are no prescribed ways of doing it. Obviously, practices and conventions (Boltanski and Thévenot 2006) can be used, but this is not to say that the profound problem of risk assessment is addressed just because one quantifies (Mennicken and Espeland 2019) the information at hand. More generally, this problem concerns the uncertainty that organisation face; how one manages firms under uncertainty, with processes that turn uncertainty into risk (Power 2007). Thus, evaluation as a term is used to cover different phenomena, including cases in which there is no objective scale against which what is evaluated can be rated. It is clear from this example that a commensurated evaluation has far-reaching consequences for those being evaluated.[11]

EVALUATION AS A DISCOURSE—TOWARDS DECISIONS FOR OTHERS

Thus far I have discussed institutions of different kinds and standards, rules as well as evaluation. The discussion refers to 'principles' that are taken for granted or objective. As such, they enable the production of states of the world. But if no objective criteria of evaluation can be used, can uncertainty still be reduced prior to the decision? From this point on, and in the next three chapters, the focus will be uncertainty reduction in cases where no institutionalized scales, and hence no knowledge of states of the world, exist.

Evaluation seen as a discourse or, put differently, as a way of labelling activities without grounding them in institutionalized standards, is essentially different from what I call evaluation. There are, consequently, two different meanings of evaluation. The primary meaning is that there are objective criteria for evaluation, use of which offers clear knowledge that can reduce uncertainty for many. Then there are other evaluations in which a group, or an individual, makes decisions on whatever is evaluated. In this latter case, the evaluand ascribes values, ranks, or merit to whatever is evaluated. Evaluation in this second sense is a discourse used to dress up subjective values in an objective and numerical language to 'enable' the conceptualization of risk, to be further discussed in Chapter 6. Most cases will be found in between those extremes. However, both 'objective' and 'non-objective' evaluations can lead to states of the world and thus to reduction of uncertainty, as long as actors acclaim them.

CONCLUSION

Evaluations can reduce uncertainty as a way of comparing alternatives against a scale to find out which option is the best, fastest, or whatever is evaluated. Evaluations can be done to test past activities, such as different treatments of cancer, to find out which was the most efficient way to save lives per monetary unit. Although states of the world are the result of historical developments, uncertainty is always future-oriented. In its pure form an actor will know the result of the evaluation immediately and directly, given that the standards of evaluation are clear as well as independent of actors' interpretations and preferences.

Only in the case of an objective scale can we speak of predictability that is generalizable and publicly known. The term I have used to capture such phenomena is 'principles'. When an evaluation is based on principles, it may be easier to obtain a result, which in some cases also can be used to calculate risks. In some cases, evaluations may be carried out without being thus labelled, and they may be done outside formal organizations and the activities of members in national evaluation organizations.

In other cases, and in all cases in which there is no objective scale against which one can evaluate, evaluations may involve transformation and commensuration, in which numbers with probabilities are assigned to different alternatives, to present the result in the vocabulary of risk, though it is still only essentially about uncertainty. Hence, the term 'evaluation' is sometimes used in cases in which there are no criteria at all. Values may nonetheless be ascribed to different 'evaluands' of human and non-human origin and thus appear as 'objective' and 'pure'. Strictly speaking, these are not evaluations. These cases can merely produce the subjective opinion of those evaluating using the discourse of evaluation. The notion of evaluation as discourse points to the second part of this volume, and the analysis of cases in which there are no, or cannot be any, principles as states of the world.

PART II

Forms Producing States of the World

Part I dealt with uncertainty reduction by principles, which include informal institutions and formal institutions, but also, for example, technical production standards such as rules for cars' carbon dioxide emissions, and competition laws that represent and result in states of the world. These principles are social constructions to which actors can orient themselves. The existence of these principles reduces uncertainty because actors can draw on them when acting, and presume that others too will act accordingly. But what if there are no principles? Here it is argued that some certainty is established when order is imposed on the world.

Part II deals with forms that produce acclaimed particular states of the world. Also, these particular states of the world can be used by actors to reduce uncertainty. Examples of particular states of the world, such as different scientific findings, economic data (for example, the daily price of Brent crude oil), who is the best-known performance artist, and who currently is world fencing champion. These facts can be used to reach ends with less uncertain outcomes. If we know that an artist is represented at a prestigious museum, for example, this knowledge can reduce our uncertainty regarding the 'quality' of their work.

Uncertainty exists in relation to identifying which candidate to choose for an open position, finding out who is the best high jumper, figuring out what competing firms will do, or evaluating who will win when my team takes part in a football tournament. This type of uncertainty also exists, for example, about which journalist is the best, which offer in the market is the most valuable, or which research proposal will get a grant. Once settled, the existence of such particular states of the world can be used to help us act with less uncertainty. Part II addresses ways to settle such states of the world. Uncertainty over what is a 'good' film is clearly not easy to settle, but 'Film festivals . . . clearly serve to reconstruct uncertainty over quality of the films and to manage it by sorting, comparing, and ranking the films that will be seen by the audiences' (Zerbib 2022: 136).

Particular states of the world refer to the condition of decisions under uncertainty for which there are no principles. That it was 23 degrees Celsius in Paris on 14 July 2020 is public knowledge. It is a historical record, and it may even accurately have been predicted one day before, 13 July. This is an example, in addition to the principles that reduce uncertainty, of a particular state of the world in the sense of established knowledge about a particular object or situation. To know the temperature beforehand is useful for those selling umbrellas, ice cream, those organizing a parade, the police, TV teams, and potential viewers of the parade on the Avenue des Champs-Elysées. To know this temperature is an example of a state of the world, typically called a 'fact', that is either true or false. Simply by knowing more, we can reduce uncertainty (Knight 1921). But this fact is not a principle. Once you wake up on 15 July, for most people knowing the temperature on 14 July becomes essentially useless.

Although facts can be disputed, they are generally not problematic. We can find out, for example, who won the world soccer championship in 1958. This is a fact—it was Brazil—and requires no further elaboration. But we do not know which team will win an upcoming championship. Hence, facts may become dated very fast. Elections occur, say, every fourth year; or a new team becomes the national basketball champion each year, and prices on traded commodities change very rapidly. This also suggests that the particular states of the world that can be used to make decisions with less uncertainty, at any given time, rest mainly on the most recent data. This is the case not least when each state of the world is simply one in a long series, such as exchange rates.

There are, in addition, many value-based states of the world that depend on judgement, directly or as part of a future-oriented decision. This is the case especially when there are no principles available, or when no principles can be established. In these cases, the notion of facts that in practice are indisputable does not apply.[1] Examples include deciding what artist and song to use in a commercial, assessing the likelihood of success of an upcoming hunting party, or working out what a good action is in, for example, a moral or aesthetic sense; or when one is uncertain about which books to be translated (Franssen and Kuipers 2013). These are examples of situations in which there are only old facts, or no facts, and when there is a need for new states of the world.

When it comes to valuing what is unique (Karpik 2010; Rekcwitz 2017), there is thus no 'objective' knowledge, or cannot be. In this case, uncertainty reduction is the result of increased knowledge concerning how alternatives are related to one another, such as rank lists, scores, quality assessment, relative status positions of actors (that is, social structure), 'winners and losers', and 'good and bad'. When a firm is selecting well-known people to front their advertisement campaigns, it is obviously important to know for what they are known, but also to know their identity, status, or rank, to make the right choice. Various ways of measuring popularity, by rating or ranking, can generate particular states of the world concerning who is 'best', 'the most rewarded', and 'the most well-known'. Public ratings and rankings offer this information. The ranking of female tennis players by the Women's Tennis Tour (WTA) is one example of a form by which outcomes that attempt to settle things in the world are produced. To win a prize at the Golden Globe awards is a signal of quality, and knowing what shows or programmes are good is also of great use to those planning to watch a series. Hence, these states of the world can be used by actors to make decisions.

Rankings and ratings matter in the economy, too, but economic value uncertainty is also addressed by market prices of different goods or services as particular states of the world. Markets exemplify forms generating outcomes—prices of whatever is traded. The making of future states—such as what the price of pork bellies will be, what is high-quality literature, or who is currently the best high jumper—are additional questions analysed in Part II.

Part II shifts the focus from the states of the world to how they are formed. Because many particular states of the world have a short temporal relevance—the price of oil a few weeks ago cannot really be used to reduce uncertainty when making decisions today—it points at the forms that make these states, rather than the states themselves. The theoretical ambition with the notion of form is to account for how the plethora of empirical instances are generated, rather than the outcomes of the forms.

Forms of uncertainty reduction generate particular states of the world, such as facts, prices, awards, and status rankings. Form (cf. Simmel 1923: 47) here refers to, but is not bound by, its use in philosophy from Aristotle to Kant (Borman et al. 1971); Kant's notion of form (of view, more *Anschauung*) determines the substance (Heidegger 1977). A **form** is a publicly recognized—by an audience—structure of roles that can mould social matters. This general and abstract definition covers different concrete forms, such as markets, contests, and rankings, and they can apply to different social spheres, meaning that there is no 'content' that is specific to forms. Social structure with roles means that there is behaviour that is expected of the incumbents of the roles, and that there are expectations of outputs, too. Because it is a social structure, those enacting the roles may be replaced over time.

Forms have temporal permanence due to institutionalization, which may be strong. How the forms come about—whether because of a process of institutionalization through mutual adjustment or decisions for others—was analysed in detail in Chapters 2 and 3. These insights make up the backdrop to Part II. A form can mould social matters, such as identities and states of the world, although the focus is here on the latter. Forms rest on a bed of general institutions, namely the abovementioned principles of states of the world. Each form also has its own cultural priming, making the forms empirically different from one another, even though they may deal with the same matter, such as different exchanges at which the same goods are traded.

Although each state of the world is, in principle, acclaimed by the audience (or not), it is in fact the form that is institutionalized, meaning that the states are normally, and without question, accepted. In this way, the form is reconfirmed, and this structuration process (Giddens 1984) is ongoing. The states of the world analysed in Part II depend on actors' acclamation. The role of the public audience in fostering by acclamation the legitimacy of states of the world is to be seen most clearly in the case of valuations. The audience is the force that ascribes status to some actors and not others, and thus to the form. This is to say that the 'outcome' of the empirically existing instances of the forms, in terms of what is 'good', boils down to peoples' 'emotions', 'preferences', or, more generally, what they value (cf. Kant 1957 e.g., 198–203). This way of establishing what is good and bad can be applied in discussions among members of a group, or by an 'audience', for example, in both markets and art worlds (cf. Bourdieu 1984; White 2002; Zuckerman 1999).[2] The chapters in Part II deal with forms that generate states of the world, and value or rank it in a process that leads to ordering of whatever is at stake.

States of the world are, to repeat, social constructions and do not have to be true to reduce uncertainty. Here it will be argued that forms are performative for the establishment of states of the world. As discussed already in Chapter 1, states of the world are often to be seen in relation to a specific public, or—more pejoratively in Douglas' term (1982: 13–15)—sects, each with its own ideas of what is uncertain and ways of reducing it. There are many examples of attempts to present forms and the states of the world that are generated as objective.

Chapter 5, 'Convaluation', refers to forms by which states of the world result from actors who mutually adjust to one another. The outcome of these adjustments can be states of the world, but this outcome is an unintentional consequence. Chapter 6 deals with forms for decisions for others that, in contrast to decisions to introduce formal institutions backed with force, as discussed in Chapter 2, are not backed by the force to implement them. Chapter 7 analyses situations in which uncertainty is 'resolved' because of a struggle between combatants by which one party 'wins' and the other 'loses'. This form is called a 'contest' and generates outcomes as a result of struggle.

CHAPTER 5

Convaluation

A ctors are often uncertain about the value of things. How do we know the quality of art? How do we know its economic value? How do publishing houses identify potential débutants to publish? How does one know the value of the oil painting I inherited? How can the value of oil in four months' time be estimated now? If there were objective and generally accepted standards against which beauty or quality—for example of paintings, talent, or creativity—could be measured, our certainty would be much greater. However, this is not the case. These examples are instances of a profound uncertainty about states of the world; this uncertainty can be called 'aesthetic', to follow Nietzsche (1911).

This chapter addresses value uncertainty. It focuses on forms that produces states of the world, and especially particular states of the world, out of mutual adjustment processes when there are no principles against which the outcomes can be determined. I call these forms *convaluations*. This refers to actors who come together and produce value as an outcome. The outcomes of states of the world are, however, an unintended consequence of actors who mutually adjust to one another. The actors, typically, pursue their own different ends, which nonetheless leads to states of the world.

In addition to the analysis of how uncertainty is reduced, the chapter shows that convaluations pertain to forms outside and inside the economy. To be more concrete, markets are instances of economic convaluations, which address economic values. But not all convaluations are economic. In practice, economic and non-economic convaluations are interrelated. This chapter uses the notion of convaluation to analyse in more detail how uncertainty is reduced within the field of so-called 'performance art', and how

Uncertainty. Patrik Aspers, Oxford University Press. © Oxford University Press 2024.
DOI: 10.1093/oso/9780197752753.003.0005

the economic convaluation of market reduces uncertainty by establishing states of the world.

CONVALUATIONS AS FORMS

Convaluations are publicly recognized social structures with a culture that establish the value of things as states of the world via actors who mutually adjust to one another. The theoretical concept thus refers to the value and convergence of actors who are occupying roles in a social structure toward a specific 'thing', which it forms.[1] A convaluation is about a 'thing' that gains value, such as the quality of performance artists or the value of stocks in a given company. Convaluations are forms that generate states of the world when there are no 'objectively accessible' underlying values. If there are objectively accessible ways to find out about value, there is no need for actors to orient themselves to one another; it would suffice to orient themselves to the rule or standard, as discussed in Part I. A convaluation concerns the specific value of a thing, which can, for example, be economic, aesthetic, moral, or political, and the result is a state of the world.

Each convaluation has a culture referring to how things are done, and a corresponding identity, as exemplified by the Portobello Road market for antiques in London, made up largely of the roles of buyers and sellers of antiques. Fashion modelling (Mears 2011) is another economic convaluation, that is, a market made up of fashion models and those who hire out their services. Convaluations, as markets, are often embedded in one another (White 2002), which is typical of industries such as fashion modelling, fashion weeks (Entwistle and Rocamora 2006), catwalks (Godart and Mears 2009), and fashion photography (Aspers 2006b). A convaluation is to some extent institutionalized—at least sufficiently institutionalized to generate states of the world. Institutionalization means that actors orient themselves to 'publicly known' forms. In this sense they are recognized and accepted by a public; it also means that those making up the audience share some ideas (cf. the notion 'conception of control', Fligstein 2001), which remain relatively stable over time and enable actors to make predictions.

The reference to the social structure of convaluations means that there is expected behaviour from the incumbents of the roles, and potentially relations between the roles. The culture—the way we do things here—of the convaluation also orders it. Both structure and culture contribute to the permeance of convaluations and also make each unique. Convaluations are characterized by roles occupied by agents who can move 'in and out' of the role. Actors are thereby free to act according to their own preferences, which means that there is no hierarchy, a key element in organizations. That convaluations are peaceful implies that the outcome is not the result of force. Ultimately, not only the convaluations but their outputs in terms of particular states of the world may become institutionalized. Science producing what eventually becomes truths is one example. The notion of convaluation, to summarize, covers many instances but is more concrete than notions such as fields (Bourdieu 2001; Bourdieu and Wacquant 2002; Fligstein and McAdam 2012).

VALUE UNCERTAINTY

Convaluations are forms that handle uncertainty of values. One important reason is that uncertainty about values—what is good or bad, for short— can hardly be determined by principles. Put differently, it would then no longer be a value. Issues of the value of art objects, and other issues that involve judgement of taste, are examples of value uncertainty. Many decisions, in the economy and also outside it, depend on us knowing what is 'good and bad'. Which art school is worth attending if I want to spend money and time on an education? How much is a photograph by Irving Penn worth if I am to invest money? Which soccer team is good enough to play in Europe so that the firm can be happy to invest in advertisement? Those making decisions are uncertain, and there are forms that may reduce their uncertainty.[2]

Ordering of people, organizations, and things are ways to reduce uncertainty. To sort things out and categorize (Bowker and Leigh Star 2000), as said, not only analytically precedes evaluation but also valuation. In other words, to be ranked means that things are brought in order, but the 'thing' must first be seen as belonging to a class or category (Hsu et al. 2009). Only then is it possible to rate, value, or rank it in a process that results in 'relative positions on an "up versus down" scale' (Fourcade 2016: 178). Categorization, and the ordering of actors, activities, and objects in all spheres of life are fundamental, not only for decision-making, but for communication and interaction. This means that who is what, when, and what is what how and when, are key questions. Far from all things have easily identifiable 'objective' characteristics. Instead, many things require categorization to be sorted and to obtain an identity. Art objects are a classic example: what is a novel (Chong 2020: 129)? It is analytically possible to separate this question from the question of what is a good novel, though in practice, these questions are often intertwined (Furst 2017). Uncertainty reduction in this sense refers to the categorization and identification of people and things.

Uncertainty reduction in this chapter revolves around judgements. This is a topic in the field of valuation studies, which deals with issues characterized by value uncertainty. More specifically, valuation studies 'denotes any social practice where the value or values of something is established, assessed, negotiated, provoked, maintained, constructed and/or contested'.[3] Valuations exist and are frequently used in contemporary society. They have always been central in social life, as Nietzsche declared: 'man designated himself as the creature that measures values, evaluates and measures, as the "valuating animal as such"' (1994:70). The centrality of valuation, both as social phenomenon and a topic of academic interest, is acknowledged by researchers. There are many empirical studies of valuations, as shown in comprehensive overviews of the field (Lamont 2012; Zuckerman 2012), and the related work by Fourcade (2016) on ordinalization.

Valuation is here defined as the form by which values are ascribed to actors or things based on peoples' views (preferences). It is thus directly contrasted with evaluation, in which value is given to actors or things based on standards that exist independent of individuals' views or preferences. In contrast to a decision that requires only one actor, valuation is a result of mutual adjustment in a process in which many actors take part. Fashion, for example, cannot be the result of a decision; it is instead the result of valuation (Aspers and Godart 2013).

The sources of uncertainty that lead to valuation are many, including, as we have seen, lack of decisions, knowledge, and standards. The valuation literature revolves around the issue of value, valuation, and evaluation, with more or less direct connections to uncertainty (cf. Lamont 2012; Zuckerman 2012). Work has been done on valuation, including actual moments of valuation (Berthoin Antal et al. 2105). Simmel stresses how selection of incumbents for positions is partly stochastic (1923: 183–185), and Stark (2009) argues that values are the outcome of dissonance. Out of this multitude of individual decisions, an order of worth crystallizes that is the outcome of valuation processes, as shown by Menger (1999, 2014). More generally, valuation is here seen as the stabilized outcome of a multitude of single decisions.[4]

One example of value uncertainty is uncertainty concerning goods' economic value (Aspers and Beckert 2011b). The best-known form by which uncertainty is reduced is perhaps the market, but let it be clear that we are talking about different types of markets. In some markets, such as currency markets or markets for stocks or derivatives, there is no uncertainty about what is traded. The uncertainty is 'only' about the price at which the objects are traded. In such markets we may often speak of risk. In other markets, such as those producer markets (White 1981) with differentiated products discussed by Karpik, and more generally in markets in which product differentiation does not occur in relation to an existing standard, uncertainty also pertains to the quality of what is traded. This means that there is sometimes even ambiguity regarding what is traded.

Quality uncertainty of individual goods traded in markets is a problem, not least due to asymmetric information between sellers and buyers (Akerlof 1970). Nonetheless, as a result of categorization, singularization, and comparisons made in trade, transaction prices emerge in public. The resulting market prices are useful to those who are actively taking part in the activities, but also—by way of signalling (Spence 2002) information— to others who potentially could take part. Prices of given products, such as timber, are an example of a particular state of the world, which, for example, pulp producers and house constructors may use when making their decisions, choosing between different housing construction materials such as concrete or wood. Prices of objects are outcomes of evaluations and/or valuations carried out by individuals in the economic convaluation called a market. However, others have shown (Aspers and Beckert 2011a; Vatin 2013) that much of what goes into valuation in markets is the result of non-market valuation processes. Next, I look closer at the logic of mutual adjustment, which gives rise to the particular states of the world, regardless of whether the convaluation came about due to organization or if it grew out of mutual adjustment.

MUTUAL ADJUSTMENT

Convaluations give rise to states of the world as a result of mutual adjustment of actors. As already discussed in Chapter 2, mutual adjustment refers to a situation in which actors adjust their behaviour to one another. Mutual adjustment is one explanation of how order comes about in social life, and decision for others (organization) is the other. The idea of mutual adjustment, which sometimes is referred to as spontaneous social process, can be traced back to the Scottish Enlightenment and the writings of Mandeville (1924), who discussed the idea of good unintended outcomes out of individual egoistic action. Drawing on this idea, Adam Ferguson, David Hume, and Adam Smith developed a social science that gives much room to unintended consequences. Mutual adjustment is also the idea used by Hayek and other proponents of the Austrian school, as well as by evolutionary economists, who claim that markets are result of natural processes. These thinkers take the individual as the starting point and look at how people act to identify the consequences at the societal level. Though few social scientists are as detailed in their approach as Berger and Luckmann (1991), and though they sometimes refer more to assumptions than empirical studies, they describe how social order emerges out of mutual adjustment.

GROWN AND DECIDED FORMS OF CONVALUATIONS

Convaluations generate what become states of the world as a result of actors who adjust to one another mutually. But how do convaluations come about? To know more about the conditions under which forms can be organized, and under which conditions they cannot, is of great importance when it comes to reducing uncertainty. If uncertainty can at least potentially be reduced by decisions, this is helpful for those analysing uncertainty reduction, as well as for those trying to reduce uncertainty. Forms do not come out of the blue, and the notion of fields (Fligstein and McAdam 2012) can often serve as a good account of the necessary background to forms and how they come about. The field approach positions actors in relation to one another, instead of assuming a state of nature (Luhmann 1995) or a fictitious starting point such as 'in the beginning there were markets' (Williamson 1975: 20).

The forms in which actors adjust mutually can, themselves, come about as consequences either of actors who adjust mutually or of decisions for others; that is, resulting from organization. These two different ways convaluation can come about have implications for how changes in form can be implementing. It has also consequences for the possibility of affecting how states of the world appear, as well as for how states of the world can be institutionalized. I first analyse convaluations that come about as result of actors who mutually adjust to one another and which, over time, become coagulated and taken for granted as institutions.

Forming the Value of Performance Art

That there is uncertainty about the quality of art and artists is well known (Bourdieu 1996; Menger 2014). Art is the paradigmatic example of how values are determined out of forms. Edvin Sandström (2018), on whose historical, but above all ethnographic, work this section draws extensively, has shown not only that convaluations generate states of the world, but also how convaluation can emerge out of mutual adjustment over time.[5]

Performance art is today generally considered as a form of art characterized primarily by visual artists who use their bodily presence as the primary tool of manifestation. The roots of the tradition can be traced to the early avant-garde movements in Europe. Performance art is not restricted to any specific space. Gradually, more and more performance art festivals have popped up in different countries.[6] Most performance art festivals are small-scale productions and organized outside the mainstream art institutions. They can take place both in traditional galleries and outside in public spaces, such as marketplaces, city centres, parks, and beaches, but rarely in established arenas of art exhibitions, such as museums.[7] This convaluation is a result of a process that began in the 1960s and has grown more stable over time.

This convaluation is about performance art, and the social structure is made up of two roles: artists and festival organizers who meet at different festivals over time. Actors gain their identities by taking part in convaluation, either as artist only, or by switching roles so that they are sometimes organizers and sometimes performance artists. The key role to be identified with is the artist, because the convaluation is about what artists perform. It is in the ongoing orientation among one another that artists and organizers gain status positions and identities. The positions and identities emerge over time together with scripts, rules, and conventions of 'this is how we do it here' that make up the culture of the convaluation. Below, the empirical focus is on the process in which this performance convaluation emerges out of actors who mutually adjust. The point is not that the convaluation describes the entire performance art world (Becker 1982), but that it is central for establishing the value around which this world revolves. Concretely is about what is 'good' and not so good performance art.

The states of the world are the outcomes of convaluations, such as what is 'good' performing arts, who is the best artist, what is the best-known festival, and which is the organizer with the highest status. The answers to these questions result from mutual adjustment of actors and the results that are generated. These states of the world can be used to reduce the uncertainty of those taking part in the 'game'; for example, who a good artist is, and consequently, which festivals to visit. Also, members of the general audience can make decisions about what festivals to attend, and curators and other 'members' of the art world may try to invite performance artists. Finally, scientists approaching the art world or performance art can use particular states of the world when selecting what to study. In a sense, an ordered art world is made up of this convaluation: what is valued, the identities of the actors, and the social structure.

Performance artists tend to view themselves as practitioners representing the avant-garde of art (Berghaus 2005:261). Performance art originates from the avant-garde tradition of Futurists in the early 20th century (Carlson 1996; Stiles 1996; Goldberg 2011).[8] The curator of a performance art festival Infr'action Venezia, who has also been distributing performance art manifestos, declares that it is an art that 'is resolutely avant-garde, creating live cutting-edge experimental art at a large number of artist-organized events all over the world. It is a counter-current, alternative, ephemeral, human scale, un-hierarchical and profoundly non-commercial. It has nothing to sell. Just to give.' This statement echoes Bourdieu's idea of art 'for art's sake' as a reversed economy (1996).

The number of artists participating in a typical festival varies from around 10 to 40. Most festivals take an international approach, trying to distribute a broad range of international artists. The audience is more difficult to characterize, and it is also difficult to count the number of people actually attending. The very nature of performance art creates ambiguity; a performance that, for example, takes place in a subway can be viewed by a dedicated audience, but seen by a lot of 'bystanders' who may or may not be aware of them partaking in the performance. The very nature of performance, of course, requires some type of 'traditional audience', but a major part of the audience consists of peers and art students. As one artist describes it in a conversation with Sandström:

> There's the audience of most of us, who've heard of each other's names or we've met each other at festivals and we've seen . . . I saw your performance in Berlin, and I saw your performance in Thailand . . . I'm doing this for my colleagues who I met, and they know something about my work, so I have something new to tell them or I have something further to explore.

This audience made up of insiders has been observed in many art worlds (Becker 1982). The other considerable audience is often onlookers in public places.

Switching Roles: Evaluating and Being Evaluated

Performance art is considered by many as an institutionalized part of the visual arts tradition. Artists themselves often describe performance art as a small world existing 'off-scene'. It is this field in which art is evaluated, positions are generated, careers take off or are stymied. It is a field that, to an outsider, may appear chaotic, but which at least to those who have been around for some time is 'natural' and taken for granted. This background can be used to investigate the role of valorization and to come to understand the processes and forms through which values are established and order the field. The social structure of the pivotal activity of the field, festivals, is made up of a set of key roles: curators, artists, and support personnel.

Although some actors tend to enact certain roles more often than others, few are identified only as curators or artists, the two key roles of this convaluation. Instead, it is common practice to switch between these two roles. This means that actors, when being curators, select and thereby valorize certain activities and performance artists, and when acting as artists, they themselves are being valorized. Status does not go in only one direction from the organized festivals to the artists; it goes in the other direction, too. However, the festivals are fewer and more established, suggesting that the direction of the status flow is from festivals—and their organizers—to the artists.

The festivals are often organized around a theme determined by the curator(s), for example, 'Body and Mind', 'Pain' and 'Spirituality'. Depending on the theme, curators select artists to represent their 'vision' for that festival. The personal ties between curators and artists are often fairly stable, and even if the curatorial theme changes, artists to a large extent follow certain preferred curators, and vice versa. But although ties of this nature are inevitable, it is too simple to say that artists and curators choose one another based only on past interactions or friendship. The selections made by curators can easily be traced by examining historical records and documentation from festivals. New ties emerge, a process that could be studied in detail by following one curator more attentively, who organizes performance art festivals in Sweden, France, and China. The general pattern observed by Sandström in his empirical study is that there is a rather stable order among this curator's artistic selection.

Curators who organize more than one festival sometimes produce a so-called 'pilot festival'. Such festivals are made up of artists included in the curator's network but also newcomers who are 'tested' for possible inclusion in other festivals; and by adding new artists, the character of the festival may change and potentially improve. Newcomers, one curator says, 'push the older generation to make qualitative work'. In contrast, 'sometimes if you invite the same artist over and over [again], they tend to be a bit lazy and the quality of their work decreases'. The testing of new 'talents' reveals that some form of 'competition' is created by the curators when they select some, but not others, for their festivals.

The inclusion of newcomers is a vital part of some performance art festivals. In this way, the festivals also change in character, and the curatorial themes adjust to the vibrations from new artists. Artists often try to go to new festivals to check out changes of context. They can follow curators, but if that is the case, they usually follow those who organize festivals in different countries. The newcomers have often been at other festivals or suggested by other artists or curators. Some artists switch sides and also take the role of curator. In doing so, they inform each other about artists they have curated or seen elsewhere. Even in their role as curators, they may sometimes be invited to be part of other festivals, and thus have the opportunity to see new artists to invite to their festivals.

As for the artists who fail to meet the curator's expectations, there are other exhibitions and festivals to try. This dynamic generates new collectives and differentiation of festivals. Furthermore, some festivals are more focused on video performance, while others might focus on public performances; some reproduce identities, while others generate new ones. There seems to be a festival for every possible form of performance, which indicates the open character of this field. Put differently, an avant-garde field has at least one side without a fence, indicating its openness and also its flux. This also means that there are many activities—performances— that are only attempts, but which are never acclaimed by the audiences.

Some festivals, of course, have more status than others. The status of festivals is often based on which artists participate, but also on the curator's status. To be regarded as a good curator you need not only to establish creative spaces and keep an open dialogue, and enable artists' freedom in choosing their performances, but also to have the skill to seek funding. As indicated, some curators are also artists, but this switching has for some paved the way for the choice of one of these roles.

Although each festival decides for others—a topic to be discussed in detail in Chapter 6—the large number of festivals means that no one of them is important enough to establish enough status to be publicly recognized as the only 'maker' of the values—the states of the world—of this art world. The resulting observed order is a combination of all the doings of the different festivals, by the festivals on one hand, and by the artists on the other, all of whom are adjusting to one another. This interaction creates status orders that resemble what can be observed in status markets (Aspers 2009). The status orders of artists and festivals are unintended outcomes that the audience—which in this case is mostly made up of artists and festival organizers, who tend to switch roles—acclaims by orientating to it. It is largely a self-propelled and thus autonomous convaluation that, once established, generates particular states of the world.

Festival Culture

An essential part of a convaluation is the culture that binds it together and makes it different from the field of art (Bourdieu 1996) or the art world (Becker 1982) at large. For performance art, the selection and exclusion of artists at different festivals reifies not only the roles, but also the identities of those who enact these roles, as well as the identities of the festivals. That some types of performance are seen more often than others because they are included—and most notably at the most prestigious festivals—brings order to the field. Even if festivals have their own cultures, there is exchange of experiences among the artists, meaning that the general culture of the convaluation made up of all festivals permeates the partial culture of the different festivals. Performers often refer to themselves as family, and it shows when they meet each other at festivals. The first encounter at a festival typically involves participants catching up. Artists have often recently met at other festivals and speak about their experiences or suggest those festivals to their peers. There is often a rather long greeting ceremony at which artists who have not met introduce themselves and ask questions about each other's work. There is usually also a lunch or dinner meeting at which the curator presents the vision of the festivals and informs artists about other necessary information.

Some festivals organize so-called 'open situations' in which artists can do 'unplanned' works. In these situations, artists frequently work together in situations that were not necessarily planned beforehand. To balance and to accept the outcomes of performances, there must be trust between the curators and the artists. Only given this trust can the parties engage in interesting dialogues and collaboration. They inspire artists to work together and construct a critical environment that is appreciated among the artists. Artists say that they learn a lot from interacting with other artists, as mentioned by a female artist from Spain: 'You know, every festival I have been to, has had an impact on my own performances. You learn so much, just being around these people.'

Values of Art: Commitment

Formulated abstractly, good performance art is valued in this convaluation. But what is this convaluation more concretely about? There is a structure that is accepted, filled with known incumbents, and there is a culture of 'this is how we do it here' in the field. What specific values emerge from the field as a result of what is selected to be present at the festivals? The primary tool performance artists use is their own body. The body is considered a universal symbol, and that is what makes performance interesting, according to the artists: 'The body functions as universal language' and 'I think that we can still learn from each other to visualize new things by exploring our corporeal identity', as an artist from Poland said. In the 1960s and 1970s, artists began to explore the body as space and experimented with its limits. Nudity and pain were often part of such manifestations, which at that time was rather provocative.[9]

Artists use the body as a mode of communication and investigate the space in-between artists and witnesses: 'The in-between is a place of value, a value of special moment', a German artist stated in Stockholm. In this space, artists use different methods to make us perceive something in a new light, he explained. Just like visual artists, performance artists work with (live) images aiming to 'challenge our perception' or just visualize the 'complexity and beauty' of the situation. In a dialogue between artists and members of the audience in China, an artist from Ireland said: 'We can only hope that the images we make stay in your heart as you grow. And if you remember us, you really teach us that art is a completely universal language. And that is simply an amazing thing.' The production of live images challenges the idea that performance art only exists in the moment (cf. Phelan 1993). Many artists find the 'objects out of action' (Stiles 1998) to be a vital part of performance because of the documentation it leaves behind. While 'it's hard to reproduce the energy from the event', yet 'some pictures really make you feel the energy', a Swedish artist explained.

But it is not only the producing of live images which motivates artists to make performances: 'You know, performances sometimes make you transform', and depending on the witnesses, 'the energy they give you makes you want to give something back', an artist from Burma said. A common reference is the notion of 'energy', which witnesses play an important part in generating. An artist who has been performing since the 1970s told Sandström that 'We can do what we do in private, but we chose to do it in front of people and it is very important who they are and where you are, it changes every single time, and it's specific, it's all specific.'

They experiment with the tensions and expectations in the given context and use different methods, such as throwing things or moving objects around to engage witnesses in the performance. A common method is also to ask for help from onlookers; in so doing, they pull them into the situation. This interactive platform they are constantly trying to create is based on five elements, according to an American artist: 'Time, Space, Body, Mind, and Concept'. He further explained that one of these elements is more or less active, and the quality of experiment with these elements is the 'uncertainty' of the situation: 'Anything can happen', he described. However, if one of these elements is used in too playful a manner, there is a risk that it will be considered 'too theatrical'. At an artists' talk in China, an artist from Switzerland declared that performance art:

> ... doesn't follow a script. And neither is it improvisation, and for me it shouldn't follow habits and the manner of theatrical things like walking in certain ways or controlling the audience in a certain way. It should be risky. It should be unknown. It should be challenging your limits, and it should be different from conventional theatre. But there are some crossovers and that's okay. But we're trying to talk about the quality of things.

What members of the collective consider good quality often has to do with their rejection of theatre as an art form. To take one example, Chris Burden said in an interview after his infamous performance 'Shoot' that occurred in 1971, in which he had a friend shoot him in the arm in a gallery: 'It seems that bad art is theatre', and 'getting shot is for real . . . there's no element of pretense or make-believe in it' (Carlson 1996: 113). In carrying out everyday activities in a complex and situational manner or experimenting with one's corporeality, artists aim to challenge our perceptions of our everyday practices. As stated by an American artist: 'Performance art is very authentic; if you suddenly get the feeling that you want to laugh then you laugh, if you got pain you show your pain, it is authentic. In theatre, you can play pain. In performance art the more important part is about honesty. If you [are] sad you cry.' Such engagement and confrontation with people has been conceptualized as 'commissure', a term 'derived from Latin *commissura* meaning to join together, and *commitere* meaning to connect, entrust, or to give in trust' (Stiles 1998: 230). Thus, performance art could be considered an art of commitment.

The analysis of performance art not only shows how states of the world come about, it also shows how the convaluation of performance art, made up of the two roles of performance artists and festival organizers (or for short, festivals), as well as its culture, gradually becomes institutionalized. This also means that identities are made, values stabilized, and status orders appear, of high-status (and low-status) festivals, as well as artists with status, and those who are essentially unknown and who make up the low-status mass against which those with status shine. In the process of constitution, there is no causal order of these elements, which mutually constitute one another. However, it is only once the convaluation is institutionalized that it enables the concrete states of the world to be formed and perhaps, over time, also a value as a state of the world. Eventually, at least theoretically, even something like a standard of art could possibly emerge. The convaluation as a form—and the values and status orders that it is made up of, generates, reproduces, and changes—is more taken for granted than any of its parts. Hence, single festivals may come and go, as do artists, but there is still a field with a culture and there are still outcomes, particular states of the world, produced: who is an artist, what festivals are important, and what is good performance art. This type of knowledge constitutes this art scene and reduces uncertainty for all of those engaged in its activities, as well as for others.

PRODUCER MARKETS AS GROWN ECONOMIC CONVALUATIONS

The convaluation of performance art is primarily non-economic, though it may have economic consequences. Markets are economic convaluations, in which actors mutually adjust to one another under the condition of competition; actors observe one another, note prices, and sell and buy things. The outcomes of markets, prices for given products or services, represent particular states of the world, which are made public on the internet, various broadcast media, and in newspapers. To have knowledge about prices is an example of uncertainty reduction for actors.

Markets function because actors can trade with one another about different property rights. However, not all markets are the same. Some are organized, and they will be analysed below, but the focus of this section is markets that emerge out of the interaction of actors in a process of mutual adjustment, namely producer markets (White 1981). The relatively detailed account of performance art serves as a ground also for this section on producer markets. There are many producer markets, and the discussion here aims at covering a range of concrete convaluations, from individual producer markets for different products or services, such as top downtown restaurants, through frozen pizzas and SUVs in Germany. As customers we take part in producer markets when we, for example, choose what supermarket to go to or to order our food from. These are so common, and also so well covered in the literature, that the empirical details shown in the case of performance art are not necessary.

The underlying idea of mutual adjustment of markets (Aspers et al. 2020)—namely, that actors adjust to one another in an ongoing interaction and observation of one another, which leads to order (Lindblom 2001)—is, as noted above, assumed by many scholars.[10] The specific literature to be used here claims that markets are the result of mutual adjustment, but stress the conditions of 'imperfect' competition (Chamberlin

1933; Greenhut 1975; Robinson 1933). Chamberlin (1933) dispenses with the assumption of homogenous goods, and argues that firms try to gain control over supply and pricing by offering products distinct from those of other producers in the market. Contemporary economists have rediscovered Chamberlin's idea of product differentiation and competition by quality niches (Bordalo et al., 2016). This view suggests that economic actors orient themselves to one another in processes in which they differentiate their offers and create niches. This leads to a stable market characterized by monopolistic competition (Chapter 7).

The economic sociologist Harrison White has discussed market-fashioning based on mutual adjustment. He suggests that what he labels 'producer markets' are a result of actors jockeying for position, through which their market identities are formed (White 1992; 2002: 266–283; 2008). This idea was presented already by Marshall, who says that 'the modern science of industrial technique deliberately standardized some products and many processes'. He goes on to say that this 'deliberately leaves many products and some processes open to varying tastes and humours,[11] to fluctuating needs, and to the caprice of fashion' (Marshall 1920: 201). The latter part of this quotation refers to economic activities characterized by product differentiation and monopolistic competition. Marshall noted more than 100 years ago that in parts of the economy, what we today frequently observe had already developed, namely that there is uncertainty about the products' 'quality' and that neither consumers nor producers necessarily want standardized products. Product differentiation—which may, as well as being a producers' strategy, also be preferred by consumers (Warde 1994)—often makes it more difficult to assess quality. At the same time, producers generate a structure of identities in markets that reduce some uncertainties.

There are economic and non-economic convaluations that address this uncertainty, determining fashion and generating prices. These states of the world do not eliminate uncertainty about what to wear or what things are worth, but they do reduce uncertainty because the sellers have status in the market, and this status order, together with firms' product differentiation, are a way of reducing uncertainty for consumers. It is this idea of product differentiation and stability of social structure (Bourdieu 1984) on which White's producer market theory draws. White's definition of producer markets is informative. Markets, White says, are 'self-reproducing social structures among specific cliques of forms and other actors who evolve roles from observation of each other's behavior' (1981: 518). White says that the specific market profile is due to the fact that 'the original indeterminacy, the Knightean uncertainty, has triggered the evolution of a profile in rivalry that is reproduced jointly between sides and severally among the producers' (White 2002: 31). The producers gain identities as a result of how the customers view their differentiated offers. The consumers, in a sense, endow them with status (Podolny 2005) by acclamation (more, less, or not at all). Status then operates as a signal of quality, and thereby reduces uncertainty (Correll et al. 2017);findings which are to some extent supported by studies on Hollywood films.[12] The social structure, culture, identities, and things traded thus gradually emerge, and eventually stabilize as a producer market. Thus, once the actors in an economic convaluation in the concrete form of a producer market have 'a shared frame of perception among its firms' (White 2002: 2), there is a market. The market is perpetuated by what actors do: 'whether an institution is explicit or implicit, practices are the vehicles for enacting and reproducing it' (White 2008: 173). Padgett and Powell (2012), for example, support White with historical evidence that market formation frequently is the result of stochastic processes unfolding over time, rather than the product of human design. Once established, however, these producer markets tend to be relatively stable (Burt 1988). Market stability is due, in the first instance, to reproduction by what actors do over time in a process of mutual adjustment. The resulting socially structured status order is a means of uncertainty reduction in cases of no clear—or the complete absence of—'quality' standards.

More fundamentally, stability is to be explained by standardization of offers, including a standard for measuring what is offered. This can function like a quality standard, or a proxy of quality (Aspers 2009). The discussion above on standards serves as a background to the idea of standard markets. But as just explained, economic convaluations can also be ordered and stabilized by social structure, typically ordered by status. In this case, it is the social structure of sellers, buyers, or both that order the market. Joel Podolny addresses the difference between objectively accessible means of knowing what is good and bad and the importance of status in relation to uncertainty: 'the greater the market participants' uncertainty about the underlying quality of a producer and the producer's product, the more the market participants will rely on the producer's status to make inference about that quality' (2005: 18). This can be stated, in reverse, as follows: the less uncertainty about what is traded, the less of a role status plays.

Godart and Mears (2009), for example, have shown how high-status fashion houses share 'hot' models, thereby contributing to their own status as well as endowing the models with status. Ordered status—in the form of states of the world—is thus an unintended outcome of the myriad of competitive and friendship relations, ties, and observations that make up the 'hive', which is so central to the fashion world.

Those who stress mutual adjustment explain ordered markets either as a result of rational egos—ready-made 'economic men'—or as a result of actors who co-evolve and become 'rational' while contributing to the making of markets. Structures in markets are, in either case, fashioned in interaction and direct communication between actors and as a result of signalling and observation. Out of the many decisions made by actors who orient themselves to one another (White 1981), and by the audience who also orient themselves to these decisions, a status order emerges. This is characteristics of convaluation. A convaluation, typically, consists of many small decision-makers, some of whom make decisions for others. This is the case with the performance art festivals. Each festival makes a decision for others about who will be included, and ranks the participating artists in a way that resembles the listing of artists at a music festival or firms brokering financial deals (Podolny 1993). Also, a producer market generates a social structure that orders actors. Sociologists in particular stress how order in markets results from actors gaining status in the process of acting as buyers or sellers, indicating that markets do not come about from 'nothing'. In reality, markets result from interaction among actors who have status positions prior to their market-fashioning activities.[13] Nonetheless, it is this order due to status that enables actors to know what they and others are. They can orient their action to the structure, and this reduces the uncertainty they face when acting.

Convaluations, non-economic as well as economic, are forms of uncertainty reduction because they produce states of the world. The convaluations discussed so far have emerged out of mutual adjustment, but never by design. In the following sections, in contrast, examples will be given of convaluations that are decided, that is, organized, but in which the concrete states of the world are outcomes that result from mutual adjustment.

CONVALUATIONS AS RESULT OF DECISIONS—ORGANIZATION

Organized fashioning of convaluations is a process in which there is an attempt (Ahrne and Brunsson 2008: 49) by at least one actor to create a convaluation. By organization, a form can be created to generate states of the world. The difference between the organization discussed here and that dealt with in Chapter 3, in which formal institutions were discussed, is that convaluations are only partially organized (Ahrne and Brunsson 2011) because the notion of hierarchy—the right to decide for others what they shall do—is not present. Moreover, though convaluations as forms can be organized, these attempts to 'organize', as it were, are only forceful given the consent of the audience. There are many examples of organized convaluations, both economic and non-economic. Two cases will be discussed: one non-economic, elections, and the other economic, exchange markets. In these cases, as discussed above, particular states of the world are generated that can used by actors to reduce their uncertainty when acting.

ELECTIONS AS DECIDED CONVALUATIONS

Elections are organized convaluations that let actors decide on one candidate among several (Harris 1932). The outcome reduces uncertainty about, for example, who is to lead, what decisions that are likely to be made, and the general direction of these decisions: are taxes likely to be reduced or increase, will labour laws be more liberal or not. As an institutionalized form of selection, elections stand in contrast to hierarchical assignment and drawing lots. Elections—ideally—reflect what voters value by selecting among the available alternatives. There are democratic political elections, and there are political but undemocratic elections (Gandhi and Lust-Okar 2009), and there are also collegial elections—as well as elections, for example for company boards, in which votes are weighted in proportion to the number of shares the voter owns. Elections are formal procedures (Luhmann 2001) based on a set of rules that may be upheld by institutions, but more frequently are upheld by sanctions, and sometimes ultimately, even by sheer physical force. Political democratic elections are organized and regulated by law, for example the laws of a specific nation-state. That there are laws means that it is a formal institution, but the political struggle in which parties compete for voters' support in elections is left to the mutual adjustment of the actors operating on the two sides of the convaluation: parties and voters. It is clear that, at one end of the continuum, an election may be nothing but lip-service to free and democratic elections, because in some cases there may be little difference between a decision on who is to occupy an office and an 'election' of this position (Gandhi and Lust-Okar 2009). But if the outcome is the result of mutual adjustment, even though organized in procedural fashion, the notion of convaluation applies.

Mutual adjustment in elections means that there is either mutual adjustment on one side of the convaluation or on both sides. There is a large literature, most of it related to political science (Dewan and Hortala-Vallve 2017), dealing with how parties and voters adjust to one another (Adams 2012). Some of these works are based on game theory, but others are more empirically grounded. Parties are said to adjust to public opinion, to mean or median voters, and the voters are said to adjust to changes in the parties' positions. There is clearly competition for the political 'space' between parties, resembling the handful of competitors one finds in a producer market as described by White (1981). Moreover, although both markets and political competition take place against the background of formal institutions, political 'cultures' differ between countries, as do the cultures of markets.

Not only the form but also the results of elections are states of the world that reduce uncertainty, once the result is proclaimed; someone gets elected and others do not, or the votes and the seats are distributed in a particular way. Some certainty is thereby created. The degree of certainty and the usefulness for making predictions of the result are conditioned on the systemic institutionalization of the election system, but also on the culture of the political system—for example, if the interaction climate is characterized by conflict or collaboration. Obviously, it also matters who is elected, or what party or party coalition comes to power. It matters because other actors can then predict what decisions can be made, and perhaps more importantly, it becomes easier to predict what type of decisions will not be made. But the latter type of uncertainty reduction builds on the systemic certainty. In more abstract terminology, the particular states of the world that are the results of elections make sense only if understood in relation to the formal institutions that regulate the political electoral system, but more fundamentally, on the bedrock of informal institutions on which a political system rests (Tocqueville [1835] 1969).

Opinion Polls and Evaluations

An election is an organized way of letting some actors—both those being elected and those doing the electing—adjust to one another to generate an outcome. The outcome, the result of the election, is a state of the world. There are also other examples of organized convaluations in which one side is given the opportunity to generate states of the world. Polls are always set up to take the temperature of public opinions and to predict the outcome of elections. Because a poll is made at a particular point in time—in practice, often over a few days—it is essentially only the voters' view that is 'measured'. The result of the poll is a particular state of the world, which can be used to make decisions, for example, by political parties. Obviously, polls are not election results, but may be reasons for politicians and voters alike even to reconsider how they will cast their votes. Political parties may, due to the results, nonetheless adjust their policies to what they believe voters, users, or consumers want, perhaps by mimicking the policies of other parties. Polls, not very different from prices in markets, communicate preferences of 'consumers', that is, voters; they may also have performative force in relation to elections.[14] The states of the world, if the results of the polls are made public, can be used by many decision-makers.

EXCHANGE MARKETS AS DECIDED CONVALUATIONS

There are different types of markets, each of which generate particular states of the world. Exchanges are organized places for trade, which organizes a process for 'managing the ambiguity and uncertainty of value by establishing social meanings and consensus' (Smith, 1989: 163). A stock exchange harbours a large set of markets for the different kinds of financial instruments traded. The prices of the shares and other instruments traded are, as in any market, the result of mutual adjustments of traders, and these prices are signals to investors. The difference discussed here is whether the market as form is the result of mutual adjustments or of decisions. Ahrne et al. (2015) have shown how organization theory can be used to understand how markets and marketplaces are partially organized. That they are organized means, above all, that the organizer(s) make decisions for others, and that these decisions constitute the markets and decide who is allowed to trade (i.e., the membership), as well as setting and controlling the rules and imposing sanctions on traders. Still, traders adjust to one another and are free to trade or not trade with the resources they possess.

To understand market organization, let us look at an empirical case: how Sweden's market for carbon emissions rights was set up. The organization of this marketplace aims at controlling the emissions of CO_2 of at least the larger CO_2 producers, who are subject to control and at the same time are allowed to trade in the market to handle their emissions by selling or buying rights to emit CO_2 from their factories. This process has been described by Martin Rosenström (2014), on whose study this section draws. For similar studies see Mackenzie (2009) and Bühler (2019), on grains and Rilinger (2022), on electricity. The idea of having a market for emissions rights can be traced back to the 1960s, but the EU first discussed this around the year 2000 (Rosenström 2014: 57). In response to the EU's decision to create a market for emissions rights in 2003, work began in Sweden to set one up by 1 January 2005. The short time period from the decision to the operation of the market is a problem in itself.

To have a market, in addition to rules and a more general market culture that guide actors' behaviour, there must be objects of trade and ways of setting prices (Aspers 2011). The objects of trade, emissions rights, are anything but natural goods. They had to be made, but how? Furthermore, if there is no interest in trading, there can be no market. In this case also the interest in trading has to be created. The interest in trading presumes a shortage—how can this be accomplished? It is clear that this 'market' did not exist, nor could it come about without organization.

In Sweden, several state agencies responded to the EU's laws and became involved in the process, first of discussing the idea of a market, and later its actual implementation. The Swedish state played a central role in this process, mainly because it passed the laws to make the market possible. Rosenström (2014) shows that there was a gap between the laws and implementation. But regardless of this, we should speak of a set of formal institutions that are used to organize the market.

The first step was to decide that plants with CO_2 emissions over a certain limit need to be enrolled in a scheme of emissions permits. Thereby the firms owning plants over a certain size became, by decision, 'members' of the market. It should be underlined that membership is not voluntary but compulsory. It is in this sense that we can speak of a hierarchical relation. It is at least partly a hierarchical relation between the trading firms and the state that organizes the markets, because the firms are forced to participate in the market. In this case the hierarchy is related to the forced creation of property rights, created shortages, and regulations, which means that firms have to purchase rights at least up to the level that 'covers' their emissions (unless they already possess emissions rights). By setting an emissions cap, the state regulates emissions but lets the 'forced' market interaction form an economy of emissions.[15] However, it is not a hierarchy in the strictest sense, because they are not forced to trade, and the firms are still independent bodies controlling their own resources. It is possible that firms in the market may 'sit' on their rights, and thereby make it more expensive for others (but each holder of rights is so small that it makes no difference). Another alternative is that 'outsiders', such as environmental associations, buy rights to increase firms' costs of production, and thereby bring about more environmentally friendly production. Thus, the market members were granted rights to emit CO_2, but they were also granted the opportunity to trade these rights. Only those firms that are included and are given rights will have a direct interest in trading emissions rights. Rights are an essential market prerequisite, and in this case these standardized rights were constructed so that it did not matter with whom one was trading; one right to emit a tonne of CO_2 is identical to another right. These firms were at the same time subject to *control* of how much CO_2 each owner of rights emitted. This control that is recorded in a form of bookkeeping is crucial to the system; it determines how many of their rights the firms inscribed in the system have used. This will determine whether they will have to operate as buyers in the market (if their emissions are larger than what they are entitled to emit) or whether they can sell some of their rights on the market.[16]

Market members will have an interest in trading only if there is a shortage; if no firm has a shortage of emissions rights, there is no demand, and there will be no trade. The precondition is that all members of the market measure their emissions. There are *rules* on how to measure emissions, there are trading rules for the market, and there is a market *culture*. But because there is no incentive for the firms to actually trade and comply with the rules, they must be subject to *control*, and there have to be (negative) *sanctions* against those who do not report on their emissions.

In this story of market-fashioning, several actors are involved, but it is essentially various state agencies that use organizational elements to organize markets for others. The setting of *prices* is yet another market prerequisite and is a consequence of the organized market in which the members may exchange rights with one another. It is, given this compulsory membership and the rules and regulations, possible to see state intervention as a forceful form of regulation. But even though these markets are organized, the organizations subject to marketization remain independent. Put differently, they are not members of the market organizer; they are only part of the market that is thus partially organized (Ahrne and Brunsson 2011).

The few cases reported here are examples of markets that are organized. But marketplaces, too, are organized. The notion of a market indeed grew out of marketplaces. Perhaps the clearest example is the stock exchange, which harbours many different markets; effectively, each listed stock is a market of its own. Yet another marketplace is the Baltic Exchange for shipping freight (Barty-King 1977). This marketplace harbours several economic convaluations (markets) and has existed in various shapes since 1744. Each different freight market—that is, each route—'is' a convaluation that every day produces public prices (particular states of the world) which can be used by everyone who has an interest. In this case, in practice it is made up primarily of members who are in this business and who also trade, as well as those interested in freight costs. The prices shift on a daily basis, but these organized—decided—economic convaluations are much more institutionalized and may remain for decades or even centuries.

It is possible to outline the distinctions between different basic forms discussed in this chapter, namely convaluations within and outside the

Table 5.1. FORMS OF CONVALUATIONS

Combinations of economic and non-economic convaluations with how they have come about, due to mutual adjustment and organization

Convaluations	Mutual adjustment	Organized
Economic	Producer market	Exchange market
Non-economic	Performance art	Elections

economic sphere on one hand, and those convaluations that are the result of actors mutually adjusting to one another, or are decided, on the other hand. These distinctions are presented in Table 5.1.

The two-by-two table suggests that there may be limitations on what can be organized. Especially issues around values may be hard to organize, and forms that have grown into institutions, as discussed in Chapter 2, may be just as forceful. But organized convaluation in particular shows the importance of both informal institutions and formal institutions for their establishment. What these convaluations have in common is that they form particular states of the world, the use of which can reduce the uncertainty decision-makers face. They produce values and meanings and thus fixate what is traded, and they produce prices, and 'past prices normally set—within certain limits—future prices' (64). Given information of prices, the costs of setting up a factory can be calculated, as can investments to reduce emissions when it is clear that emissions are 'regulated' in markets that offer a price of the right to emit CO_2.

CONCLUSION

This chapter focuses on the form known as 'convaluation'. Convaluations are forms that address value uncertainty by the production of states of the world resulting from actors who mutually adjust to one another. In this sense, this chapter relates to the discussion in Chapter 2, in which mutual adjustment leads to institutions. It is clear that not only convaluations but also values may become institutionalized, which means that they become taken for granted. Democracy is a value that is taken for granted in some countries, but not others. Other values indeed change more rapidly, for example, what is currently a fashionable tie for men, what is cutting-edge contemporary art, as well as economic values such as the current price of gasoline. These values too are particular states of the world that are outcomes of convaluations, but they change rapidly.[17]

Convaluations resemble the other forms discussed in Part II. They are social structures of roles, publicly recognized by an audience, that mould values as a result of actors mutually adjusting to one another. Status and standards are the two opposing ways through which convaluations are ordered (Aspers 2009). In standard convaluations, as in markets with homogenous products, the outcomes are prices of standardized goods or services. In status markets, the goods or services are consequences of the status order(s), so that high-status producers offer more highly valued products. In both these two economic convaluations, states of the world are produced that actors can use to diminish the uncertainty they face when acting. A more detailed discussion of the relations between specific forms and states of the world would be possible. Such a discussion would not change the main message of this chapter, and it is therefore located in the Appendix.

A convaluation is institutionalized. Thus, both those who are actively involved in the convaluation and their audience normally acclaim the output without thinking too much about it. Convaluations can either result from a process of mutual adjustment or be organized. If they are organized, the concrete states of the world that a convaluation generates still do not result from decisions for others. As a matter of fact, no one has made the decision; it is an outcome of actors' interaction. Obviously, a market can be organized with the intention of reducing uncertainty and introducing prices, but price levels are typically not organized. Therefore, and in contrast to attempts to decide states of the world discussed in Chapter 3, and decisions for others, which will be discussed in the next chapter, no one can be held directly responsible for the states of the world generated by convaluations. In cases in which a convaluation is organized, there is someone responsible for the form, and that it exists, but not the concrete states of the world that are the outcome.

In reality, most cases are not to be found at the extreme ends, between completely organized and completely unintended. If ratings are quantified, they may appear more objective. Rankings can also be made using algorithms. In a study of sex workers offering their services on platforms, the ranking turns out to be based on an algorithm (Velthuis and Van Doorn 2020). Although the outcome is not a direct result of those who decided about the algorithmic solution, nor by users who directly vote; it is a sociotechnical device for ordering the suppliers that has been deliberately put in place. This is an example of interplay between decisions about conditions without steering the details, but it is also a decision that limits the agency of buyers and sellers to influence the outcomes, because it results from mutual adjustment.

Scientific truths, to take another example, are neither discovered nor decided centrally, though there are many who make decision for others within the scientific field at large, including those hiring professors, those funding research, and those reviewing articles, to take a few examples. Ideas are gradually accepted by people who start to use and practice this new knowledge. After some time, such knowledge can become taken for granted and seen as truth (Kuhn 1962). Knowledge, seen in the light of sociology, is then social, and much of its production can be understood as an outcome of convaluations. Many individuals may try to make truth-claims, essentially based on their own preferences, wishes, and ideas. But only a few claims become 'knowledge' by being acclaimed by the public audience of the 'scientific community', typically those connected to and based on other statements that are already accepted as states of the world. There is a form of 'competition between alternative explanations offered by scientists' (Dahrendorf 1968: 249; Mantzavinos 2016: 152). Science is the paradigmatic example of public uncertainty reduction by means of generating knowledge: 'Science is always a concert, a contrapuntal chorus of the many who are engaged in it. Insofar as truth exists at all, it exists not as a possession of the individual scholar, but as the net result of scientific interchange' (Dahrendorf 1968: 242–243). The establishment of scientific knowledge is, hence, an outcome of the mutual adjustment of scientists (Mantzavinos 2016), in a stable social structure that, out of a multitude of small studies, produces particular states of the world (i.e., convaluation). This means that there are no decisions made, hence no one is responsible for what is true and not true. It is only the trust in the scientific community as a whole that is used to legitimate a certain statement because of its being acclaimed. But since science is an ongoing process, it may take some time until a state of the world is more clearly established. The openness and lack of central authority opens up the field for interpretations, but this is unproblematic as long as one is aware of the procedures and never-ending processing and production of the scientific community. It becomes a problem when actors select one finding from the scientific community without regarding others, or problematize its limitations. Even worse is when a group of people reject the scientific community altogether in favour of their own knowledge.

In other spheres of society, or in certain arenas, it is more difficult to produce knowledge. The internet, to take an example of an arena, is full of opinions—and although some gain recognition and may eventually become states of the world, most simply go unnoticed. It is the same in public debate. Indeed, some actors have sufficient status to become recognized for what they do and say. But this freedom must necessarily lead to an established consensus, especially because anonymity is present, meaning that one does not have to lose face in public. People whose views have more impact can include bloggers, influencers, well-known politicians, and many others, as well as large groups of anonymous actors and organizations who, with financial means or state resources, try to influence what is 'right'. Their claims are made in relation to other claims, and there is thus competition between those making claims to be acclaimed by the audience. In the language of Part II, such claims are made within a form in which these claim-makers have a position. A fashion influencer who is wearing something special, such as specially cut jeans, gains influence when followers (and perhaps even more so, other influencers) adjust their behaviour and also start to wear a similar cut of jeans. But such trendsetting is typically done by bloggers who are already established and who have many followers. Thus, they already have status in the social order of a convaluation.

Furthermore, this chapter shows the structural similarity between economic and non-economic convaluations. Put differently, markets have been presented as economic instances of convaluations, and although sociologists would probably not claim that the existence of markets eliminates uncertainty, it is easy to agree with Arrow, who says that 'the absence of markets implies that the optimizer faces a world of uncertainty' (Arrow 1984: 160). This has a concrete consequence in that it connects economic and non-economic valuation processes (Aspers and Beckert 2011a). The example of performance art shows how aesthetic values are set, which describe what is good performance art and who is a good performance artist. These states of the world can be used by museums setting up exhibitions of performance art. Thus, the status of performance artists can be turned into a financial asset. Similar processes have been shown among fashion photographers (Aspers 2006b), who gain status in the convaluation of magazines, for which there is little money, but this status, once acquired, can be their ticket to well-paid advertising jobs. At a more general level, economic and non-economic convaluations, both of which generate particular states of the world, are conditioned by one another, such as when the state finances research to enhance the competitiveness of a nation.

CHAPTER 6
Deciding for Others

The analysis of value uncertainty, which began in Chapter 5, continues in this chapter. Here the focus is on fashioning states of the world that can reduce uncertainty resulting from decisions for others. **Forms of decisions for others** are publicly recognized social structures with a culture that produces states of the world by decision. Each individual form is then characterized primarily in terms of what decisions are made, but obviously also its culture, and the concrete set of incumbents of the three roles, some of whom may even be individually recognized. Essentially, three roles and their interrelated permanence over time make up these forms: those making decisions, those for whom the decisions are made, and the audience acclaiming decisions. Hence, a given public acclaims the form and its outcomes. How the decisions are made in these forms may differ. The decision may be the result of a jury (group) or made by a person after discussion, interpretation, or negotiation. However, a detailed analysis of this decision procedure in which actors are involved is not the focus here. The point is nonetheless that the accepted decisions become states of the world that can be used by many actors who make their decisions with less uncertainty.

Forms of decision for others appear in numerous empirical examples, but they are often set up by organizations trying to decide for those who are not members. The Oscars jury makes decisions on actors and others' performances. Many people orient themselves to these decisions which include, say, the best picture of 2020 'Parasite', directed by Bong Joon-ho. Such decisions are seen as states of the world by such actors as film producers, who, for example, select composers for the film music of upcoming productions (Faulkner 1983). Directors who have been awarded a prize

Uncertainty. Patrik Aspers, Oxford University Press. © Oxford University Press 2024.
DOI: 10.1093/oso/9780197752753.003.0006

may also be given more opportunities and larger budgets to make films. It also guides directors when casting roles, although other aspects matter, too (Zuckerman et al. 2003). Not least, an award may direct people in the industry towards what is 'good'.

In science, a Nobel Prize, such as for medicine, exemplifies decisions for others made by a committee, which has been delegated this task by the Nobel Foundation. The concrete decision is about who shall be given the medicine prize, with its status and financial reward. By this consecration of values, the scientific community not only celebrates itself and creates an aura of importance, but it also signals what is good science and, indirectly, what is less good science. Non-scientists may also orient themselves to this. Additional examples of forms of decisions for others are attempts to set up an award for the best young entrepreneur, to pick the national soccer team, or to 'evaluate' pig-farmers' animal-friendly production based on certain (and contested) values. There are of course even more examples of value questions that can be addressed by forms of decision for others: who is the greatest soccer player of all time? What is a good wine? Which university is the best?

Both Chapters 5 and 6 deal with value uncertainty. The main difference between them is that while Chapter 5 analyses forms from which states of the world result, ultimately, from mutual adjustment, Chapter 6 studies forms by which attempts are made to decide for others. This latter includes attempts to decide what is 'good' and 'bad' by using rankings and ratings. It also includes, as foreshadowed in Chapter 4, what are called 'evaluations'— but only those which lack objectively accessible standards of evaluation, meaning that it is nothing more than a practice reflecting the discursive use of the term 'evaluation'.

Instead of decisions backed by power, a standard, or an objective rule of an evaluation (issues discussed in Chapters 3 and 4), I here analyse forms whose outcome is an attempt to make decisions that are accepted by a public audience.[1] Hence, decisions for others are attempts whose 'success' is ultimately due to the audience's level of acclamation. These attempts are all made by actors, and it matters who these actors are: both who the decision-makers are, and who makes up the audience. The views of those who make up the audience matter because there are no standards or rules, nor the possibility to implement these decisions with force.

When decisions about general principles become legitimate, such as laws, they are enforced so that they have a lasting and large impact on several conditions and actors. But when a group of academics come together to decide on which submitted proposal is going to be funded, this decision reduces the uncertainty of those involved—some get money, but others do not—but it does not necessarily lead to the establishment of general principles. In the next period, another decision will be made about which projects will be funded, meaning that it is an ongoing activity, although not constantly. In other words, each of these decisions has limited scope and is bound in time. This form of decision for others is institutionalized, but the results in terms of particular states of the world are not. The form is typically institutionalized because it and its decisions are repeatedly acclaimed. Thus, in contrast to decisions of formal institutions, there is no power that backs up this form. The outcome of the forms, nonetheless, are states of the world that reduce actors' uncertainty.

This chapter begins with a presentation of decisions for others that are called 'evaluations' but for which there is no objectively accessible standard on which to base the decisions. This type of 'evaluation' is here treated as an attempt to make decisions for others. Next follows an analysis of valuations, evaluation as a discourse, reviews, ratings, prizes, rankings, and predictions. Although all of these attempts to decide are oriented towards the future—because the decisions have not yet been made—the actual object of the decision can also be events that have already elapsed, or facts that have existed in the past. It will be shown how the different labels are more like a discourse, and how the explanation boils down to attempts to make decisions for others.

VALUATION ARISING FROM DECISIONS FOR OTHERS

When there are objectively accepted states of the world, they can be used to take actions with considerable certainty about the outcome. When it is known that one must jump 7.80 metres to get into the final of the men's long jump competition, this is clear and cannot cause uncertainty. It means that anyone who is taking part in the qualifying round and makes it can also jump in the final. In other cases, there are no standards. Large domains of social life are characterized by a lack of such stated standards; this is also a domain in which uncertainty is rampant. What is good and bad is essentially a normative issue, or, expressed in a Nietzschean way, a matter of taste. Nonetheless, many try to take decisions, and there is also a demand for guidance—expressed by readers of restaurant reviews, for example—and more generally a demand for ideas about what is good taste and what is right (Bourdieu 1984).

There are many aspects that increase the role of forms that settle value uncertainty. The fewer strict norms, the less taken-for-granted knowledge, and the more 'views', 'opinions', and decisions that we make based on 'aesthetic' judgement, the more relevant forms of uncertainty reduction to adjudicate among all these opinions become. Forms for decisions for others can be seen as attempts to address issues of value uncertainty. Convaluations are forms that can either be decided or grown, but actual states of the world are outcomes that actors have fashioned in a process of mutual adjustment. Forms of decisions for others, in contrast, are attempts to decide directly, as it were, on states of the world for others. In both cases, states of the world require acclamation from an audience made up of actors who can say 'yes', but they can of course also say 'no'. Such acclamations can be made more easily if principles of justification are employed (Boltanski and Thévenot 2006). In other words, only if people orient themselves towards, and in a sense accept a decision, will it result in an ordering. Consequently, not just anyone deciding on what is good and bad—such as when one decides to have a cup of tea instead of coffee—will directly lead to an ordering of the world; it is only decisions that are made to affect others in the public realm that stand in focus here. In reality, different attempts to decide for others will compete with one another to be acclaimed by the audience in order to be legitimate. The more who try to make decisions for others, the stronger the competition for acclamation is, the closer one gets to the form called convaluation. And the less competition and more monopolistic the conditions are, the closer one gets to the ideal-type form of decisions for others.

VALUATION AS AN EVALUATION DISCOURSE

Evaluation was discussed in Chapter 4 as an activity for comparing something against objectively existing standards, or more generally, measures something in an 'objective' way. This is a condition for objective evaluations. However, without a standard, outcomes are hard to predict. It may be difficult to predict for those being evaluated and for the public in general, but also for those enacting the role of evaluator (when there is more than one person, it must be a joint decision). The problem of value uncertainty is difficult to address because it is unclear against what the evaluation is taking stock, or because there is so much room left for interpretation and negotiation, or there are no external 'evaluation standards'. If it is unclear what is to be evaluated, this of course increases the uncertainty. The reason is obvious: if one cannot predict outcomes, it is difficult to prepare oneself for such an evaluation, and it is hard to develop a strategy to improve and to score better on the next evaluation because the values are not made explicit or fixed.

Activities called 'evaluations' but which do not meet the criteria laid down in Chapter 4 are in fact decisions. When a decision is made but is called an 'evaluation', actors can still orient themselves to this state of the world, and it may thus become effectual. But regardless of the terminological confusion, decisions for others that are called 'evaluations,' or anything else, may have a much stronger impact than evaluations proper.

There are many examples of forms of decisions for others that are institutionalized and which produce states of the world, although the activity is labelled 'evaluation'. Here I draw on a study of evaluations of theatre companies in Poland by Lewandowska and Smolarska (2020). Their study is about funding decisions made by an evaluation panel for the funding of Polish theatre companies. These funding decisions are based on what panellists see in terms of quality in the companies' public performances. It is the theatre companies' repertoire, what they show to a regular audience (into which the panellists blend), that is evaluated. This study is a clear case of evaluation of art that illustrates 'evaluations' based on weakly institutionalized standards. Although there are some common ideas of what not-good theatre is, terms such as *quality* are hard to concretize and may differ between panellists in ways that are incommensurable. This contrasts with cases with clear-cut standards, such as evaluation of pole vaulters, which essentially measures how high they can jump. The evaluation of theatre companies is an example of person-dependent evaluations, and therefore, to avoid bias, the panel is composed of different types of specialists who represent the different views and interests of the theatre in Poland.

Panels set up to evaluate theatre companies consist of seven members, and to be included in the evaluation, the theatre company's productions must be seen by at least four members. In the study, 30 panellists were interviewed, the majority of whom perform this role in addition to their other roles in the theatre world, such as critics, as well as in academia or as employees of public theatres. The theatre productions are scored over the season, and the panel comes together to make the final decision on which company will 'win' the competition, as well as the rank order of the competing companies.

As has been shown in other cases, the decision-making process involves elements of haggling and trade-offs among the panellists. It is thus clear that decisions are not 'rational' and oriented to standards, but neither are they random, because those involved have been socialized in similar ways and share many values. The decisions by the panellists—states of the world—are communicated publicly and, given the institutionalized financial support system, are largely seen as legitimate. Furthermore, in this case there is essentially only one organization that decides on financial support for theatre companies in Poland. Once the support opportunity is there, Polish theatre companies orient themselves to it and its decisions, making it important and thereby acclaiming it.

The decisions made by the panel have consequences most directly for theatre companies, the main audience of the evaluating organization. The outcomes are states of the world, but, as has already been underlined, states of the world do not have to be true to reduce the uncertainty for actors when they make decisions; the notion of 'true' states of the world lacks meaning here. Orientation is possible also for theatre companies that did not obtain support, which adjust their programmes in ways they believe will increase their chances of receiving support in the future. But also, critics, actors, and the general audience are affected by the decisions and orient themselves towards them, directly or indirectly. Moreover, the financial support for theatre companies enables many actors to perform and audiences to see plays, and thus maintains an art world in which the audience, to a substantial extent, is made up of other actors and insiders (Becker 1982).

Paradoxically, without the financial support that is the practical outcome of the evaluation, in one sense there would be more 'certainty' because each company would know for sure that they had been left to their own devices. But as discussed above, a decision—in this case to have an organization that hands out financial support to theatre companies—reduces uncertainty concerning how support is given, but it also creates uncertainty because it is unclear which companies will be supported and which will not. However, in this case, few theatre companies would say that it would be better not to have the possibility of support just to be certain (that there is no money).

In other cases, an organization tries to make decisions for others, namely those who are not members of the decision-making organization. This attempt is essentially made without having the authority to implement the decision. Examples are evaluations of what garment producers pay their workers. The organization Clean Clothes Campaign organized an evaluation of the wages garment-producing firms pay their employees under the aegis of what they called 'Fashion Checkers'. The knowledge they generate by publishing their results enables not only customers but also politicians, for example, to make decisions on whether to buy or not to buy from a certain garment company or make decisions about supply chains for garments. Fashion Checkers carried out a survey of garment manufacturers, and based on the results (or lack of results) from the survey, these firms were evaluated according to various values, such as supply chain transparency. Concretely, the evaluated firms are given commitment scores for showing a 'public commitment' to develop an 'action plan' (to increase transparency) and to make publicly available (disaggregated) their suppliers' labour costs.[2] Each of the three dimensions of evaluation can be scored 'yes', 'partial' or 'no'. Ultimately, the results only matter if they are 'acclaimed by the audience', thereby making them a state of the world.

Fashion Checkers is an organization that is separate from those evaluated, but which 'forces' the latter to participate in the evaluation. Regardless of whether one wants to take part in an evaluation or not, one has to relate to its 'verdict' (Mears and Finlay 2005; White 2008).[3] Fashion Checkers' independence also means that as the evaluators, they and their results enjoy considerable autonomy. Autonomy is an important aspect of the organization's legitimacy in evaluating, rating, giving out awards, and developing rankings. It can be achieved if these organizations are separate and independent from those subject to the evaluation. This is important for the trustworthiness of the organization, as well as their outputs in terms of 'evaluations', ratings, awards, or rankings. Rankers, for example, should not have an interest in who is ranked top and who is ranked low; this 'business model' is supposed to provide useful information that can be translated into money. Obviously, such information could be sold to individual actors exclusively instead of being made public. The performance of evaluations, regardless of whether they reflect reality more or less completely or correctly, can generate states of the world, also when those who organize the form only try to create states of the world for others, and only with the means of making a proposition with the hope that it will be acclaimed.

Science too, is a form, though well supported with resources, which also 'only' make propositions, out of which some become acclaimed. As noted above, acclaimed scientific outputs—states of the world—are the outcome of a process of mutual adjustment. But the whole field of science rests on many organized forms that contribute to these outcomes. Research funding (Roumbanis 2017) and reviewing academic texts are two examples of decisions for others. To act as reviewers, academics switch roles for a limited period—for example, from researcher to scientific reviewer for scientific proposals or articles. Reviewing is an institutionalized practice, and there are organizations that are set up to distribute research funding—typically national research foundations—which use researchers to make evaluations, which simultaneously is also a way to reduce the uncertainty of other researchers, who then can get indications of what gets support and who gets support.

Scientific work is often considered to be objective, and when we look at the empirical research on scientific evaluation it is evident that the output of grant applications—that is, the relevant decisions—refer to objective standards. In reality, however, these evaluations reflect the views of those evaluating, suggesting that one cannot speak of evaluation of scientific work against an objective scale (Lamont 2009; Merton and Zuckermann 1971; Roumbanis 2017). Consequently, the selection of reviewers is a political issue, indicating that it matters who does the reviewing. Obviously, some objective dimensions, such as the number of citations a researcher's publication has generated, how many grants a person has received, the number of graduate students they have supervised, and other things, can be and are used to evaluate candidates. But there is no formula for the objective commensuration of these different dimensions, especially given the future-oriented potential of the researcher and project that is to be valued. Moreover, in these evaluations, typical non-numerical dimensions also matter, such as quality, creativity, and independence. This means that there is no one, objectively commensurated scale for the evaluation of grant proposals, nor for positions or awards given to scientists. This case is a good example of an evaluation in which there are both objective measures and objective scales, but these are influenced by actors' views, meaning that subjective elements are also involved. The decisions of research foundations—states of the world—are published, and other scientists can orient themselves to what they perceive to be the 'right' strategy for the next round of evaluation. But clearly, this 'guesswork' shows that the predictive value in cases when a new panel is put together is limited, which indicates that the situation is not characterized by evaluations according to standards.

It may be concluded that at one end, there is a continuum with evaluations with no standards and nothing but the views of those deciding what is 'good' and 'bad', and at the other end, evaluations grounded in conventions such as scientific standards. However, many of these depend, in practice, on persons and personal preferences, and it is an open affair to what extent the persons enacting the roles can resemble an 'objective' standard or if the decisions they make are completely erratic and, as such, not contributing to reduction of uncertainty for decision makers. others.

REVIEWS

The term *reviewing* is frequently used, also in everyday life, and typically refers to an evaluative statement—but, in contrast to ratings, normally without 'scoring' whatever is reviewed. Blank (2007) referred to restaurant ratings as cases of connoisseurial reviews of restaurants, for which objective criteria are normally not the main means of differentiation. Connoisseurial reviews also occurs in art worlds, and partly because the kind of review, and partly because artistic activites frequently are closely related to the personal identity and their existential being, artist may be severyl affected by reviews.

Reviewing reduces uncertainty because states of the world can be produced. But how is reviewing done when there are no standards? Chong (2020) has analysed the role of uncertainty faced by those reviewing novels. This is a role that few occupy permanently; many switch roles (Aspers 2011), such as that between reviewer and author, with most of them identifying as the latter. Chong mentions that there is an association for reviewers, but hardly anyone identifies as a reviewer. As Chong shows, there are plenty of people in the United States who do reviews, but perhaps only 12 'full-time critics left in America' (Chong 2020: 106). This means that there is less organizational certainty, but in this case also no institutional certainty in this art field. Chong does not focus on the uncertainty reduction that the reviews potentially bring about, nor on the work and uncertainty of authors and editors (Childess 2017; Furst 2017), but on three distinct uncertainties that reviewers face. The first is epistemic uncertainty, referring to the uncertainty of the objects in question—the novels to be reviewed. The second uncertainty is social, by which Chong means how the review will be received and the consequences it may have for the reviewer, most of whom identify mainly as something else, occasionally reviewing books for magazines. The third uncertainty to which Chong refers is institutional uncertainty. This refers both to formal institutions on reviewing and to informal institutions related to what it is and how reviewing should be done, and its value and role in the literary community and in society at large.

Chong's study provides a concrete phenomenological understanding of the uncertainty actors face, and the means of uncertainty reduction in this study can be used to reduce these uncertainties. A review is itself a means of reducing the uncertainty of the text published, both its content and, above all, its quality. It is a convaluation out of which values of 'quality' and status hierarchies are partly constructed. Such a hierarchy is also made up of sales, publishing houses, different awards, general media attention, and the like. There is a status hierarchy among reviewers, but there appear to be few 'superstar' reviewers (Rosen 1981). Thus, in the convaluation of reviewing, the uncertainty that an individual reviewer may face nonetheless translates into less uncertainty for authors, publishing houses, and readers when reviews are published. Furthermore, the publicness of the review process partly also addresses the two other uncertainties that Chong brings up, social and institutional.

Though Chong rightly points out the social uncertainty, the fact that a range of reviews are written and publicly available diminishes this uncertainty for reviewers. The reviewers, in a sense, are not alone. Moreover, she shows that a lot of institutions known by the reviewers are in practice known to reduce this social uncertainty. These include 'playing nice' rather than being brutally honest and critical, and to only 'punching up, never down', meaning that reviewers only criticize those above them (Chong 2020: 83–97) on the status ladder, as superstars are like 'tanks' who cannot be seriously hit by negative reviews. Taken together, a culture has emerged in which a neutral review can be seen as critical, and in reality, only an overwhelmingly positive review signals the 'quality' of the book.

Finally, institutional uncertainty is also there, but at the same time Chong shows that the reviewers themselves are quite aware of the norms, values, and conventions that guide reviewers. The golden rule of reviewing, she informs us, is 'Review as You Would Want to Be Reviewed' (Chong 2020: 72). There is also a fairly unanimous perception of what aspects a reviewer should consider, namely: how the characters of the novel are presented; language or prose; plot and structure; themes and ideas; and the extent to which the expectations of the genre are met (Chong 2020: 42–43). Because being an author—or failing to become one—are major issues for those involved in writing novels (Furst 2017), these decisions are all deeply existential. The more committed an individual is to a specific social outcome—for example, a career as an artist—the closer failure is to actual death. Consequently, the centrality of uncertainty differs by individual, and so does the need to reduce existential uncertainty.

RATINGS

Evaluation tends to cover many different things, many of which lack clearcut standards. Also, ratings may cover a whole range of practices, and it is not uncommon that the rating is preceded by an evaluation. In analogy with what was said above, in the case of rating, first and foremost, something is classified *as* something, such as 'being a sports car'. In many cases there are rules on how to evaluate, and there is an attempt to create 'objective' conditions for rating. When rating is based on a publicly available standard, then it is in fact an evaluation. The rating in focus here covers cases in which value is ascribed to something (Stark 2020) where no objective scale exists. This activity covers some of the observations that in everyday language are called evaluations. Hence in this case, rating is carried out when there is no standard, and the outcome is thus the result of a decision. As soon as interpretation becomes the main issue, and when group dynamics are paramount for the outcome—and thus when valuation is involved and, more generally, when those who are rated cannot predict the outcome—it is reasonable to speak of attempts to make decisions for others. However, even when standards are lacking, a rating may nonetheless have performative power and may generate states of the world because it orders things in the world.

Espeland identified the relations between evaluations and ratings, but also between evaluations and rankings, in 'Formalized Evaluation: the Work that Ratings Do' (Espeland 2020). The research by Espeland and Sauder(2007) shows the complexity of rating, and also illustrates how what are here called states of the world come about. The construction of the score is central to whether a rating is publicly acclaimed by an audience. Espeland studies the consequences for actors of the states of the world. Moreover, Espeland's work lends itself well to an analysis both of states of the world and of how they reduce uncertainty.

Rating scores can be used for evaluations. Blank (2007) has analysed evaluations of restaurants and of computers. Obviously, knowing what restaurants meet one's preferences reduces uncertainty for those selecting which restaurant to go to, or from which to order something to eat at home. When buying a computer, which people do only infrequently, the complexity of the different components, and how they are combined in different computers, may be hard to overcome for a layperson, so a commensurated value (example.g., a 'best buy' or a score) reduces the uncertainty for computer buyers. These two objects of rating are obviously different, but illustrate well how procedural reviews for computers can use objective criteria, and how in others, such as connoisseurial reviews of restaurants, objective criteria are normally not the main means of differentiation (Blank 2007). Connoisseurial reviews may include a commensurated rating, or ratings of several different dimensions, such as ambience, food, and service, which are not commensurated (Karpik 2010). Blank, who analysed several restaurant ranking systems, describes one by which the star ratings 'reflect the reviewer's reaction to food, ambience and services, with price taken into consideration' (Blank 2007: 45). But there are also restaurant rating systems that are procedural. Blank describes the process of evaluating restaurants, which starts by selecting a restaurant and proceeds by trying different dishes at several different visits to the restaurant over time. The review has to be written, and the different components being reviewed are often commensurated to one overall score. The study by Blank shows in detail how complicated the reviewing process is, and how many actors, including restaurant owners, editors, and readers, have a direct and indirect influence on the actual review.

Trust in the review is one important dimension. The trust and the credit an audience gives a review is due partly to the reviewer, but mainly to the outlet publishing the rating. The rating is then embedded by a trustworthy source that has gained status over time. To recall, status is relational, which means that ratings that come from high-status outlets are institutionalized and generate states of the world, at least until the next round of reviews. Restaurants that have earned good reviews over many years, and of course have had many satisfied guests, become institutionalized and may even withstand occasional bad reviews. For a new restaurant that is slaughtered in a review, it may mean the end. The uncertainty for customers is diminished by the states of the world that the reviews generate. This theoretical idea is supported by Blank, who has empirically also investigated the reactions and value of reviews and ratings for the audience. It has also been shown that films revies are useful in the eyes of the film audience (Reinstein and Snyder 2005).

We have seen that credit ratings of countries, and activities at least partly using different indexes, have been seen as procedures by which uncertainty is repackaged as risk. Credit scores of individuals are a way of presenting rankings; originally, estimating people's 'moral character' played a role, but gradually such scores have become a function of standardized procedures and measures relying on existing data (Carruthers 2013). The scales of risk are not just at the ordinal level, but at least at the ratio level. Another aspect of that rating described as valuation is that it implies commensuration. This means that the different dimensions, each of which may be at least reasonably 'objective', are brought together into one common metric. In this commensuration, meaning is lost, and new meaning is created. But the main point here is that as long as there is not one common metric to which everyone in the field can relate and consider as the standard, rating is not objective; it is a decision for others about value. Ratings, to make a last point, are absolute, meaning that all those that have been rated may, in theory, get the highest score. This does not mean that the states of the world—that is, the rating scores—should not be transitive to other settings. The result of ranking, nonetheless, is order, which means that uncertainty decreases. *Rating* is a term that presumes some form of objectivity of the scale used for rating, though in reality, such a scale is lacking.

PRIZES AS INDIRECT COMPETITION

A prize is awarded by making a decision in favour of one candidate over other alternatives (English 2005). In this sense, order is proposed and, if acclaimed, states of the world that can reduce uncertainty are the result. Awarding a prize may include an orientation to an explicit and concrete thing, such as the selection of the winner in a rap battle. But there does not even have to be an existing value that the awards reflect; the decision, together with the winner or what is winning, may instead be largely performative, as in architecture competitions (Kreiner 2020). Prizes may be awarded based on what has been discussed so far, for example, reviews, and ratings, both of which may be done according more or less to a standard. In most cases, a prize is given to someone for an accomplishment. The decision on who or what organization is rewarded, and for what accomplishment, is normally decided by the discussions of a jury or the equivalent of a jury. The Noble Prize is the mother of all prizes (English 2005). It is also probably the highest status prize, and the lack of a Nobel Prize in a certain area can be a justification for setting up an additional prize. Prizes are organized, and how they are organized—for example, open to all or only to a limited group of members—has implications for how they are received and their impact (Edlund et al. 2019).

The Oscars is an example of an indirect competition, which yields a list of winners, all of whom are credited with recognition, publicity, and status. Even an Oscar nomination 'serves as a signalling device, indicating which films are viewed by industry experts as being worthy of recognition' (Nelson et al. 2001: 1). The status that the prize confers on those awarded it can be used by film directors and production companies to make sure that their productions get high recognition, although great commercial success cannot be guaranteed. The giving out of awards—as when the Academy of Motion Picture Arts and Sciences announces the 'best actress' and other awards at its official Academy Awards, known as 'the Oscars'—means that states of the world are created. Not only is the award ceremony organized, but the entire selection procedure is laid out in a detailed 38-page document.[4] The procedure for membership is far from easy. The Academy, made up of different branches, only allows new members by sponsorship: 'The Academy's membership process is by sponsorship, not application. Candidates must be sponsored by two Academy members from the branch to which the candidate seeks admission.'[5] This suggests that the Academy is autonomous.

There are other competitive prizes, such as design awards.[6] Awards are also given out in scientific disciplines, such as the Hans L Zetterberg award in sociology conferred by the University of Uppsala:

> The prize is to be awarded yearly to a young researcher, Swedish or foreign, who, with his/her scientific work in sociology, preferably through the fruitful

combination of theory and practice, has moved the research front forward. Through his/her published works, the nominee should have reached an acknowledged academic position but should not be at the end of his/her research career.

The upper age limit for nominees for the Zetterberg prize is 40 years (the year the prize is awarded), and each winner gets 100,000 SEKR (about €10,000). Sociologists can be nominated to this prize by anyone, but the prize committee can, in principle, give it out to candidates it deems worthy. This is one example of a scientific prize that attempts to bring some order to the world.

In some cases, there is an awareness of the competition around a prize, as in that among those who have chosen to take part in an architecture competition. In other cases, such as the Nobel Prize, there are no official lists and no way to register to take part. The jury is essentially free to pick anyone as prize winner. Although recipients of awards are essentially determined by a jury, there may be fierce competition, such as in architecture competitions (Kreiner 2020). The architectural bureaus that have been selected to take part in an architecture competition—an 'architects battle'—do so without directly 'turning against each other' because everyone is 'performing in isolation' (Kreiner 2020: 34–35). Once the proposals have been submitted, each architecture bureau has to await the jury's decision. Although there are rules on how to make decisions, it is also clear that the jury can overrule them.

Some awards only mention the winner, but others also mention runners-up. There is a wide variety in terms of nominations, eligibility criteria, and many more aspects, all of which are important but nonetheless do not change the concrete fact that the prize awarded is given for some reason to one person (or organization). In contrast to ratings, awards give the prize to only one winner. This means that the spotlight is on one only, and this also means that the impact on the winner can be great. The most obvious effect is of course for the winner, who may gain money, status, or a combination thereof.

Competitions and awards may of course have a major impact on those who win, and on those who do not win. Competitions for classical musicians may nonetheless reduce the uncertainty for musicians, who thereby are exposed to a competitive situation, which may help them as musicians (MacGormick 2020). Competitions in terms of awarded prizes are often indirect, because in many cases, such as the Nobel Prize, a person may not even know whether they are a potential candidate.

Awards are frequently built into a narrative, and there are sometimes donors who stand behind the prize. In most cases the award has procedures to elevate and draw attention to their value (Espeland 2020: 108–109). These factors further the award and make it more likely that it will be recognized and that it can be seen as a form that generates states of the world, to be used by actors to reduce their uncertainty. The value of an award, from the perspective of this study, is the reduced uncertainty about what is good and bad for actors in the domain for which it is a reward. The decision on the award may manifest itself as an acclaimed state of the world.

Although in science the Nobel Prize is not the only prize, it is so dominant that it is almost a form of decision for others in its own right. In some areas, there is only one form due to regulation, such as honorary awards provided by the state to foreigners. In other fields, such as culture, there are more awards 'than our collective cultural achievements can possibly justify', and in US literary circles there is a standing joke by Gore Vidal saying that 'the United States has more prizes than writers' (English 2005: 17). If prizes come to be plagued by inflation, hardly any decision has any meaningful impact. It is simply cognitively impossible to keep track of prizes, especially if none stands out from the crowd. In such cases, one can commensurate the different prizes in numbers and start counting how many prizes one has, rather than listing each of them.

RANKINGS

Rankings (Ringel and Werron 2020, Ringel et al. 2021), according to Espeland, are 'devices for "monitoring" performance over time' (Espeland 2020: 105). They emerged as a means to measure performance in areas of competition (Ringel and Werron 2020). In contrast to ratings, rankings must by necessity create a hierarchical order (Levi Martin 2009: 127), because all those subject to a rating can be deemed 'excellent' if they meet the relevant criteria. Rankings, thus, are relative, at least on the ordinal scale of measurement, and the ordering is vertical. In this section, I rely much on the work of Espeland (Espeland and Stevens 1998; Espeland and Sauder 2007), and in particular 'Formalized Evaluation: The Work That Rankings Do' (2020) to give an account of rankings.

There is no doubt that rankings can be used by actors to make decisions with reduced uncertainty. Rankings define 'excellence in a particular way' (Espeland 2020: 105), and those ranked are ordered in accordance with something. This 'something' may be a very strong and institutionalized standard, or, in contrast, nothing but the views of those performing the ranking.

The form of valuation because of ranking is made up of the three relevant roles: those ranking, those being ranked, and the audience. The form, as mentioned above, is the institutionalized role structure that orders its environment. The output is, as in the case of evaluation, numbers or the rank order of whatever is ranked. By ranking or valuing a 'thing', a value is created by the actors who are enacting the roles of the form.

Taken overall, besides being simplistic, rankings can be obscure, often inaccurate, and subjective. Nevertheless, rankings provide some certainty in a context of uncertainty for actors making decisions (Esposito and Stark 2020), a finding also shown by Espeland (2020). Moreover, Espeland (2020: 101) points out that the first university rankings in the United States were issued by *US News and World Report*, which started in the 1980s. The first reports were marketed as 'consumer information for prospective students and their parents' to be used 'for making decisions' about which university to attend (p. 101). In its narrow usage, this is almost like private knowledge, known only by those who know about the service and pay for it. But once this is relayed in the media, and because 'media competition spawned rankings and continues to propel it' (p. 102), the outcomes of rankings become public, and this means that states of the world, or public knowledge, is generated. This ranking practice expanded to other areas, including 'community colleges, hospitals, doctors, diets, health plans, jobs, mutual funds, realtors, even countries' (Espeland p. 101). The point here is not that all these rankings are, or must be, 'correct' and that true states of the world are produced; the point is that there is an audience that, by acclaiming these rankings, made them 'real'. In this sense, rankings are performative. Their impact may be so great that even those who are ranked—for example, universities—are willing to pay for the information to be better able to adjust to the criteria laid down, and thereby hopefully to climb in the rankings.

Both those who evaluate and those who are evaluated orient themselves to the value called standard. In fact, a standard may become more institutionalized than the order of the identities of the actors evaluating and being evaluated. Take the QS World University Rankings as an example, which rank universities and also disciplines at universities. The top universities, such as Cambridge, Harvard, Oxford, and Stanford, are currently more institutionalized than the ranking. Gradually, academics have learned about this and other rankings, and at some point this may become more institutionalized than the universities' 'tacit' or 'known' rank order, especially among older scientists mainly socialized prior to the emergence of university rankings. Many different actors perform rankings, including bloggers and influencers, not least in the form of different lists, such as the best chainsaw (without relying on any objective testing), best band ever, or best holiday resort, to take a few examples. The scope of rankings varies. Rankings can be local—say, all doctors in a community—or global, such as a ranking of all the countries in the world on how democratic they are.

Any type of ranking suffices to bring order because it generates qualitative differences between what is (e)valuated. Forms of uncertainty reduction imply the use of quality schemes (Podolny and Hsu 2003) to facilitate actors' decision-making, thus making better decisions among alternatives. Given that there are categories and that there is (e)valuation within these categories, there may also be comparisons that result in rank orders (Zuckerman 1999) that facilitate decision-making. Rankings, however, do not have to be stable (Esposito and Stark 2020: 138). In addition, the more of them there are, the less each can contribute to enhancing the certainty of decision-makers, because each can orient itself to 'its own' favourite ranking outcome. Because of the interest in special segments—for example, not just horror films in general, but horror films with vampires— there is a need for additional rankings, and a list of 'best vampire films'. There is an analogy here to producer markets, in which the audience, in this case made up of consumers, can only make meaningful distinctions if the different producers, who compete in a market by offering similar but not identical products, do not exceed a handful (White 1981).

PREDICTIONS

If no one had the slightest idea of what would happen in the future, uncertainty would be almost unbearable. But given the informal institutions that are simply taken for granted, and the large number of formal institutions that guide us, uncertainty, so it appears, is manageable. But given the fact that the future cannot be known, it may still be of interest to form the future.

There is a large literature on predictions of the future, but as Morgenstern pointed out (Beckert 2016: 227), any prediction about human behaviour will become part of social life. Thus, actors' adjustment to a prediction alters the conditions in which it was made. But this, as Beckert shows in his review of the literature, has not stopped actors attempting to predict the future.

Surely, 'The best way to predict the future is to invent it,' as the informatics developer Alan Kay has stated. Still, the complexity of a prediction, its time horizon, and its precision will strongly influence the degree to which it will be correct. Hence, a prediction that there will be an election in

Switzerland in the future can be wrong, but given that elections are institutionalized, that is highly unlikely. The prediction that on 29 October 2035, there will be a referendum about abolishing the cantons in Switzerland is much more precise. There is nothing pointing towards it, however, and it is so precise that no one would bet on it.

For a prediction to become real, the audience must orient themselves to it and, by 'taking action', make it real. This corresponds to the idea that states of the world do not have to be true; it is enough that they are considered 'real', following the Thomas Theorem, for actors to use when acting. Depending on the exact statement, the authority of the person who made it, its precision, the exact time period, and procedures (Austin 1986: 14–15), it may be more or less likely that the audience will take action. It is hence the legitimacy or the perception that a statement is right or good—that is, 'what I would like to see materializing in the future'—that matters if actors are to orient themselves to it or not. Thus, as mentioned above, states of the world can create reality. Performativity in economic sociology (Callon 1998) is much broader and refers also to the making of reality based on theory, which implies causality between the 'statement' (theory) and the outcome.[7]

Jens Beckert (2016) stressed the role of and need for expectations, that is, the 'future results with the course of action they are contemplating' (p. 35), for a capitalist economy. These expectations are fictional, meaning that the expectations are contingent on future conditions. Beckert starts his analysis at the individual action level. It is indeed possible for individual actors to have fictional expectations and that these drive their actions, and that the common view about the future reduces uncertainty. Beckert has also argued that 'imagined futures' are a key activity of organizations under conditions of uncertainty (2021).

A special characteristic of projections is that they make sense, have an impact, and reduce uncertainty only if they are public. If an actor is powerful, rules for others can be decided, and in this sense some states of the world for the framing of the future can be decided by force. But given the lack of force that is the condition of Part II of this book, it is when others also act in accordance with the statement that it can become reality. It is thus only if these expectations become public, and if actors orient themselves to them, and in this sense they are acclaimed by an audience, that they can become states of the world. Even states of the world about the future can reduce uncertainty, not least if compared with a situation characterized by uncertainty and without common stories or narratives that bind actors presently acting together with a common and less uncertain future. To gain credibility, that is, to 'inspire belief in a specific future'

(Beckert 2016: 273), narratives may be socially created to generate shared perspectives.

States of the world can, for example, be generated when organizations such as the World Trade Organization make predictions about how trade will develop in the near future. This type of projective statement may become 'real', and they may to some extent resemble self-fulfilling prophecies if enough actors orient themselves to them. Examples of this kind of future-making include the narratives created in social movements (Fligstein and McAdam 2012) or when markets are created (Donald and Yuval 2003).

Komarova has analysed the making of narratives in art markets in India and Russia, showing how these narratives create 'projections for the future that can serve as a source of certainty and create stability in the market' (2017: 347). Komporozos-Athanasiou (2022) argues that what he calls speculative communities create imagined futures that bring people together to address uncertain conditions. To imagine a future is of course not something new; the typically religious idea of prophecy is its root (Weber 1946: 285). In line with the arguments presented here, narratives do not necessarily create certainty—not least given the large number of contingencies that always exist for future action. But narratives to which many actors orient themselves may become states of the world that can reduce uncertainty because they are acclaimed in public, and may become self-fulfilling prophecies (Merton 1957).

CONCLUSION

When no objective scales of value exist, actors may try to decide for others what is right. Decisions for others about what is right and wrong, or good and bad, are typical examples of how states of the world are generated. Such decisions can be about many things, and be temporally oriented to past events, the contemporary situation, or the future. These states of the world can be used to reduce uncertainty when acting. Though they come under different labels, their underlying logic is similar. They are all forms that can generate states of the world.

Over time, a series of decisions may form more general values of what is good and bad, which means that forms of decision for others are able gradually also to generate informal institutions, if they become taken for granted. This can be the case if decisions are consistent enough for an underlying value or standard to gradually emerge. This is to say that over time, states of the world have become informal institutions that may continue to exist even without the support of the form that initially fostered it. When this happens, there are similarities with the informal institutions discussed in Chapter 2. Forms for decisions for others also share many similarities with decisions for others about rules. But the decisions here are not about rules—principles that apply to many cases—but about particular events. There are, moreover, no negative sanctions that can be implemented by force (as discussed in Chapter 3) to impose these decisions; instead, they require public acclamation.

'Inflation' is a general problem that may occur if there are too many attempts to make decisions for others. When there are many different ranking lists, or too many awards, this tends to create 'inflation'; it also makes it more difficult for the audience to keep focused on one award. Both hinder the establishment of states of the world. It may be that there are so many attempts to make decisions for others about values, in each instance confined to a limited audience, that no states of the world can be established. In the case of one decision-maker being challenged by others, such inflation generated by competition may turn the form of decision for others into a convaluation. Hence, although each individual attempt to create a state of the world may reduce uncertainty, problems arise when there are far too many, none of which can produce states of the world. Stark summarizes this general problem: 'There are so many best movies, best movies 2016, best movies ever, best movies about football, samurai, surfing, that it is implausible that each of them can become a reference' (Stark 2020: 17). White (1981) takes the view that only a small number of producers make up a market because it is impossible for actors to separate out a larger number into distinct identities, creating the nucleus of a market in which competition may be fierce. A similar logic exists with prizes, ratings, and rankings: for actors to meaningfully distinguish them, there can only be a small number, perhaps a dozen.[8] When there are many competitors, so that it is no longer possible for the audience to keep track of them, in practice we have a convaluation.

Consequently, and ideal-typically, when there is only one in a domain who can make decisions for others, it represents a perfect case. Thus, if a single form becomes dominant—such as a performance art festival, which is in fact a situation similar to a monopoly—then what this festival decides to show becomes an instance of the form of decision for others. In contrast, if attempts to decide on rules for others—what in the literature is called institutional entrepreneurship (Garud et al. 2002)—occurs when there are many small actors, and as an attempt to decide for others, it is a convaluation.

This chapter has shown how states of the world come about because of decisions for others. But these decisions are not backed by force, and are consequently 'attempts'. The forms have, due to institutionalization, sufficient status to generate decisions that are acknowledged by the audience. There is then a sense of, if not agreement, at least acceptance of the decision as 'valid' and thus worthy of consideration. The social activities leading to states of the world, discussed in Chapters 5 and 6, are peaceful. However, these decisions rest on a bed of other states of the world, including both informal institutions and formal institutions. But what if there are conflicting ideas about values, norms, and even directly opposing interests? In the next chapter, the formation of states of the world out of direct interaction by parties with opposing interests is in focus. This is to say that the outcome that may reduce uncertainty for those making decisions is not one of negotiation but of conflict among contestants.

CHAPTER 7

Contest

Uncertainty, it has been argued, can be reduced in public using different states of the world. In most cases, states of the world emerge in an orderly fashion as exemplified so far. Although formal institutions can be implemented despite conflicting interests, and even despite resistance, this is normally not an open conflict between one making decisions and the other being subject to the decision; it is simply one party making a decision that has the legitimacy to do so, such as states.

How are states of the world generated when the different parties cannot settle what is 'right' and 'wrong' peacefully? What happens if there is struggle for something that both parties cannot have, such as winning a swimming race? What if there is a conflict over basic institutions or values, and neither informal institutions, formal institutions, nor peaceful forms of uncertainty reduction offer solutions? How do the forms that produce particular states of the world come about?

Following the logic of the two preceding chapters, this chapter too focuses on how states of the world come about. The main difference between this chapter and the other chapters in Part II is that the analysis here is about states of the world that are the result of a contest between actors with different interests. Match racing between sailing boats is an example of a contest, as is the final of the world chess championship. Two pugilists who fight in the ring is another example. The outcome of contests results in states of the world from a direct interaction or even confrontation by contestants. Although many contests are about values, they can really be about anything. There is thus no specific empirical domain or 'content' of the form called a 'contest'.

Uncertainty. Patrik Aspers, Oxford University Press. © Oxford University Press 2024.
DOI: 10.1093/oso/9780197752753.003.0007

The cases discussed in Chapters 5 and 6 are all, essentially, peaceful interactions that lead to particular states of the world. Dahrendorf is clear about the role of uncertainty and conflict—'uncertainty demands variety and competition'—and he thinks that with the 'assumption of fundamental uncertainty about what is right, there follows the necessity of conflict' (1968: 240). Dahrendorf concentrates on peaceful conflict, but contests are not necessarily peaceful. As will be discussed in detail below, the classic duel—as a direct and physical, often organized, conflict between two parties—was a way of settling states of the world that has its roots in the contestation of claims. Wars, battles, and duels are examples of how contests settle issues directly. Though it is less frequently used today, the history of humankind is unthinkable without conquers, war, and even fighting about what is right and wrong. The stabilization of nations, borders, and disputes using violent means has in one sense reduced the uncertainty in the world. The costs for those involved may be very high— ultimately people's lives are at stake. With the lack of objective ways of knowing the outcome prior to the contest of opposing parties, and without indirect ways of reducing uncertainty, such as the use of the form called 'decision for others', or a lack of institutions that may prevent direct conflicts, hostilities may be the only way left open.

This chapter begins with an analysis of the most central concepts of the chapter, focusing on contest. Then follows a discussion of the transition from peaceful interaction to a setting in which there is direct conflict. A key point here is that much of the uncertainty reduction is not accomplished as a result of more knowledge; the historical case of battle shows that the legal process was not set up to determine truth, but rather to provide what is here called particular states of the world. The chapter analyses cultures of contest, and points to the existential dimension of uncertainty.

CONCEPTS OF CONTEST

Contests are a publicly recognized social structure that produce states of the world resulting from struggles between contestants, by which one wins at the expense of the other(s). The unique forms are recognized by their respective cultures, that is, informal institutions, and by their specific formal institutions. As in the other forms, the roles, the contestants, and the audience make up the social structure that, together with its culture, constitute it. Contests are frequently organized, and when they are not, they occur against a backdrop of institutions. The organizer can be one of the contestants or someone else. Although the word *contest* has slightly different meanings, I here refer to it as a 'fight'. The notion combines the root of *con*, meaning coming together, and *testify*, meaning 'bear witness to' or 'affirm the truth of'—in other words, as a form of direct conflict resulting in states of the world. The word connotes competition, the desire to win, but also the idea of 'contesting a statement'. A contest (or contestation) establishes 'true' states of the world that can be used by actors to reduce their uncertainty when acting.

The very point of a contest is that one wins at the expense of the other. This is what, with Simmel (1955: 59), could be called direct competition (Levi Martin 2009: 123). It is a direct form, in contrast to bidding in a market, where a lower bid may simply be ignored. A knock-down, for example, is impossible to ignore. In a market, it is not necessarily the best outcome to 'win' an auction; the price may be considered by the great majority to be much too high. After the fight, as with other types of 'competition', order is achieved as a consequence of its outcome; when one team wins 5 to 0 is definitely over. In contrast to status (Cooley 1894) however, as was discussed in relation to convaluations, those engaged in a contest are not just clearly adjusting to one another, they are fighting one another and face the consequences. There is thus no decision about the outcome; if so, it would not make sense to speak of a contest.

There are of course many contests, from a small dispute between two pupils on the school yard that turns physical while their peers look on, to an organized fencing game, or war between nations. But they all share the characteristic of a direct conflict between two or more contestants (Weber 1922: 20–21). But obviously, not all outcomes of contests lead to states of the world, such as when it was not public. Two drunkards who start fighting over something in an empty alley at 2:30 at night, which neither of them will remember the next day, exemplifies this.

As in the other chapters of Part II, outcomes of contests depend on their acclamation by an audience as being relevant. A world championship boxing match is relevant to many, including those who pay to watch it at home, to those betting on it, as well as journalists reporting on boxing. Obviously it matters to other boxers, but primarily to the two fighters (Øygarden 2000). The contests may be acclaimed already prior to the actual event, but a sudden event may also become a state of the world after it has occurred. Whether it will be a state of the world or not ultimately boils down to whether the contestants are acclaimed or not, meaning that the interest, will, and preferences of the audience matter. The exact outcome thus depends on these empirical issues, and though important, these are beyond the scope of this study.

It is the outcome of a contest that settles things and may generate states of the world. In a contest there are rules determining what is to be done to achieve what is good and what is not so good. Ideal-typically, only those battling directly affect the outcome: others' views, ideas, and arguments do not matter. In reality, of course, things are less clear. A typical example is boxing (Øygarden 2000). Before the match, uncertainty about the outcome may be high, and the stakes for those involved are extremely high. Uncertainty is both the reason for the match and what causes the hype, with speculation, betting, verbal assaults ('sledging'), and the enormous emotional charge that is often recognized between boxers in a title match and among those in the audience. If one boxer has the great majority of supporters shouting his name it is likely to affect how he performs—but no matter how much they shout, if he is knocked out, the match is indisputably all over. The shouting crowd and many other things, too, will affect the judges and the referee. Even when there is a knockout, or the judges decide the outcome on points, the notion of contest still makes sense; the interaction is direct, and the outcome follows from the contest.[1]

In boxing there is also a referee, a role that was already part of the organization of boxing in ancient Greece. The role of the judges is to decide, in terms of scores, who is the winner in cases where there has been no knockout.[2] In a way, boxing is set up as a contest with a jury, whose task is to score according to rules, a form of standard. But boxing judges may not always behave as if they are merely scoring against a standard; instead, it may turn into to something like award-giving, that is, a form of decision for others. More fundamentally, because it is a direct contest, the score—the number of punches landed, among other things—depends on the skills of both boxers. The contest, though it may be played out in many different ways, diminishes uncertainty. One participant loses; the one whose hand is raised, or the one still standing after a boxing match, is the winner. Provided that it is perceived that the rules have been followed, the result of the ordering cannot be undone, and the outcome is publicly known.[3] Boxing is an example of how uncertainty is an opportunity: for the boxers, especially for the challenger, and for fans, organizers, and betting houses.

A contest is a concept with many siblings. Combat is a direct way of settling uncertainty between those taking part. Other 'siblings' are more recent and include more peaceful ways of interaction by which uncertainty is reduced. Combat, duels (Ciklamini 1963), or war, by which uncertainty about the strength of the parties is settled, are, however, particularly notable examples because life is at stake.[4] The outcome of the struggle is uncertain prior to the contest or the combat. The notions of struggle and conflict are correlates, and above all discussed in terms of their forms and consequences by Georg Simmel (cf. Simmel's notion of *Kampf* (struggle); 1923: 186ff). Simmel did not, however, focus on the issue of uncertainty.

Several contests that are tied together in a system of rules represent a tournament. The origins of tournaments are probably to be found in games in 8th-century France (Van Creveld 2013; Elias 1994). These games, in which casualties were 'natural', were organized, and there were rules (Bumke 1986: 342ff). There are today various forms of tournaments using the round-robin format (everyone involved meets at least once), such as the soccer Premier League in the United Kingdom; or elimination tournaments in which only the winner stays in the competition, such as the US Open in tennis. In tournaments the players meet and 'fight' directly with one another to settle, normally according to rules, what (or who) is good and what is not so good. The result is order that can be states of the world. The soccer World Cup is a contest that in the end produces certainty about the quality of the teams: the cup and gold medals go to the winning team, the silver to the team that comes second, and so on. Moreover, a formal ranking list with all member nations is represented by FIFA (Fédération Internationale de Football Association). This ranking is not the result of a decision, an evaluation, nor a valuation, but results from the outcomes on the pitch.[5] Though each contest may be said to reduce uncertainty, it is strictly speaking wrong to associate the value of the sport with the reduction of uncertainty; it is much more the ongoing uncertainty and the never-ending game characterized by uncertainty that attracts the audience.

'Contest' covers the notions of combat, and even war, as a state of violent conflict with weapons by means of several battles over time between groups (states) (Janssen et al. 1987: 703), ultimately including kind of a 'war of all against all'. Some computer games use a multiplayer online combat arena in which different players or teams of players are involved in the combat. The combat usually ends when the opponents' bases have been destroyed or when there is one party still standing. The teams can be ordered according to their scores, or one can create tournaments of different types to let more than two actors engage in combat. Contests are typically between two contestants, and the direct nature of the contest means that the results are intransitive.[6]

Outcomes of wars become states of the world. Today's boarder between Denmark and Sweden is not only formally regulated, it is also taken for granted; it is a state of the world. It is nonetheless the outcome of the more than 10 wars between Sweden and Denmark. The knowledge gained of a war is not just certainty about who won, that there may now be an end to the fighting, and thus it may be possible to make predictions again. In addition, the different military tactics and also the 'success' or 'failure' of different weapons systems will be evaluated. To give weapons for free during an ongoing conflict, if the weapons are deemed successful, beats any type of advertisement; it is reduction of uncertainty due to real-life combat of different weapons that is the real test. Decisions will be made by other armies concerning what they will do, what type of weapons they will purchase, and also from which firms. The development of new systems of weaponry commonly proceeds after observations of the outcomes of real wars. States of the world can thus be used by many decision-makers to reduce uncertainty.

FROM VIOLENCE TO PEACEFUL CONTESTS

There is a link between peaceful and violent contests, not just in history. A contest may start as a negotiation and end with violence, such as combat, or vice versa; in both cases the actors are in opposition. War is the ultimate example of a violent fight, which also creates states of the world. But warfare cannot be explained solely by uncertainty, as classic anthropological studies make clear (Wood 1871). Nonetheless, if outcomes of war were certain, wars would be less frequent because it would make no sense if one party knew that it did not have a chance, and the other party was equally certain it would win. This is clearly stated by Van Evera:

> War is a trial of strength. If its result was foretold, the weaker could yield to the stronger, achieve the same result without suffering the pain of war. But often relative strength cannot be measured without a battlefield test. If states agree to their relative power, this test is unnecessary, but if they disagree, a contest of arms can offer the only way to persuade the weaker side that it is the weaker and must concede. (Evera 1999: 14–15)

That there is prior uncertainty may be a reason to wage war. Thus, a war or a fight can be due to several reasons, including that one does not know one's own status—strengths and weaknesses—nor the status of the other contestant or contestants. Concrete uncertainties can be the exact costs of war, the moral status of the two parties, uncertainty about the different alternatives, and other reasons (Fey and Ramsay 2011; Ramsay 2017).

War, including private wars between people and families—not to forget direct fighting between tribes, civil war, fights between gangs, and many other types of violent activity—are examples of physical contests between, normally, two contestants. The duels of the Middle Ages and after are perhaps the best example for displaying the intimate relations between contest, uncertainty, and states of the world. These duels involved one person who had made a statement that was contested by the other person. It could, for example, be one person accusing another of lying about him or his family. If both parties uphold their claims or accusations—potential states of the world—one may challenge the other to a duel. Hence 'the declared intention was to put an end to, or at any rate reduce, the number of false accusations by making both parties back up their claims by their lives' (Van Creveld 2013: 98). So, the conflict is about knowledge in an awkward sense, who is right and who is wrong about the accusation. The driving force behind a claim is thus that there was no way to objectively, or justly, find out which statement is true and which false; instead, a contest settles it.

A trial by combat is thus a means of reducing uncertainty about the 'true' state of the world, typically in cases when the peace or 'oath' does not suffice to settle the issue; what is required is a 'decisive test' (Foucault 2019: 128–129). It was 'a substitute for trial' (Van Creveld 2013: 103), and in many countries it was regulated by the law, including early Nordic law such as Icelandic law (Ciklamini 1963). Combat for trial, or one of its predecessors, the Scandinavian *Holmgång*, was a regulated way of settling issues in a direct physical fight, thus without having a court decision.[7] Thus, knowledge about what is 'right' is established by direct contest and constitutes a state of the world. Obviously, such states mean a lot to those in combat, but also could mean much to third parties, such as a woman over whom the contest is being fought. One could, of course, decide not to accept the challenge, but that would entail accepting that the opponent's statement was 'true'. The larger picture is that these contests were essentially about social status, and to withdraw would mean to lower one's status. This type of duelling was regulated and organized, but was clearly a battle, and Foucault calls it 'private wars' (2019: 129ff). The duels were normally settled by either fencing or shooting. Before the duel it was made sure that the ground was even, that none of the contestants had the sun in their eyes, that the weapons were similar, and many more details to ensure that none of the contestants had an advantage. A duel did not have to be public, but both being right and maintaining status or credit in society (Crowston 2013) were of course public phenomena. The outcome, to in any way settle the issue and to make it a particular state of the world, is because it becomes a public matter (Foucault 2019: 116–117). Therefore, duels were sometimes advertised and were, in general, popular events, ensuring that there would be an audience. In this way, the claim of the victorious contestant would prevail and become a state of the world. This is an example of how the duel's result is also publicly acclaimed. Many duels would not be very useful unless there was an audience, and the legal procedure was in many cases limited to its confirmative role as the end of an ongoing battle.

There is perhaps not much rationality behind the outcomes of duels, and the results they generate could scarcely be described as 'true,' but duels nonetheless generate states of the world. The outcome for the participants may indeed be lethal, even for the participant who is in the right 'on the merits'. The outcome of a duel is a potentially a state of the world, but no principles are established, only a particular state of the world. Gradually, and for several reasons, duels were replaced (on the continent of Europe) by Roman law. The practice of duelling was never entirely abandoned, however. One may argue that the role of duels as a way of reducing uncertainty in society were never very central socially. However, if people were prepared to die for honour and status, they must have been important in some sense. More peaceful 'duels' still exist today, such as the so-called 'rap duel' (Lee 2009), but as noted above, the outcome of such a duel is decided by the bystanders, not directly between the contestants.

Contestants may disagree or fight over who is right or wrong, or they may fight over values or material objects. If there is a conflict between two or more parties about states of the world, this may lead to a contest. Peace, or the establishment of a state of the world, is achieved when there is an agreement. In some cases, the conflict between those who were set to duel was resolved peacefully prior to the duel.

Next, I look at organized games, zooming in on the field in which peaceful contest is paramount, namely sports.

INDIRECT CONTESTS AND COMPETITION

Contests tend to be organized, and in some cases organized to maximize the uncertainty of the outcome. Violence is not a necessary component of contests, though there are many cases of precisely this. War games—that is, organized games that replicate wars or fighting—are an example of a contest. Such games have been played since time immemorial. The fights between gladiators in the Roman Empire are well known and have been the subject of countless films and stories. There are written records describing what it was like, including statistics, but many of the details must be inferred. I here rely on the works of van Creveld (2013), who refers to the fights of gladiators as war games, a notion also used by Simmel.[8] The reason for organizing gladiator games was not the reduction of uncertainty. The real reason, in contrast, was to increase uncertainty, to show the might of the organizer of the game, to draw attention from other matters, and to entertain the people (Van Creveld 2013: 72).

However, these games have a lot to do with uncertainty. The uncertainty created by gladiator games is obviously a deeply existential matter for those who were forced to fight, and those who also took part of their own free will. The fights or even battles were organized to create uncertain outcomes by pairing gladiators in such a way that they were as evenly matched as possible (Simmel 1923: 342). This also made the games more entertaining. The uncertain outcome of the games is of paramount importance also to organize betting, which went along with the games (Van Creveld 2013: 70). Who the contestants were was not decided until shortly before the game, to maintain the tension and uncertainty (Van Creveld 2013: 69). Furthermore, a lot of actions were taken to adjust weapons, armour, and the like, to create fights that were more 'appealing' to the audience, which often meant making sure that the outcomes were uncertain in addition to making sure that much blood would be seen. Many gladiators were well-known figures in public, and though uncertainty was created, so were the states of the world in the form of the results. With the decline of the Roman Empire and the rising cost of slaves, these deadly games disappeared.

There are, in addition, plenty of organized games with little violence. The field of sport shows many examples, also of attempts to replicate some of the more violent games. Fencing is today a sport, as are wrestling and boxing. Sport is probably the domain that shows most clearly that contests are organized, and how. Although the outcome of sporting contests reduces uncertainty as such, the organization of games aims to create uncertainty. Sport as such thrives on the fact that the outcomes of events are uncertain. There is thus a path paved for entertainment that leads from the deadly games of ancient Rome to contemporary sport, and uncertainty is central to these games. Put in one sentence: combat games were created to enhance uncertainty to a level that it could absolve people to the degree that they would forget or neglect the everyday problems they faced.

There are numerous empirical examples of outcomes of contests that result in reduced uncertainty. E-sport or competitive gaming, tennis matches, and boxing matches, for example, generate order resulting in rankings, prizes, or the like. By means of contests uncertainty about who is good and who less good is reduced or even settled, at least temporarily. Games have a temporal structure; as soon as one game ends, the focus can shift to the next. Associations capitalize on this insight to run leagues and not just single matches. The invention of the league, which was a major shift in English football (Döllinger 2021), meant that every game mattered. Obviously, games are not only entertaining because of the uncertain outcome; the performances, too, are valued. It is undeniable that competitive elements and the correlated uncertain outcomes are pivotal for the huge interest in sport.

Ice hockey as it is played in the US National Hockey League is a good example of an organized direct contest. In addition to some general rules about wage caps, for example, there is the famous draft system, which aims at equalizing teams over time. Each year a large number of new players are ranked and made available to the teams of the NHL. The teams that made it to the playoffs for the Stanley Cup (championship) are not even allowed to pick from the list of ranked newcomers. Indeed, the team that ranked lowest in the previous season gets its pick of the top players.[9]

But the game is organized not just to make it more exciting because of uncertainty about the winner. It is also organized—and sometimes changed—to make it more entertaining and more uncertain, not least to achieve surprise (Hutter 2010). A match with very few goals is arguably less entertaining than one with quite a few goals. To increase the number of goals per match, in July 2005 the NHL decided to reduce the size of goaltenders' protective gear.[10] The changes reflected the interests of fans, players, teams, and others.

Some sports are defined by being direct contests, such as football, tennis, or boxing. The results of football championships are not transitive, and there is consequently no world record in football. Although competitions are often organized (Arora-Jonsson et al. 2020), they need not be organized as direct contests. Sports are frequently organized as indirect contests, as already noted by Simmel (1923: 323). It is indirect because it is not about winning by destroying the opponent or defeating the other contestants in a direct struggle. Quite a few sports are best described as indirect. Examples are sports decided on the track between athletes, who are not in direct conflict with one another. When all athletes start at the same time, such as the famous Vasaloppet, the one who crosses the line after 90 km cross-country skiing in classic style is the winner. This is very competitive, but it is indirect.

Some sports, such as high jumping, pole vaulting, and swimming, have official world records. These world records are transitive, and there is no direct contest, although there is certainly rivalry. However, this indirect way of determining the world champion, or winning the gold medal at the Olympic Games, may be as uncertain and as exciting as a direct contest. The differentiation entailed by the analysis of ways of uncertainty reduction means that activities in the field of sport, for example, are not identical. Some competitions are organized events at which rivals come together. At the field and track world championship, one of the disciplines is the women's high jump. The rules are decided so that there will be only one winner, namely the person who jumps highest in that competition, qualified by certain conditions if two make the same height. In this case one contestant gets or takes something that the persons who do not win cannot have, namely victory. The contest is organized, and the winner is decided according to a protocol (i.e., a formal institution) and measurement using standards. Though there is no direct fighting between the contestants, the psychological game and the obvious fact that there is no decision, but that it will be decided depending on how the contestants perform and not as a judge decides, means that it is a competition. The weightlifting 'battle' in Atlanta 1996 between the two main contestants—the Greek challenger Leonidis and the two-time Olympic gold medallist Bulgarian-Turk Süleymanoğlu—ended with victory for the latter in the very last round, when Leonidis failed to set what would have been the fifth world record in this competition.[11]

Other sports, such as diving and figure skating, are competitive too, but the outcome requires decisions made by a jury. Umpires are frequently part of the organization of almost all sports, but their role is often marginal, and in such cases the task often consists of checking equipment, making sure that the rules are followed, and making calls about the winner. However, if everyone involved—in particular the audience, the jury, and those taking part in a given sport, such as divers—view the decision-making as fair and correct, and in a sense as 'objective' as high jumping, then diving is a contest that depends on the athletes' performance. Thus, by having independent and experienced judges who heed the rules, the score may resemble a ranking according to a standard.[12] However, in the early years, the Olympic Games organized competitions also in art. In this case, as has been analysed previously, there are no standards, and it was clearly an instance of decision for others. In artistic competition, there is no 'objective overall value' that is apparent to the parties (Simmel 1955: 59). Thus, reality is often a combination of pure forms. The more important the role of the jury, the closer the contest gets to the form of decision for other. Big wave surfing is yet another example by which contests with judgements are key. It is an example of an activity that is about searching and overcoming danger, risk, and uncertainty that brings order among those who are seen as insiders of the most advanced clique of surfers (Corte 2022). In this case there is no external jury; it is essentially the narrations of insiders, judging one another in process of mutual adjustment that result in states of the world out of process similar to convaluations, though contests are arranged (Corte 2022: 204). In all these cases the outcomes are states of the world that reduce uncertainty.

THE CULTURE OF CONTEST

Each specific form has its own unique culture. Not even the most brutal fight is without rules. Simmel noted that many institutions are necessary for contests to occur (Simmel 1923). Such insights, though, are almost tautologically true because a lack of rules is also informative to the parties in conflict. In most wars, each side follows some norms, and there may of course also be general norms applied by both contesting sides. There are today rules of war, which is to say that informal institutions, together with formal institutions of war, provide a base for activities that ultimately are about defeating the enemy.

Contests generate states of the world that can be used by actors to reduce uncertainty. The forms of contests have, as was shown to be the case with convaluations and forms of decisions for others, specific cultures as well as their own histories. Margaret Mead, for example, says that war among the Manus had three themes: headhunting, the capture of enemy women, and various economic considerations (1937: 233–234). Thus, the contest is not purely fighting for the sake of winning, and consequently, throughout history, the reasons for war have been numerous and varied. The outcome of a decisive battle between two parties clarifies the situation and produces a state of the world (or many) within the framework of which one can speak, do business, and much more.

In many traditional cultures, violence is an integrated part of social life. It is, in other words, institutionalized. However, the lack of other institutions and formal institutions may lead to fighting. Let us look at the role of war in some native Australian tribes (Wood 1980 [1870]). There may be several reasons for direct fighting, but it is 'almost invariably the possession of some territory', and this is often connected to trespassing 'on the district of another [tribe], especially if it is one in which game of any kind is plentiful' (p. 58). The uncertainty of ownership is settled by the fight, which takes place in accordance with a specific set of rules and practices that apply from the declaration of the fight, during it, and until it ends.

Nonetheless, fighting is common, and 'every tribe is at feud with its neighbour' (Wood 1980 [1870]: 58). The fighting is not a war, but disputes are settled by battles, which in itself is institutionalized. A battle is the result of one tribe challenging another. The next day, and after 'taunting their antagonists with cowardice and want of skill in the weapons', and after having 'worked themselves up to the requisite pitch of fury, they begin to throw spears, and the combat becomes general' (p. 59). Each of the warriors stands on a line. While standing on the line, each combatant seeks out one contestant from the other tribe, and the battle is more like a series of duels in which spears are thrown. Women and children may watch the ongoing fight from the bushes. Although such fights can sometimes be 'very bloody' they usually end when 'one man is killed' (p. 59). The fight is not quick, because the warriors are skilled, though many are wounded and may be crippled for life—for example, by boomerangs—during the combat. Brutality is part of the game, and 'like most savage nations, Australians mutilate their fallen enemies' (p. 59). Taking a trophy was called 'taking fat', in the course of which they 'open the body, tear out the fat about the kidneys, and rub it over their own body' (p. 59). Being a good warrior and showing courage was one of the few means of excelling in this society, and fighting and killing enemies was key to this. It is not even the case that the 'victorious warrior . . . waits for the death of his enemy before taking his strange war-trophy' (p. 60). Thus the defeated warrior may, lying on his back, still be alive and 'doomed to see his conqueror adorn himself before his eyes' by rubbing the disabled man's body parts 'until his whole body and limbs shine as if they were burnished' (Wood 1980 [1870]: 60).

This cruel description represents a form of resolving uncertainty about who is a victorious warrior and who is not. The form called a contest is a means for men to become someone in the community. Prior to taking part in this form, one is a member but not fully accepted, and certainly not a 'warrior'. The form—as a concrete empirical instance, it is here called 'fighting'—is clearly institutionalized. It has a very distinct culture, made up of practices and rules for how things are done. In other words, the cruelty and associated virtues are institutionalized, and in this sense 'taken for granted', which means that the moral burden of killing is taken from the shoulders of the participating individuals. This is not only about reducing uncertainty, and fights may settle disputes of land and also bring some order to communities. Some warriors are valued as good, others die, and others provide a backdrop for those who are celebrated. There can be no doubt that contests produce states of the world. There can also be no doubt that contests are existentially meaningful, and the result of the serious matches are states of the world manifested as social status. Geertz has analysed Balinese cockfighting, and though the contests are organized, and cocks may die that have been brought up with much care and effort by their owners, it is only 'apparently' cocks that are fighting; actually, 'it is men' (Geertz 1973: 417).[13] The analysis shows that central existential questions of 'who I am' are tied to the public social structure. Thus, uncertainty is reduced because people are positioned in the social structure and gain identity. Hence, the social order is central for reducing uncertainty.

THE MAKING OF FORMS OF CONTEST

The form of contest that reduces uncertainty can be the outcome of mutual adjustment, such as when a war is fought, largely without any rules, or organized, such as a world championship boxing match, which is regulated by the relevant organization. The ways in which the contests are arranged say nothing about the brutality of the actual contest. The organized gladiator contests at Rome's Colosseum and other arenas in the Roman Empire were as lethal as a fight between two gangs fighting over a block who happen to run into one another at a gas station. Football hooligans meeting up to have a fight at a field may be as organized as a boxing match. The difference between these examples is simply between contests that are organized and those which are due to mutual adjustment.

Contests that are organized are by definition planned, and information about them is more likely to be spread; they are therefore also more likely to generate states of the world. The main reason is that contests, if they are institutionalized, deliver outcomes that in a sense are expected states of the world. A World Cup Final in football occurs every fourth year, and the fact that one team will be champions is much more predictable than which country will actually win.

Organization of contests are common, but it may appear somewhat paradoxical that much violence in society is at least partially organized and regulated. This is indeed the case with regard to how states of the world based on contests come about; most contests are organized. Many conflicts occur between two or more parties, without any party actively trying to organize the conditions or the event. Furthermore, a conflict may unfold if no other means are available to resolve a dispute. A war between nations is an example of a contest that is not organized, and there is no institutionalised form for it but war, meaning that each state of the world that is the outcome of a war is unique. Each such state may be of major importance and dominate the memories of those who took part, their relatives, and all who were affected. But the implications reach far beyond this group because a war may affect other nations, people, the way wars are fought, the type of companies that will strike deals based on the 'success' of their armaments on the battlefield, as well as civil construction companies and many more.

CONCLUSION

Contests frequently are, but must not be, organized, but they do produce states of the world. Contests may revolve around either direct or indirect struggle. What are here called contests, not least the classic variant of which anthropologists and historians have given plenty of examples, settle uncertainties about status, and in many cases about what is considered right and wrong. The values are set in public—be it in a small village or a larger domain—and states of the world are thereby established. Although contests may result from mutual adjustment—for example, war between tribes—many contests, including war, imply a large degree of at least partial organization (Ahrne and Brunsson 2011). This chapter has given ample evidence of organized contests—also contests in which actors have been forced to fight. Some of these have been organized for the sake of 'entertainment', others to create a 'diversion' from the problems of real life.

Increasingly, informal institutions and formal institutions have guided humankind towards a more organized way of life, leading to reduced uncertainty. It is clear, however, that over time, contests such as war games, games, and sport have become *more* organized, and more peaceful, but it is unclear whether violence and war have declined across the globe, however much its forms have been transformed over time (Mann 2018). These are today created largely as entertainment, of which the world of sport is the most salient example. As noted, some contests have a logic similar to convaluations.

This chapter ends Part II. In contrast to Part I, its three chapters deal with value uncertainty. Although already discussed in Part I, it argues that a state of the world does not have to be true to be valid. The states of the world discussed in Part II are in most cases not institutionalized, though they can be. The forms generating the states of the world, in contrast, are by definition institutionalized—but it is also clear that new forms can emerge and others fade away if the audience no longer attends to them. This chapter, more than the other chapters of Part II, makes it clear that states of the world arising out of interaction do not have to be either 'true', right, or 'fair'. The sociology of knowledge perspective stresses that it is enough that people agree on 'what there is', namely, states of the world. An underlying distinction that was announced in the preface, of how states of the world come about, can now be clarified: namely, emergent states of the world resulting from mutual adjustment of actors, and those states of the world resulting from decisions for others.

Emergent and Decided States of the World

Two ideal-typical ways in which states of the world come about have been identified: mutual adjustment and decision for others (Hayek 1973). A grown order is an unintended outcome of actors who orient themselves to one another. The actors do not have to either aim for the result or be aware of making a result. The order, as it were, emerges as an outcome of an orientation to others over time. Informal institutions were given as one example of emergent states of the world.

The empirical form that today most clearly generate states of the world, primarily out of a process of mutual adjustment, is science (Nowotny 2016). As a form it is not a machine that is perfect, but typically an instituted convaluation whose culture implies reflexivity, the making of tentative states, and a search for new questions. Science is largely a publicly existing convaluation in which actors take part. Hence, science is not democratic; there is no parliament and no voting, and no majority decision arena or a principle of majority. The scientific states of the world are not results of decision for others. The rationale of science and its procedure of knowledge production is not political, and its order results from mutual adjustment by actors who hold certain virtues. But even considering its shortcomings, science production is arguably the best way to reduce uncertainty reduction that there is.

In producer markets the social structure is based primarily on the status order of the sellers (Aspers 2009). Concrete examples of this type of market can be observed in the wine industry (Humphreys and Carpenter 2018), the financial industry (Podolny 1993), and fashion photography (Aspers 2001). An ordered social structure obviously also orders any particular actor who is positioned in this social structure. The individual actors' decisions are facilitated and can be made with less uncertainty because the form is ordered. This is because this public order informs decision-makers of what or who is good, and what is not good.

Mutual adjustment cannot be planned. It is a profound insight that public uncertainty reduction is due to informal institutions, which by definition cannot be organized. Moreover, there is nothing that by necessity implies that informal institutions must be rational or that a coherent structure of institutions will emerge. Elias, referring to Parsons, says that informal institutions, a social structure that Elias calls 'tissue', result

> from many single plans and actions of people [that] can give rise to changes and patterns that no individual person has planned or created. From this interdependence of people arises an order sui generis, an order more compelling and stronger than the will and reason of the individual people composing it. (Elias 1994: 366)

This basic 'tissue', which is the unintended result, Elias says, is neither rational nor irrational.

A decided order, in contrast to a grown order, implies that a decision is made about an outcome. A decision for others about what is good or bad is, in practice, only an attempt to create states of the world. Decisions, however, can either be supported by formal power to make sure that they can be implemented, or require acclamation from an audience. This insight into how orders leading to uncertainty reduction come about has consequences. One consequence is that uncertainty can be reduced by organization; it is possible to make decisions for others that reduce uncertainty for many. But other states of the world, and especially the most profound—the informal institutions—cannot be changed easily, and not by decisions.

CHAPTER 8
Making and Reducing Uncertainty

Uncertainty is a condition of human life that gives rise to both opportunities and problems. Complete certainty would mean that life comes to an existential standstill. To be a human being means to live, act, reflect, hope, have wants, try to achieve things, but without knowing the outcome. However, seen from the subjective side of an individual actor, one may want to reduce the uncertainty one faces in most domains, almost as much as possible.

Uncertainties—in everyday language, some of them are called 'risks'—can be due to many causes, including climate change, nuclear power, war, famines, atomic bombs, erratic leaders, and pandemics, all of which add to the mundane uncertainties we face. Many uncertainties have been reduced because of societal developments; for example, because of democracy we have better health care and, generally speaking, more knowledge. With access to the internet and the algorithmic toolbox, much of this knowledge can be accessed and implemented by more people than before. This advancement is not only due to scientific work; in fact, institutional conditions are the most profound and most important reason for uncertainty reduction. And this uncertainty reduction and the possibility of making better decisions, to plan and thus to make strategic decisions with some certainty, are important for the prosperity, wealth, and health, from which many human beings today can benefit. The Inuit example presented in Chapter 2 reports on a way of life that probably few would prefer to what they currently have. Famine and lawlessness still exist, of course, but in most cases this was a larger problem in the past when there was less knowledge and fewer resources to counteract these events. The contemporary Inuits' situation is in many respects less uncertain,

Uncertainty. Patrik Aspers, Oxford University Press. © Oxford University Press 2024.
DOI: 10.1093/oso/9780197752753.003.0008

largely due to scientific findings but also due to collective state-based solutions like welfare systems. However, scientific development has led to production, emissions of substances, as well as the melting of ice that is the traditional locale of the Inuits' life and culture. And they are also facing problems because their own traditional knowledge is eroding (Oosten and Frédéric 2002).

Scientific knowledge rests on a bed of institutions, and the ordering of the world by informal and formal institutions has reduced the uncertainty people face. In other words, the order in social life has not always been accomplished by rational decisions—this is obvious due to the variety we can observe between different societies—but rather by a long process of establishment of institutions. Considering all things, and even all possible contingencies, it is probably fair to say that people are more certain today about many things than in the past. This means that uncertainty seen from an objective perspective has decreased, but that does not necessarily mean that the experienced subjective uncertainty also has decreased. It may very well be that subjective uncertainty is an existential constant, not least since we cannot commensurate uncertainties to only one uncertainty.

As discussed in the book, it is often problematic when risks are created based on commensuration of uncertainties. Nonetheless, all risks are outcomes of some kind of commensuration, but not all processes of commensuration are problematic. The focus here is on those that are problematic (e.g., when information is neglected), and other commensurations that involve judgements, or when it is not based on standards or accepted facts. Though commensuration is often correlated with quantification, it is not the latter that is the concern, but commensuration that implies a reduction of complexity in order to present something as risk, when the decision conditions in fact are characterized by uncertainty or even ambiguity.

This final chapter summarizes the findings from the preceding chapters, and then addresses some more general questions. After briefly mentioning the variety of uncertainties we may face, I connect back to Chapter 1, and turn to uncertainty as an opportunity and a discussion of how it is organized. The final issue, to be further studied in the future, is how our being is connected to uncertainty and uncertainty reduction. Central for our being is how we manage the public and handle both its large supply of knowledge, and the visibility of our shortcomings that it produces.

THE MAKING OF MEANS OF UNCERTAINTY REDUCTION

Assuming uncertainty, each individual actor is likely to use the available means of uncertainty reduction, both private and public, to reduce their uncertainty. Given that an individual may be better off facing less uncertainty, there is no surprise that actors invest much time, resources, and effort in reducing the uncertainty they face. Strategies of individual uncertainty reduction are a common research topic in the social sciences, not least in business studies. The analysis of public means of uncertainty reduction complements the much larger research on individual strategies for reducing uncertainty, to thus find public solutions to what may appear as individual problems.

The notion of 'states of the world' is developed to account for the knowledge that can reduce uncertainties for many actors. It is different from individual knowledge. For a state of the world to exist, it is not enough that one or a few believe something to be 'knowledge'; it must be accepted by a larger audience to be public knowledge. The concept of 'states of the world' is defined in a way that clarifies that not all knowledge can reduce uncertainty; only publicly available knowledge can reduce uncertainty for many.

The basis for all uncertainty reduction is made up of the essentially taken-for-granted informal institutions on which actors draw, often unconsciously, when acting. On this cultural basis, many other states of the world rest, including formal institutions and standards. Formal institutions, such as laws, can easily be changed simply by new decisions. Individual means and strategies of uncertainty reduction are built on the foundation of informal institutions. Formal institutions such as laws are always explicit but can, over time, become taken for granted. Standards make advice available on how to act and how to coordinate activities, and evaluations can be made according to standards or rules that are known and independent of actors' views. Rules or standards are supra-individual and do not depend on the interest of single individuals, who are all parts of the social world. They are in this way 'objectively accessible'. States of the world can be principles, meaning that once they exist, they are applicable to many cases and can be used to reduce uncertainty for many.

In addition to the principles of states of the world, three forms have been discussed: convaluations, decisions for others, and contests, whose states of the world are acclaimed by an audience. All three refer to the making of particular states of the world, such as a single historical fact, a decided law, or a result of a competition. For analytic purposes, three forms are presented—but it is also shown how, in many cases, reality is a blend of these three ideal-types. Convaluations generate states of the world as a result of mutually adjusting actors. Decisions for others are attempts to shape the world, but these attempts only become real if they are acclaimed by an audience. Finally, contests are outcomes of struggle, most typically direct struggle between parties. Forms generating states of the world are more entrenched than the statements they generate, because these forms are institutionalized. The results of the forms (states of the world) exist, and actors orient themselves to them. But actors also orient themselves to the forms generating the states of the world. States of the world may appear to be static, but they can refer to a process, or be used in a dynamic process. In some cases, there is an almost endless and rapidly changing flow of concrete states of the world by forms—as when markets generate prices.

States of the world do not downplay the great complexity which confronts actors. The ultimately subjectively perceived and experienced uncertainty may be hard to manage, or even unsurmountable, for some. The practical side of how to make use of the different states of the world, how they can be combined with private means of uncertainty reduction (private knowledge), and how to create states of the world to improve the situation in a domain are of course very important, but they are beyond this study. To integrate, or at least to relate the findings of this book to the decision models under uncertainty presented in the first chapter of this book, is a major task. To some extent it may also mean to switch the focus from individual decision-making that implies an adjustment to existing conditions, to also include decisions that are about how to change the environment and the conditions of decision-makers. There are plenty of more concrete management solutions which address actors who operate under uncertainty (Courtney et al. 1997). Though these models do not advise how to actually decide, they provide tools for the process of making decisions. Many of these solutions imply the role of prudence, a virtue which has been with us since the dawn of Western rational thinking.

It is knowledge that reduces uncertainty. But as has been argued, knowledge of social processes is difficult to use because of knowledge's double nature; in other words, the fact that it changes its own premises when being used. But as mentioned, knowledge itself is not just an object, nor are we, those who 'know'.

ADDRESSING UNCERTAINTY

Uncertainty is a result of us not knowing, and there are many things that we do not know that we do know. The old and naïve view that we can 'uncover' the 'underlying laws' of society and social life and thereby control it lingers in many social science disciplines even today, long after it was initially conceived by Comte. Still, it is clear that, although not even the natural sciences produce absolute truths (Kampourakis and McCain 2020), much progress has been made, and today many states of the world are produced by research that help actors to achieve their ends in decision-making situations. As mentioned, the complexity of our socio-technological fabric also increases with more knowledge, which is used in a multitude of combinations, sometimes without knowing the consequences, in addition to the field of unintended consequences (Elster 1989). The combined use of different states of the world may be uncertain. This is to say that an effect of a certain action must be traceable, *ceteris paribus,* to a cause. In our complex reality, this 'tracing' may be far from easy. Furthermore, it may often be difficult to isolate and 'measure' the contribution made to a decision by a single state of the world. Put differently, the reduction of uncertainty is always a moving target (Nowotny 2016).

That our means to uncertainty reduction are typically insufficient frequently causes problems. But the attempt to reduce uncertainty is always related to the horizon of relevance (Schütz 1971) of actors, which points to the fact that not only do the interpretations of the world differ, but also what is relevant and the extent to which uncertainty is more like an opportunity or a nuisance. Actors may approach uncertainty differently and do not necessarily have to try to seek more knowledge. They may try to assess the uncertainty they face, or they may simply copy what others do. Still, these approaches do not affect the cause of uncertainty, which is lack of knowledge.

Though actors perceive uncertainty for many different reasons and may have different preferences for how much uncertainty they want, reduction of uncertainty by means of states of the world implies that actors can achieve their ends more easily than if they lacked the relevant knowledge. To have knowledge of the available means of uncertainty reduction, as stated throughout the book, is not easy. Clearly, some states of the world are results of decisions for others, and yet others emerge in processes of mutual adjustment. To account for these two processes is also key to understanding their role in the public. Put in one sentence: public awareness, and the possibility to make strategic use of states, including the active use of states of the world, are intimately connected with how these states come about. But, as mentioned in Chapter 1, uncertainty is also an opportunity.

THE OPPORTUNITY OF UNCERTAINTY

Uncertainty as opportunity (Esposito 2013) is present in the works of Knight and Keynes, and in the business literature (O'Malley 2004: 3–4). Uncertainty represents, among other things, opportunities for profit by entrepreneurs or speculators (Pareto 1935), who do not know the outcome of their actions (Schumpeter 2000) and who exploit uncertainty (Stark 2009: 14–15), or who use it as an asset for creative collaboration (Ibert et al. 2021). The tensions and dissonance (Stark 2009) needed for creativity are siblings of uncertainty.[1]

Luhmann (2000: 186) says that organizations thrive on uncertainty. With certainty, much of their activity and their defining decision-making traits would cease to exist. In this way, opportunities due to uncertainty are key to the dynamics of social life. Pierre Michel Menger (2014) addresses the issue of uncertainty management, in the sense of how actors exploit uncertainty. He suggests that the creation of uncertainty deserves more attention, and opens up a discussion of how change is a prerequisite of uncertainty (Knight 1921: 312).

Much effort also is made to create or enhance uncertainty. To create uncertainty about future states is a means of making money in the domain of entertainment, which includes the world of sports. TV amateur cookery competitions and sport thrive on uncertainty; a football match is interesting to a large extent because the outcome is uncertain, and that it is emotionally charged. It is the excitement about the uncertain outcome that triggers the audience to go all in as a fan, to be thrown into an emotionally excited state, strengthened by being together with others. Moreover, as a performance artist pointed out above, the 'uncertainty' of the performance situation in which 'anything can happen' is part of what makes it cutting-edge. There is in these cases a wish to be surprised (Hutter 2010), and this may explain why people actively seek out uncertainty and challenges, including extreme sports. But this form of search for uncertainty also typically occurs within a frame or regulation, control, and, ultimately, certainty. It would require rather extreme measures, such as joining an ongoing military conflict as a volunteer, to put oneself in a situation of existential uncertainty.

Sport is about knowing that someone will win, but not knowing who. To put it differently, sport creates controlled uncertainty in a highly certain context. To accomplish a situation of uncertainty requires a real competition. To have complete certainty is like playing pool with oneself; it is obvious who will win. Neither is it possible to create a duel between one's two fists, or have a running competition between one's two legs. Though uncertainty in the early days of football essentially was an issue only for those taking part and a few locals, it soon became an issue also for a growing number of supporters (Döllinger 2021). Initially, only one-off matches were played, with no organized tournaments. With the introduction of tournaments and leagues, uncertainty could be maintained throughout the season. Though each match produces a score—indeed, a particular state of the world—the uncertainty is perpetuated by the way the season is organized. And as soon as the uncertainty concerning which team is best is settled, at the end of the season, there is always the next season to look forward to. Moreover, each game may be quickly forgotten, but the form—the organized contest—is institutionalized.

There is no doubt that this organized uncertainty also has major economic consequences. The turnaround in the field of sport is large, but to this one should add betting. Betting is an organized type of 'meta-uncertainty' that exists only because there is an underlying uncertainty on bookies' offer odds, such as in football matches. Odds come with likelihoods and thus appear as risk. Clearly, the numbers are expressed as a ratio, but there is no underlying objective reality. The odds transform uncertainty into risk. The betting industry, in a sense, tops up the uncertainty of the game itself, but also transforms reality by making it 'calculable' in a way that resembles how credit scores are determined. Betting undoubtedly increases the economic importance of sport. During the Covid-19 crisis, when essentially all sports activities had to be paused, bookies started to arrange bets on e-sport, such as e-soccer. Thus uncertainty, not risk (as in a lottery with objectively known probabilities) is the essence of betting, though it is presented in terms of a discourse of risk.[2]

It would be too simple to reduce all activities to a matter of uncertainty. That one can gain pleasure from watching a film, or even a game of soccer, despite knowing the outcome, suggests that these activities are not only about uncertainty. However, in terms of uncertainty, the difference between watching the upcoming Super Bowl final and one that took place five years ago is considerable. Even though both refer to particular states of the world, there is a clear difference between, on one hand, future-oriented uncertainty, the result of which we cannot know before it has unfolded, and on the other hand, events in the past, which we can know or can at least find out about. This difference in the temporality of uncertainty of sports activities can also be translated into money; it is clear, for example, that one cannot bet on past games. Moreover, people's willingness to pay to see these two games, live or on replay, differ considerably.

In relation to what was said above on decision-making and knowledge, decision-makers may also see uncertainty as a resource for avoiding responsibility. By displaying uncertainty about the causes of pupils' problems, counsellors have been found to distribute and partially avoid responsibility for taking action (Iversen and Evaldsson 2020). Although some aim to create uncertainty, and some actors exploit it, from the narrowly defined perspective of individual actors often less uncertainty is preferable to more.

Or put differently, being exposed to unwanted uncertainty is something to be avoided. It is truly uncertain whether one can climb to the summit of the mountain K2 during the winter and come back alive, but it is not difficult to avoid this uncertainty.

It may be clear that actors want to reduce the uncertainty they face, but there are many situations in which they prefer that their competitors or enemies act under uncertainty. In other cases, actors may want to create uncertainty to have more excitement for themselves and others. This drive may be more critical because we have managed to reduce uncertainty in general. A life with total certainty and complete predictability because of complete knowledge about the future, a theme reappearing in fiction, is of course not possible. It would also be a boring life.

EXISTENTIAL UNCERTAINTY REDUCTION

Uncertainty can be about many things, including one's own existential uncertainty. This is the first as well as the ultimate uncertainty, because it is about the life and death of my own life. Existential uncertainty is about questions like: Who am I? What will happen to me? How will my life unfold? When and how will my life end? One can essentially eliminate all uncertainties by knowing that one will die tomorrow. But this uncertainty reduction is absurd, and underlines that uncertainty is an essential aspect of life. It is certain that we will all die, although we may not know when and how (Heidegger 2001: 258). But because it is your life, and the only one you have, it is the hub of all uncertainties. It is this 'private' problem that is the phenomenological (Husserl 1989, Heidegger 2001) starting point for the other uncertainties discussed in the book.

Sometimes uncertainty leads to existential concerns. This is the case for those whose life is at stake, but it can also be about identity uncertainty. Who one is and the possibility of becoming what one wants are aspects that must be coupled with the issue of uncertainty, as mentioned above. The historically dominant institution that has provided comfort, hope, and in a way, certainty, is religion. Religion may also be comforting in times of war, illness, and death—even your own death. That something external to the individual can offer comfort may be important to counteract the individual responsibility of facing uncertainty and having to make decisions. But with enlightenment, the 'unquestioned bond' to religion was turned into an 'optional extra' (Dahrendorf 1985: 45). Religion can function as an interpretative shield that offers meaning to events over which one has little control. In cases we do not know, and when actors have little control over their own destiny, uncertainty prevails, though the religious comfort may embed one's destiny in hands of a mighty God. This is an example of how individual problems may be addressed by public solutions.

PRIVATE TRUTH CLAIMS AND THE PUBLIC

This study is grounded in phenomenology, informed by the sociology of knowledge and the 'antifoundationalist' pragmatist treatment of knowledge we find in the works of Dewey, Wittgenstein, Quine, Sellars, and Davidson (Rorty 2009: 317). States of the world that exist in the public potentially offer knowledge to many who deal with uncertainty in our complex world.

To reject the search for and hope of absolute knowledge (Popper 1972), and aim for consensually and pragmatically based knowledge in terms of states of the world, is to direct the searchlight towards informal institutions and a whole range of forms of uncertainty reduction that need not be centrally decided or administrated by one and the same authority. The phenomenological approach presented here grounds knowledge in taken-for-grantedness and practice, but without arguing that this is the only aspect that matters. To acknowledge this foundation of informal institutions, which are historically grown, moreover, is a rejection of the postmodern idea that the world is like a surface of things that can be easily shifted.

The states of the world that reduce uncertainty when used in decision-making are public social constructions and as such, available to anyone. The public is central already in Kant's ([1783] 1964) notion of *Aufklärung* (enlightenment) as a project of reasoning. To generate these states of the world requires collaboration in the public, and consequently orientation to others—known individuals, but also those who are generalized others. The public, to go back to what was stated in the first chapter of the book, requires and implies openness to allow actors to exchange views and to access information and knowledge. Thus, and despite all of the psychological and sociological caveats mentioned above, the condition of a public discussion is to give and take, in which arguments (and not propaganda) are both practised and cherished (Popper 1963: 355–358). The public also implies the cultivation and care for this public. The public, say as concretized in the form of academia, implies that people have the right to express themselves, but also have the requirement to respond to what others say and do. What grows out of public social interaction is ideally centred around arguments that are neither overdetermined by power or money, nor governed by sanctions (Habermas 1987). One must listen to those who possess knowledge, but those with less knowledge or who challenge this knowledge cannot be excluded. The publicness requires also, in many cases, collaboration and much organization, as has been shown, in addition to what emerges spontaneously. The 'objectivity' that can be reached in the public, for example regarding scientific findings, is due to the 'social aspect of scientific method,' namely the 'friendly-hostile co-operation of many scientists' (Popper 1966: 217) that largely is public.

By following the sociology of knowledge tradition, and make use of Popper in a 'pragmatic' fashion, the states of the world that emerge must neither be individually rational nor, viewed as a totality, coherent. This means that the public is not like a machine that produces 'correct statements' in a rational way, leading us closer to the truth. The public is characterized by liberal virtues, but it is neither 'naively liberal' nor 'inherently rational', because it is grounded in the more or less taken-for-granted and unreflectively existing virtues, practices, norms, and values that make up the bedrock of what we call informal institutions. Thus, there is a kind of 'conservativeness' of the public because of this bedrock of informal institutions, which obviously is different for different publics. In other words, the informal institutions, such as religious convictions or democratic values, provide a base that is not easily changed, but which has a profound impact on what people do.

The Private Responsibility

No matter what their level of knowledge, actors are considered responsible for what they do. States of the world is the term here used to represent knowledge. This knowledge has, over time, grown, and the more public knowledge in the form of states of the world there is, the more we can act by drawing on this stock of knowledge. Consequently, if one knows little, one is to only a limited extent responsible for one's own actions: this is the case of children and those who are intellectually disabled. In contrast, with the historically growing stock of knowledge, we know more. This also means that more responsibility than before is located within us. A consequence is that—in a scientific context, largely devoid of forces that take the burden of responsibility off the individual's shoulders—the existential uncertainty is increased. Under such conditions, responsibility is not taken over by a God but is largely carried by the individual, implying that one is, to a high degree, responsible for one's actions to make the 'right' decisions. The public awareness of the existing stock of knowledge can be used as a benchmark also for demanding that we ought to take responsibility for our actions, because we 'should' at least be aware of the potential consequences of those actions. Actors can more easily be evaluated if they are considered to be responsible and held accountable for their actions. This may also put more stress on actors in the public. Politicians and other leaders are frequently scrutinized in the public, and even the smallest wrongdoing can be blown up in the media. This scrutiny in public may lead to increased subjective uncertainty and may even lead to an escape from the public.

The Escape from the Public

The level of responsibility becomes high for a person who lives and to a large extent is observed and evaluated in the public. The 2000-year-old Western ideal of living—act, perform, and live in the public—also means that the public is a demanding arena to operate within. It is perhaps not surprising that some people do not want to play along with the public game.

Given these circumstances, the public, seen from the perspective of the individual, can become a burden and perhaps even a danger. It may be a threat to what one 'is' and 'wants to be' (Aspers 2015). This suggests that many may seek to find ways of coping with the demanding public life, and avoidance of it is indeed one way to handle the situation. There are many routes that lead people away from the public. Weber (1946, 1978) wrote about the centrality of sects, which is here to be interpreted in a broader fashion than strictly religious, as a way to develop ideas that are secluded and at the same time implying abnegation of the public. To be a member of a secluded sect based on its own values, and alleged 'states of the world' that are not exposed to the scrutiny of the public, may reduce complexity of the world and make one's life 'easier' to manage. Under these conditions one does not have to find things out, and one does not have to let one's own ideas be challenged by others. To be a member of a sect—or to use a virtual modern form, an echo chamber—is to deny the knowledge and corresponding demands of the public, because the sect may try to reverse the knowledge. This denial comes with the advantage that complexity, accountability, and responsibility are reduced. Moreover, that the alternative (i.e., private) truth claims are offered by the secluded sect or within a closed internet community means that one is no longer responsible to act according to what is valued in the public. The sect offers protection from being exposed to the scrutiny that comes with making decisions in the public, both the direct exposure and the historical record of the acts that exist online. As a member, one is protected because what one is exposed to does not challenge or put oneself in much uncertainty. Many of the facts and states of the world are excluded or rejected and replaced by 'alternatives', such as when 'alternative' claims about election results are presented as truths in some communities. This escape from the public is a strategy to in a highly selected way combining parts of the life-world parts of the system world to manufacture an alternative 'truth'. It is in many ways a reversal of the process called modernization (Habermas 1987).

If the public primarily becomes an arena for ex post judgement of decisions and the character of decision-makers against the standard that each single act must be correct according to the different states of the world that exists, then public life becomes almost unbearable. To be in the public requires, according to Arendt, that we can 'make and keep promises' (1988: 237) to clearly be accountable for our actions. At the same time, she says, the only redemption from the irreversibility of making decisions in the public is the 'faculty of forgiving'; this may sometimes be necessary for breaches of formal institutions, but also of bad decisions drawing on, or failing to draw on, states of the world. Forgiving, however, is not a principle that can be decided, but a virtue that must be practiced.

A Typology of Convaluations

It is possible to summarize the above discussion in a typology based on ideal types of different convaluations. This appendix presents the sub-categories of convaluations by building on what is general in all of them. These different categories mirror the variety of coordination by convaluations. In relation to these, we can predict what types will be fashioned under what conditions, and predictions about their consequences. It was argued that in a status convaluation, the rank orders of the two sides are more institutionalized social constructions than what is valued, whereas in a standard convaluation, the value underlying the standard is a more institutionalized social construction than the rank orders of actors of the convaluation. In other words, order can be either a function of value (standard) or a function of social structure (status).

I described the main points above, but it is possible to draw an additional distinction between two types of convaluations, called assembly and reflector, which are distinguished by role structure. Both can be ordered according to status and standards. An assembly refers to a group of actors, all of whom have the same role, who come together or are brought together to interact openly, for a shorter or longer time. This is the case, for example, when development-oriented NGOs observe each other's behaviour and evaluate development projects. Some NGOs may be evaluated as being more virtuous than others (cf. Gourevitch et al. 2012), thus generating an order among NGOs.

Convaluations based on status also cover the valuation of members within a group. The consequence is differentiation among them, but it often also 'ranks' them, as, for example, the 'best soldier in the platoon'.

Selection of recipients of grants or academic positions is an example well known to academics (Lamont 2009), which they may think of as a standard, but most have evidence that rather suggests that it is a status convaluation.

A reflector, in contrast, links actors from two different sides, each made up of different roles with different interests. On one side are those who are doing something, thus being valued or evaluated. On the other side are those who endow the 'performers' with value, namely the audience. Each side is oriented to the other side, but there are usually also relations—as rivals or as collaborators—among actors on the same side. The incumbents on the 'audience' side make the calls and judge what those on the 'stage' side do or offer, and thereby affect the actors on the stage side. In empirical cases, the roles of stage actors and the audience may not always be that clear, because both can affect what is going on (cf. Kennedy 2005). There may, in other words, be a mutual exchange of 'e/valuations', that is, a form of reflection. Markets can exist only as the reflector type, because there must be two sides (buyers and sellers), which empirically are characterized by different interests. Assemblies and reflectors can be ordered according to the two principles discussed above, status and standard, as shown in Figure A.1.

		Assembly Actors have the same roles	Reflector Actors have different roles	
Typology of convaluation				
			Actors have a role only on one side in the reflector (Fixed roles)	Actors switch roles in the reflector (Switch roles)
Principle of order	Standard	Stockbrokers ranking each other depending on how much money they make in the market	Producers of garments evaluating the offers of input material from suppliers	Lawyers representing buyers or sellers of properties
	Status	Designers 'gossiping' at a fashion cocktail party about who is the best designer	Musicians are positioned depending on who has been on the cover of *Rolling Stone*	Academics deciding on research funding for other academics

Figure A.1. Typology of six types of convaluations.

We can further divide a reflector into two types: fixed-role and switch-role structures. The fixed-role structure sets identities for the role on one side of the convaluation. Most real markets are fixed-role markets (Aspers 2011). Shoe manufacturers, for example, only have the role of producers of shoes in this economic convaluation; they do not also operate as consumers or buyers of shoes. In such markets, shoe manufacturers operate as buyers in many business-to-business markets, where they buy commodities such as leather, glue, and other components needed to produce shoes. These they buy from suppliers, who are located upstream in the production chain. Actors, consequently, can have different roles in different convaluations.

What makes the switch-role structure different from the fixed-role structure is that actors, organizations, or individuals switch sides (roles) in the convaluation. The review process in academia, as we know, is organized as a switch-role structure. When we submit academic papers, we do this in the role of authors, but we frequently switch roles so that we are also reviewers in academic convaluation. In this convaluation there are two roles, but few of us identify with the role of reviewer. Incumbents in switch-role structures are not directly identified with one of the roles of the convaluation, but with the more general role encompassing the two sides (roles). This means that those on one side—for example, evaluators—may be drawn from the same group or category as those who are evaluated, such as when we academics submit papers to, or review papers for, journals. Art directors of advertising campaigns, who peer-review each other's works and hand out awards, are another example of a convaluation in which those on the stage and those in the audience are drawn from the same category. Traders and agents of garments, or traders in a stock exchange market who switch roles between being buyers and sellers, also exemplify the switch-role structure of the reflector. Thus, from a strictly role-analysis perspective, there is no difference between switch-role and fixed-role structure; in both cases, actors come together and enact roles. One difference is that identification in switch-role convaluations involves a more general role that encompasses the roles of the two sides. An important consequence is that there will be no conflict between the two sides (as we typically have in labour markets) or an organization that represents one side. It is possible to exemplify and relate the different types of convaluations; below they are presented in Figure A.1.

NOTES

CHAPTER 1

1. This knowledge definition addresses, in a broad sense, the elements of uncertainty that have been identified in the business literature: '(a) lack of information, (b) general uncertainty of causal relationships, and (c) time span of feedback about results' (Downey and Slocum 1975: 563). It will be shown in Chapter 7, however, that under certain circumstances, narratives may create states of the world due to performativity. Discourse in general, however, is too broad a category, in that it does not even have to refer to knowledge.

2. For something to be a state of the world, the cost of access must be low or at least accessible. The cost of buying a newspaper or paying a subscription for physical or electronic services, or purchasing a media license, such as the annual fee for having a TV set—all of which are low enough not to block entrance for the large majority—still allows knowledge to be called public.

3. More generally, the idea presented here about truth comes close to the classic definition of knowledge as 'justified true beliefs', but rejects the notion of absolute 'truth' and thus leaves more room for sociological variations of degree in what counts as knowing. It does, however, lead to the idea that many scientifically rooted virtues, such as objectivity (Daston and Galison 2007), are deeply institutionalized and offer a firm basis for knowledge-based reasoning in our world. Knowledge, in many ways, differs from other beliefs only in graduated fashion; some, for example Quine and Ullian (1970: 6), see knowledge as 'sober' belief. Over time it is uncontroversial to speak of increased knowledge that can be used to predict actions (Pareto 1935).

4. This basic assumption is not different from what we assume about other people in general. If we did not assume that people are largely rational (Davidson 2004), we could hardly interpret, relate to, and interact with them.

   The decision theory literature is immense. There are even journals dealing with this matter. The *Journal of Risk and Uncertainty (JRU)* (1988) 'welcomes original empirical, experimental, and theoretical manuscripts dealing with the analysis of risk-bearing behaviour and decision-making under uncertainty. The topics covered in the journal include, but are not limited to, decision theory and the economics of uncertainty, experimental investigations of behaviour under uncertainty, empirical studies of real-world risk-taking behaviour, behavioural models of choice under uncertainty, and risk and public policy'. (https://www.springer.com/journal/11166/aims-and-scope)

5. It is of course possible to speak of collective uncertainty, economic uncertainty, environmental uncertainty, and many other empirically related terms. This would be a type of classification. The focus here is on the relations between what brings all of them together, uncertainty and knowledge. The results can then be applied to all the different possible empirical instances.

6. Uncertainty reduction is a general theme (Bonss 1996) in this literature, but it is rarely discussed concretely. Luhmann's (2001) work on reduction of complexity, both by decisions and by process (in German 'Verfahren'), is an example of uncertainty reduction. Transparency could arguably be one form of uncertainty reduction. However, although some transparency generally improves things, merely trying to be very open about everything (including everything that is not knowledge) does not in itself reduce uncertainty. What this largely sociological literature on 'risk society' refers to is a societal development stage in which the distribution of risks becomes more important than the distribution of wealth (Bonss 1991: 259–260).

7. This is to say that the epistemic problem of uncertainty presumes that there is no ambiguity, since with ambiguity there can be no certainty. Only when we know that there is such a thing as a firm, a potential investment or a set of competitors, to take some examples from the economy, can we speak of uncertainty with regard to how to act. Ambiguity is more profound than uncertainty and opens the door to ontological questions.

   Ambiguity is an ontic problem that addresses the question of what category an entity belongs to, for example by using a test; that is, 'an orchestrated attempt to reveal an entity's potentially unknown properties or capacities' (Marres and Stark 2020a: 420). It refers to the condition in which we do not know whether there is a state of the world at all.

   Ambiguity, however, can occasionally be eliminated as a by-product of uncertainty reduction. If a process of uncertainty reduction leads, for example, to the emergence of a market, this social form—the market—comes into existence. There is then no doubt that there is a market, and as a consequence, not only is ambiguity reduced but also uncertainty.

8. Economists, following Arrow, tend to see uncertainty as a state to which probabilities apply, while ambiguity (or to make it even more confusing, what some economists call 'radical uncertainty') is seen as an epistemic state.

9. To make probabilities, the metric must be at the ratio scale, that is, the scale with equal intervals between the scale units and zero as the starting point of the scale. Although uncertainties are sometimes at the ordinal scale—meaning that they are transitive and can be ranked—this is not enough for calculations of probabilities. I am grateful to Pierre Michel Menger, who emphasized this in personal conversation.

10. Although Knight was clear about the fact that in reality we are never informed about everything or have 'perfect knowledge', in part two of his book *Risk, Uncertainty and Profit* (1921) he discussed the situation of a world with no uncertainty. This part is called 'Perfect Competition', dealing with circumstances in which there is perfect knowledge, and in which alternatives can be handled under risk, using probabilities. It constitutes the bulk of his analysis, and this part codifies the thinking and teaching of the neoclassical model in economics. The ideas he presents suggest that actors have perfect knowledge (Beckert 1996: 806), although this model has gradually been abandoned by economists.

The model developed by Knight, however, was supposed to show how hard it was to achieve a state of risk, and that uncertainty is the normal condition.

11. Generally speaking, machine learning (Fourcade and Johns 2020) can be applied to gain more knowledge, and although this knowledge is inherently neither private nor public, it is clearly companies and states that tend to profit from AI development in terms of reducing their uncertainty. Algorithms are obviously an important way to find out things about, for example, customers and users, and can be used by firms and other organizations as well as individuals. But given the opacity of algorithms (Christin 2020), it is, as a phenomenon, to be included as a private means of uncertainty reduction and will not be further discussed here. Machine learning is the more general term and is defined as 'the practice of automating the discovery of rules and patterns from data, however dispersed and heterogenous it may be, and drawing inferences from those patterns without explicit programming' (Fourcade and Johns 2020: 804).

12. There is no point here in discussing 'logical states of the world' at length, including for example the fact that 35 + 52 = 87. To perform such operations is a capacity an actor has or does not have, in short. The specific state of the world that 35 + 52 = 87 is not important; the point is that one knows the procedures of mathematical calculations and can use them to get results; this knowledge of states of the world is not empirical. Much of the different kinds of knowledge held by different individuals may help them as individuals to act in different ways (Hayek 1945). Me knowing that I did not empty my garbage bin in the kitchen this morning means that I can predict that it may start smelling. It is a concrete instance of the general knowledge that garbage starts to smell. However, the fact that I know something about the world—in this case about my garbage bin—means that only I know something, but it is not institutionalized.

13. Douglas and Wildawsky (1982: 5–6) discuss the situation in which there is certain knowledge but not consent, which may lead to coercion or more debate, and the case of uncertain knowledge but with consent, meaning that there can be agreement to launch more research. Finally, there can be a situation in which there is neither certain knowledge nor consensus—which may cause an unstable situation. Douglas analyses the important question of how societies deal with risks, given the alternatives outlined. The solutions adopted in each society thus do not have to be rational.

14. My focus is thus not on how one comes to know certain things (Hardin 2009), nor the discussion of certainty or truth (Bonatti 1984).

15. The way scientific truths are established in the first place will be touched upon in Chapter 5. Once such truths have been established, they may very well be institutionalized, to be discussed in Chapter 2. Accepting the sociological insights about all things that condition and limit knowledge, knowledge is here used in a pragmatic-sociological way (James 1955), which means that it refers to what the relevant public count as knowledge: scientific knowledge is defined by scientists. Though we no longer speak of natural laws (Levi Martin 2011: 321–350), and though we recognise that scientific knowledge does not offer absolute certainty (Kampourakis and McCain 2020; Nowotny 2016), there is no doubt that science has provided much knowledge that orders the way we think and know the world, and thereby our possibilities of acting in predictable ways in the world (Hacking 1990).

16. The social world is here perhaps an epistemic exception. The task of reducing uncertainty for social scientists is thus in many ways harder than for a natural

scientist. The reason is that humans can and will use the knowledge produced by the social sciences to ask questions about themselves and use it to alter their behaviour. This reflection and questioning is central for the human being (Heidegger 2001). This special status of humans has been pointed out by many, including Elias (1956), who says that we are both the 'subject' and 'object' of scientific investigation; in addition, people have an interest in shaping the world in various ways.

This subject and object of the investigation may have become more rational because of the increased knowledge available. The approach taken in this study means that only some basic assumptions about actors need to be made. The first is that they are ontologically constituted as 'being in the world' (Heidegger 2001), and we cannot, therefore, consider them as atoms who only later and occasionally become 'social'. Actions are primed by socially generated institutions. Individuals may use knowledge differently and may act rationally in different situations; this study looks only at the publicly available states of the world that can be used by actors to reduce uncertainty. The practice of actors is beyond the scope of what is studied here.

17. Keynes, famously, speaks of the problem of a competition 'in which the competitors have to pick out the six prettiest faces from a hundred photographs, the prize being awarded to the competitor whose choice most nearly corresponds with to the average preferences of the competitors as a whole'. This setup means that 'each competitor has to pick, not those faces which he himself finds prettiest, but those which he thinks likeliest to catch the fancy of the other competitors'. Obviously, all competitors in this competition 'are looking at the problem from the same point of view' (Keynes 1973: 156). This points to the problem of, in this case, three levels of interrelated anticipations.

18. For a society, the existence of many ties may nonetheless lead to reductions of uncertainty, for example if they make up a dense network (cf. Putnam 1993). In societies with weak institutions and/or a weak state, people have networks as an antidote; but distrust between people in different networks may be rampant, leading to a systemic effect of very high uncertainty.

19. The formation of organizations is a general strategy that essentially is about incorporating the uncertainty of the environment and thereby reducing it (Luhmann 2000: 183–221). The idea is that decision-making, by selecting one 'way' and rejecting other options creates a bar and pointer for members, for example employees of the organizations as well as those orienting themselves to it. Formal organizations are clearly capable not only of reducing transaction costs but also the uncertainty that the constant negotiation of contracts would cause (Coase 1988; Williamson 1981). This may lead to the internalization of the coordination process, which results in evaluations or valuations taking place inside an organization. One example is hiring. This can be done on the open market, or it can at least to some extent take place as a form of internal labour market, typically resulting from a vacancy chain (White 1970). At the same time, much evaluation and auditing take place within organizations. This means that forms of uncertainty reduction are used not only for addressing issues of coordination between organizations and individuals, but also within organizations.

20. This establishment of public knowledge, which was done by businessmen and academics, was central for the emergence of a public domain (Habermas 1962). In the business world, information and knowledge is key. Habermas (1962) has

shown that the information and knowledge that individual businessmen could obtain through, for example, correspondence about prices, gave them an edge when doing business. Thus, some businessmen knew more than others (Braudel 1992a). The fact that essentially all knew that this private knowledge existed, but only some had it, caused uncertainty for those who did not possess this knowledge. This certainty that some had could be used to make better decisions and to make more money than those with less knowledge.

Prior to the emergence of a public, in the mid-seventeenth century little public information was available. Information and knowledge were private and could be exploited. The great possibility of arbitrage was evident in the wealth of tradesmen. An individual may thus prevent others from gaining this knowledge. Uncertainty is, under these conditions, reduced for the individual but not for others. With the introduction of newspapers in which prices could be published, information could reach a larger number of people. With fixed places of trade, rights but not necessarily goods could be traded, and information could be published in publicly available newspapers (See 1968: 27–30). Thus, once the originally private information system became public (Habermas 1962: 34–35), as exemplified by publicly announced prices of stocks and products, uncertainty is reduced for many.

Today this knowledge advantage for some actors may still exist in practice, but attempts have been made to implement formal rules. Contemporary efficient marketplaces, such as stock exchanges, have detailed regulations on when information must be given to the public, and also what centrally placed actors are allowed to say. These decided rules make sense and play a role only if those who are supposed to follow them do so. Thus, the virtues and the institutions on which this trade rests are crucial for ensuring that the system does not fall back into bribes, corruption, and lies. Nonetheless, publicness of information is a guarantee of uncertainty reduction in the economy.

21. Reduction of uncertainty in public facilitates individual decision-making and makes coordination possible. If an actor has no idea what others will do, or when actors do not share any knowledge, it will in practice be impossible to coordinate any affairs. Individual strategies and knowledge presuppose some predictability of others' behaviour. Knowledge of others is never just individualized, but draws on the knowledge of average others (Heidegger 2001), for example their behaviour and their values.

22. Daipha's (2015) study of how weather forecasters make decisions under uncertainty is a good point of departure to connect private decision-making and the collective means used in decision-making. She acknowledges the institutional context and shows how actors' decisions, in a pragmatic fashion, draw on much of what we know.

23. Uncertainty reduction in relation to states of the world points to the sociology of knowledge, in the sense of trying to give an account of processes of knowledge and what counts as knowledge in each context, which is a general problem of knowledge. The idea of increasing knowledge, often couched in terms of development, was present at the birth of sociology. Comte analysed history as developing in three stages: the theological, in which we had little knowledge of the world, and observations were explained by supernatural forces; the metaphysical, in which attempts to obtain knowledge of the world were rational, but essentially determined by an external God; and the positive, in which the rational scientific method can justify observations and explain them in terms of

general concepts and law. The final stage is the scientific, characterized by laws of sociology that are built on laws of other disciplines. This is a simplified view of historical development, but it is informative, not least regarding the scientific ambition to understand our own development of more knowledge; the role of science is, of course, paramount for understanding reduction of uncertainty.

Weber (1978a), for example, writes about rationalization and the possibility of calculability based on institutionalized procedures and the law. He shows that increased predictability is associated with the aggregation of institutions. At the same time, there is a process of social differentiation of society from one community to different spheres, each with, increasingly, its own set of values (Boltanski and Thévenot 2006; Weber 1946), which increases the complexity and limits the range of many institutions, such as their virtues, to one sphere only. Taken together, however, the reduction of uncertainty for a single actor does not have to imply reduced uncertainty for others.

CHAPTER 2

1. This distinction reflects the discussion by Montesquieu (2001: 26, 28), who, in book 19 of his *Spirit of the Laws*, 'Laws in Relation to the Principles Which Form the General Spirit, Morals, and Customs of a Nation' (§12, 14), used the terms *institution* for decided laws, and *custom* for grown tradition. Similar ideas can be found in Aristotle and De Tocqueville. Others used it later (Czada and Schimank 2000).

2. The notion of institution is of Roman origin and refers to the formalization of inconsistent Roman law. The formalization took place in the Justinian era, which started in 527 AD, and the notion of 'institutions' refers to the different elements of the newly formalized law. The term's origin can be traced back to judicial decision-making about laws. David Hume (1711–1776) used the term for law and, for example, order (Hume 1826: 447), indicating that the term has been broadened considerably since its introduction.

   The use of the term in social sciences has been different (see Hasse and Krücken 1999; Joas and Knöbel 2004, e.g., 748ff; Schülein 1987;, and Scott 1995 for presentations of the concept of institution in sociology and other disciplines. See also Nee 1998 for an account of development, with a focus on action-oriented theories in economics and sociology).

   Political science and political economy offer similar positions on institutions in relation to sociology and economics (Hall and Taylor 1996). Also, political philosophers lean more towards decided rules (Emmenegger 2021; Rawls 1971: 55). Despite variations, it is clear that sociologists' views on institutions are generally much broader than those of political scientists or economists.

   In sociology, the notion of institution appears already in the works of Spencer (Schelsky 1980), Durkheim, and Weber, using the term *convention* (Weber 1978b), and the term has been used by many sociologists (Gronow 2011; Herranen 2020; Joas and Knöbel 2004). Despite different meanings in different disciplines, the social sciences—generally speaking—agree that institutions are important and profound, and that they reduce uncertainty. Durkheim, who saw sociology as the science of institutions, speaks of the notion as meaning 'all the beliefs and modes of behavior instituted by the collective' ([1901] 1982: 45). Streeck and Thelen propose a very general definition of institutions as 'building blocks of social order' (2005: 9). Beckert argues that 'institutions stabilize actors' expectations by indicating what constitutes legitimate (and likely) behavior' (2016: 88). Giddens (1984: 24) sees institutions as providing 'solidity' across time and space. It is, however, Berger and Luckman (1991) and the new (organizational) institutionalism that are the most important sources for the contemporary discussion, although the latter lack awareness of traditional studies on institutions. This reflects a neglect of Parsons, who was strongly connected with the tradition (Joas and Knöbel 2004). Parsons' notion of institutions, however, is quite broad and refers to values, highlighting socialization and the shared symbolic level that produce coherence, thus reducing uncertainty concerning others' behaviour (Parsons and Smelser 1956: 102–103). Parsons and Smelser also acknowledge more concrete economic institutions, such as the 'contract' (Parsons and Smelser 1956: 104ff).

3. Williamson says: 'The confession is that we are still very ignorant about institutions' (2000: 595). He continues, the fact 'that neoclassical economics was dismissive of institutions and that much of organization theory lacked scientific ambition' (Williamson 2000: 595) is among the reasons why the field has not been very much developed theoretically.

4. The group of Ammassalik Inuit studied in 1884 consisted of 371 individuals, and though they shared some of the traits of other Inuit, they were defined as a group by dialect and by being 'natives of the same territory'. Essentially, however, they were characterized as lacking some of the traits of other Inuit (Mirsky 1937: 61). The Ammassalik were wanderers who lived in relative isolation, and 'look at the sea, for from the sea come their food, their clothes, their shelter, and their means of intercommunication' (Mirsky 1937: 52). See also the study by Birket-Smith (1948), who studied the Inuit (Eskimos) in the 1920s, as well as the study by Boas (1884–1885). Boas' analysis of social order and law indeed points in the direction presented by Mirsky, but is less critical.

5. Put differently, the economy was never 'embedded' (Polanyi 2001)—because that presumes that it could be treated as separate from other parts of society—it was simply one whole.

6. Although phenomenologists generally agree, while Husserl speaks of an ecological primary ground (*Urboden*) (1992: 49), Heidegger (2001) talks about being-in-the-world (*In-der-Welt-sein*) by stressing practices, and Schütz (1976) starts with the empirically given social world and our mental orientation to it. It is a world that is to be studied with scientific tools, as it is composed of institutions, cultural elements, and thereby includes concrete values such as norms of beauty or ugliness (Schütz 1976: 36; 1975: 119–120, 131). People are born into the world and, through socialization, they gradually learn how to use institutions, 'forget' them, and thus take them for granted. It is primarily in practices that institutions are used. Taken for granted (*das Fraglos gegeben*) is defined by Schütz as 'the particular level of experience which presents itself as not in need of further analysis . . . until further notice' (1976: 74). The lifeworld is the foundation of more theoretical reflections and codified knowledge, is where the primary (and in many cases secondary) socialization and internalization occur, and it is therefore deeply rooted. Socialization refers to the 'integration of the expectations of the actor' (Parson and Shils 1951: 20) regarding what to do and what to think. It is the background of everyday life activities and used for interpretations (Garfinkel 1967: 36–37). The lifeworld, Schütz says, is 'constantly pregiven' ([1966] 1975, 5, 116–132), and though it is not fixed, it is relatively stable.

7. The issue of performativity—that is, the idea that a theory is the blueprint for the world and that actors use this theory to make the world according to the theory—is much facilitated when some form of institutionalization of the theory in question has occurred. The performativity of neoclassical economic theory (Callon 1998) is a process of institutionalization that has reduced uncertainty for many.

8. What is in fashion (Aspers and Godart 2013), to take one example, cannot be institutionalized, but fashion in itself is an institution. Creative actions and outputs of creative processes and actions are not institutions, although creativity itself may be an institution. Individual preferences, views, reactions, actions, and much more are also examples of what is usually not institutionalized.

9. If a guest at a huge gala reception to honour a newly elected chair were to go around and shake hands and introduce themselves to everyone present, this would be an example of using introductions by handshake in an incorrect way. This would make us aware of the institution, and such behaviour may lead to sanctions, now or later. If someone were to come to a very small private party in someone's home and not introduce themselves, this would be an example of not using an institution. Learning how to do business in another country, which of course starts with the acceptable and normal behaviour of the country in question, is a clear example of how institutions are important.

10. Asaf Darr has, in several works, analysed the micro-interaction between tradespeople (2003) and between sales staff and customers (2006), and shows that an entire social infrastructure of institutions is used.

11. Reflection may of course be triggered when institutions are used wrongly, are not used, or malfunction. Generally, reflections are facilitated by switching (Aspers 2015; Mische and White 1998); one example is when a businessperson is abroad and observes that things are done differently than at home. Reflection may lead to discussion of criticism and debates, but if no problems are identified with an institution, it is less likely to change. Sometimes a grown institution is so firmly institutionalized that even identification represents a major difficulty. In such cases a more complete deconstruction may be required (Heidegger 1994: 118).

12. The way to trade properties is part of the housing market of a specific country. These institutionalized patterns, rules, and practices are rooted in historical processes (Kohl 2017). Foreigners buying properties in France can be certain that the system is stable and that people in general behave in a way that is right and correct, meaning that fraud and so on is limited as long as one plays the cards as they are supposed to be played. This institutional stability allows people, even though they do not know the language, to buy properties in France.

13. An economic sanction is simple and direct: a trade relation, ultimately, is ended, or the interaction does not lead to a deal. Even in many cases in which decided rules are present in the form of legally binding documents, it may be easier and/or less costly simply to terminate an ongoing relationship than to take the counterparty to court, especially where the court system is less developed. This has been shown to be the case in, for example, the garment industry (Aspers 2010).

14. Institutional entrepreneurship is defined as 'activities of actors who have an interest in particular institutional arrangements and who leverage resources to create new institutions or to transform existing ones' (Maguire et al. 2004: 657).

It is somewhat paradoxical to speak of entrepreneurship, however, because if institutions are taken for granted, entrepreneurial actions cannot, so to speak, plan that others will 'forget' about them. At most, we can speak of a critique of existing institutions, connected with the use of a new or already existing practice.

Other notions, such as institutional work, refer to 'physical or mental effort aimed at affecting an institution or set of institutions' (Lawrence et al. 2011). Moreover, establishing a new institution is a process that occurs over a longer period, involving several actors who interact—but such a process does not follow a blueprint. When sanctions kick in to preserve what is at stake, it is possible to speak of institutions. Only then would a 'new' institution be established. Institutional entrepreneurship and institutional work are, in contrast to the grown order of institutionalization, attempts to create a decided order. Hence, to have any meaningful use in discussing a change of institutions, these terms should be employed only for decided rules by means of decisions. This literature, consequently, fails to acknowledge the stability of institutions, and also thus does not realize at what profound level grown institutions may reduce uncertainty. Yet another concept from the neo-institutional school is 'institutional logic', a term used already by Berger and Luckmann (1991: 82) but which does not bring much clarity to how institutions work or reduce uncertainty. Institutional logic, say some centrally placed neo-institutional researchers, 'has become somewhat of a buzzword. Buzzwords are overused; as a result, their meanings often get distorted and overextended and they burn-out of existence' (Thornton and Ocasio 2008: 99). Thornton and Ocasio defined institutional logics as 'the socially constructed, historical patterns of material practices, assumptions, values, beliefs, and rules by which individuals produce and reproduce their material subsistence, organize time and space, and provide meaning to their social reality' (1999: 804).

An approach that actually addresses changes of institutions is French convention theory (Diaz-Bone 2015, Boltanski and Thévenot 2006). This school is sometimes described as a form of 'pragmatic institutionalism' (Diaz-Bone 2012: 64). It argues that conventions play a role when rules and institutions are seen as 'incomplete', or when they fail (Thévenot 2015), which requires that actors must find ways to use them or to make 'appropriate interpretations' (Diaz-Bone and Salais 2011: 9). These situations are also the origin of the very conventions used in these situations: 'Conventions emerged historically from interactions wherein actors had to solve coordination under the condition of uncertainty on how situations, persons, objects can be evaluated in a shared way. Without shared evaluations, no coordinated collective intentionality would be possible and any interaction would fail' (Diaz-Bone and Salais 2011: 9). Hence, institutions exist, but conventions are used pragmatically to cope with situations, in particular when they fail. Put differently: 'Conventions run the economic process in its dynamics, not institutions' (Diaz-Bone and Salais 2011: 13). It can be problematic that the convention school claims that it 'understands institutions as multi-layered sediments of conventions' (Diaz-Bone and Salais 2011: 11), because it blurs the distinction between convention and institution. It is clear that by stressing the pragmatics of actors in situations, the convention school gives weight to action and agency, and does not run the risk that 'almost every pattern or structure' is labelled 'institution', which is the case in the neo-institutional school (Diaz-Bone 2012: 68–69). If too much weight is given to the pragmatics of situations, there is a risk that the normal everyday business, in which actors are engaged in their mostly institutionalized activities, is downplayed. This is not to deny that institutions are questioned (Habermas 1981: 188–189). David Stark has argued that the order of worth (conventions) of Boltanski and Thévenot is 'not about the application of rules, and hence differs from "institutions" either in game theory or in new institutionalism' (Stark 2009: 15n3).

15. Human beings' behaviour is related to the language they use; quite often, a switch in language correlates with a switch of cultural register.

16. Searle also adds one important thing: 'but we need to distinguish the statement of this fact (which is institutional) from the fact stated (which is not institutional)' (2005: 3). This distinction comes from Searle's basic premise that there are 'observer independent' (1995) features of reality, which he calls 'brute facts', referring to knowledge produced in natural science. The social world, and the objects of study for the social sciences, is essentially made up of features that are 'observer-relative'. According to Searle there is an underlying logic of society, social-institutional reality (2008b: 31), which rests on a firmly established knowledge based on the natural sciences. This view draws, from a sociological point of view, on the futile idea of knowledge presented by Popper (1972), who demarcated 'objective knowledge' as existing in a human world independent of other forms of knowledge.

    Searle's notion of institution is rationalistic, essentially tied to language and performative declarations of linguistic propositions, but it neglects practice and the coagulation of meaning resulting from mutual adjustment. To Searle, all institutions require language, though language does not require institutions (2008a: 28). But this approach means that he cannot account for firmly rooted and taken-for-granted institutions, because states are always codified in language. His analysis of institutions, and more generally states of the world, is thus at best partial.

CHAPTER 3

1. Legitimacy can come from the belief in a legal order, which can be based on, for example, knowledge or grown institutions, or the belief in a specific person: either someone who has gained the position by tradition, as discussed in Chapter 2, or by charisma, personal traits, or traits given by God. These different grounds for the acceptance of decided rules can of course be combined. A person or organization may propose an institution that comes into use because of the status (cf. charisma) of the organization and because it is well in line with already existing institutions and rules. A decision made with an attempt to affect others by setting a rule about what is right and wrong may become an institution if it is accepted by many and becomes taken for granted over time. Decided rules may thus be put in use because of the power of the issuer and the fear of sanctions, or because they are legitimate. What is not discussed explicitly by Weber is that an actor trying to impose a formal rule may gain legitimacy, even though there is no legitimate authority when the attempt is made.

2. There are many examples of decisions that attempt to reduce uncertainty. A head of department may decide which faculty members shall get some of any extra research time that might be at their disposal, and the coach of a soccer team decides who gets to play in the final. Promotion of potential candidates within a bureaucratic organization after a vacancy may cause uncertainty about who will

get the position. This, in turn, may lead to stress, interaction, and attempts at positioning among the candidates. A decision by a superior may diminish this uncertainty. Actors then react to the decision and adjust their behaviour. This means that the decision has consequences.

3. An organizational culture may emerge due to the interaction of members of an organization, but this interaction is likely to be the result also of the interaction with actors from other organizations, such as those in the same field. An organization may also decide on rules that further certain behaviour by its members when interacting with members of other organizations. Organizations may observe one another and make decisions that form, eventually, a 'culture' of an industry. Such a culture is a consequence of organizations making decisions for their own members—for example, rules, strategic decisions for itself, such as how it acts in a market, and attempts to make decisions also for others.

4. https://www.dwds.de/wb/sitzen.

5. Obviously, they cannot know this. But actors know, at least, that this is against the law and that there are punishments for those engaging in cartels.

6. This stood in stark contrast to the United States which, as early as 1890, enacted the Sherman Act to prohibit price-fixing agreements between firms. To counteract such agreements, the law was changed to foster competition between firms and thereby ensure that US customers did not end up being the victims of powerful firms. Later, some German academics at the University of Freiburg become attracted by the idea that cartels impair fair competition, leading them to call for state intervention (Quack and Djelic 2005: 258). What is more, they suspected that the 'inability of the German legal and political system to prevent the creation and misuse of private economic power had contributed to the disintegration of the Weimar Republic' (Quack and Djelic 2005: 258)—a conviction shared by the Allied forces after the war. But it was only with the end of the Second World War that these ideas made any substantial difference in Germany. These liberal ideas emerged in the post-war era, and their impact decreased only in the 1960s or 1970s (Brunnermeier et al. 2016: 63), leading to substantial institutional change. This change occurred due to the aforementioned American economic policy, which ran counter to the German tradition of cartels by circumscribing market concentrations and instead emphasizing fair competition. It is important to note, however, that the US legislation was aimed at preventing price fixing because it was considered to be at the customers' expense. Mergers—and the concomitant effect of creating larger and larger organizations—were not forbidden, and instead became common in US corporate history (Perrow 2005; Chandler 1962).

7. This de-concentration policy particularly affected heavy industry firms, such as Krupp. With the onset of the Cold War, however, more far-reaching plans for deindustrialization were scrapped. Instead, the Allied forces decided to establish Western Germany as a bulwark against the perceived threat from the Soviet Union (Quack and Djelic 2005: 259). This entailed that Germany would have to rebuild its economic landscape. At the same time, the Allied forces were adamant that this rebuilding could not happen along the lines of the old German economic tradition that rested upon cartels. Instead, the German economy was reorganized in accordance with the US economic tradition. This is to say that the US forces made decisions about crucial aspects of the legal framework of the German economy. This change, obviously, created uncertainty for some, leading to more certainty for others.

8. The US authorities decided the agenda for the reorganization of the German economy, but the codification of these decisions into actual law was left to German lawmakers.

   Because of the different legal traditions, US antitrust law differed substantially from its German counterpart, at least in some respects. For example, while US law allowed private antitrust lawsuits, in Germany this was restricted to official authorities (Quack and Djelic 2005: 262). Notwithstanding these differences, sanctions—legitimately derived from the codification of antitrust law—played a pivotal role in the reorganization of the German economy.

   Initially, attempts to implement the new legal antitrust framework in Germany met with stiff resistance from German heavy industry, which feared that this seriously threatened their historically strong position in the German economic and political landscape (Quack and Djelic 2005: 260). These apprehensions were shared by the German Industrial Association, which likewise resisted the changes at first (Quack and Djelic 2005: 260). This resistance was unsuccessful, however, managing only to delay the implementation of competition law for two years.

   The German parliament passed it in 1957 as the Act against Restraints on Competition (*Gesetz gegen Wettbewerbsbeschränkungen*) (Quack and Djelic 2005: 262).

9. The political pressure that led to the abolition of these exceptions came from other countries in the European Union (Quack and Djelic 2005: 264). The starting point was when plans for the European Coal and Steel Community (ECSC) were first proposed in 1950 (Quack and Djelic 2005: 262). These considerations immediately raised concerns on the part of the US authorities, as they feared that the new Community might become a Europe-wide German–French cartel (Quack and Djelic 2005: 262). Even after the United States overcame its initial hesitation, however, the French and German authorities by no means agreed on the details of the legal framework concerning competition issues that was meant to underlie the ECSC. Only after lengthy discussions that required the intervention of US High Commissioner John McCloy was an agreement reached (Quack and Djelic 2005: 262). The results of these intense discussions were laid down in the Treaty of Rome, which 'laid the groundwork for the operation of a European competition law system' (Quack and Djelic 2005: 265). For the ensuing decades, the Treaty of Rome constituted the basis for the institutionalization of European antitrust laws, a process that turned the European Competition Authority into a major global policy player (Quack and Djelic 2005: 264). Quack and Djelic (2005) couch this astonishing development in the following terms: 'When the Rome Treaty was signed, Germany was the only member state with a competition law––and even there it was only emerging. Today, all member states have competition regimes, shaped and inspired, in one way or another, by the European Community competition regime' (p. 271). Thus, they conclude, the emergence of competition law presents a case of 'transnational institution building' (p. 272).

10. Vereinbarungen zwischen Unternehmen, Beschlüsse von Unternehmensvereinigungen und aufeinander abgestimmte Verhaltensweisen, die eine Verhinderung, Einschränkung oder Verfälschung des Wettbewerbs bezwecken oder bewirken, sind verboten.

11. Marktbeherrschung, sonstiges wettbewerbsbeschränkendes Verhalten (2), Anwendung des europäischen Wettbewerbsrechts (3), Wettbewerbsregeln (4) and Sonderregeln für bestimmte Wirtschaftsbereiche (5).

12. The German original text reads:

> Ein Unternehmen ist marktbeherrschend, soweit es als Anbieter oder Nachfrager einer bestimmten Art von Waren oder gewerblichen Leistungen auf dem sachlich und räumlich relevanten Markt 1. ohne Wettbewerber ist, 2. keinem wesentlichen Wettbewerb ausgesetzt ist oder 3. eine im Verhältnis zu seinen Wettbewerbern überragende Marktstellung hat.

13. Furthermore, the highest federal authorities according to the respective federal law are also defined as responsible for the enforcement of cartel-related laws.

14. The original German text reads:

> Leitet das Bundeskartellamt ein Verfahren ein oder führt es Ermittlungen durch, so benachrichtigt es gleichzeitig die oberste Landesbehörde, in deren Gebiet die betroffenen Unternehmen ihren Sitz haben. Leitet eine oberste Landesbehörde ein Verfahren ein oder führt sie Ermittlungen durch, so benachrichtigt sie gleichzeitig das Bundeskartellamt.

15. The responsibility of these different authorities is shared in accordance with Germany's federal principle. Transgressions concerning individual states are handled by the respective federal authorities, while the Federal Cartel Office is responsible for nationwide infringements of the law.

16. The federal government subsequently has to submit this report to the German parliament, the *Bundestag*, which can then give its opinion on the report:

> Das Bundeskartellamt veröffentlicht alle zwei Jahre einen Bericht über seine Tätigkeit sowie über die Lage und Entwicklung auf seinem Aufgabengebiet. In den Bericht sind die allgemeinen Weisungen des Bundesministeriums für Wirtschaft und Energie nach § 52 aufzunehmen. Es veröffentlicht ferner fortlaufend seine Verwaltungsgrundsätze.

17. In German:

> Die Kartellbehörde kann alle Ermittlungen führen und alle Beweise erheben, die erforderlich sind. Für den Beweis durch Augenschein, Zeugen und Sachverständige sind § 372 Absatz 1, §§ 376, 377, 378, 380 bis 387, 390, 395 bis 397, 398 Absatz 1, §§ 401, 402, 404, 404a, 406 bis 409, 411 bis 414 der Zivilprozessordnung sinngemäß anzuwenden; Haft darf nicht verhängt werden. Für die Entscheidung über die Beschwerde ist das Oberlandesgericht zuständig.

These proceedings necessarily have to include three parties: the regulatory body itself, the defendant parties (namely, corporations, cartels, and/or associations), and relevant third parties, such as individuals or collectives affected by the behaviour of the accused parties. Usually, these parties are permitted to make an official statement on the proceedings. However, after this procedure the cartel authorities are entitled to collect and even seize evidence to make their case. This includes, among other things, witness interviews and expert views on the case. To buttress their role, the regulatory bodies are also entitled to confiscate whatever evidence they deem pertinent to their investigations. If the authorities decide that a violation of cartel law has occurred, they have the right to issue regulations to correct this situation. The relevant regulation has to be announced in the *Bundesanzeiger*, a federal gazette published by the German Department of Justice (*Verfügungen der Kartellbehörde nach § 30 Absatz 3, § 31b Absatz 3, §§ 32 bis 32b und 32d sind im Bundesanzeiger bekannt zu machen*).

A recent case that exemplifies this procedure concerns developments after the bankruptcy of the German airline Air Berlin. After depending for years on the financial support of a former competitor, Etihad Airways, Air Berlin was forced into bankruptcy once Etihad shut off the tap after continuous losses in August 2017. Subsequently, the German carrier Lufthansa signalled its interest in buying parts of Air Berlin's operations. This, however, was prohibited by the European Commission and the German authorities unless Lufthansa made concessions. In order make the desired purchase, Lufthansa had to concede some take-off and landing slots at Düsseldorf airport to keep its market position in balance with its competitors. Only then, after the cartel authorities had determined that Lufthansa's acquisition of certain parts of Air Berlin would not diminish what was considered to be fair competition, could Lufthansa proceed to finalize purchase. Hence, the bankruptcy and subsequent sale of Air Berlin is a clear example of how rules set by regulatory bodies at different levels (national and European) organize markets.

18. It must be noted that the reduction of uncertainty as a result of the German antitrust law was directed primarily at final consumers, and that the institution—the law—was imposed against the will of those it was intended to govern. Put differently, for the firms subject to the decision, it did not diminish uncertainty but only meant that they had to adjust to another institutional landscape that forbade them from collaborating in certain ways. It nonetheless reduced uncertainty for customers. Hence, the actors know what they can do, and they also obtain ideas on how others will behave because of decided institutions, which is to say that uncertainty is reduced.

19. https://www.cen.eu/work/ENdev/how/Pages/default.aspx

20. https://www.cen.eu/Pages/default.aspx

21. The concept of partial organizations refers to social orders that are not complete, as discussed above, yet incorporate components of complete organizations. These components, to repeat, are *membership, hierarchy, sanctions, rules,* and *monitoring* (Ahrne and Brunsson 2011: 86). The idea of partial organizations can be used to describe the cucumber standard as a partially organized order, that is, an order that relies on components of formal organizations, which was defined above, without being identical to a formal organization. This becomes clear with regard to the fact that the cucumber standard made use of rules, membership, sanctions, and controls, yet lacked the hierarchy component, as discussed in the case of decided institutions.

22. Class I cucumbers must:

> be reasonably developed;
> be reasonably well shaped and practically straight (maximum height of the arc: 10 mm per 10 cm of the length of cucumber).

This class, however, allow some defects:

> a slight deformation, but excluding that caused by seed formation;
> a slight defect in colouring, especially the light-coloured part of the cucumber where it touched the ground during growth;

slight skin blemishes due to rubbing and handling or low temperatures, provided that such blemishes have healed and do not affect the keeping quality.

23. Within the EU, controls are carried out by national regulatory bodies. In Germany, for example, due to its federal system, the *Bundesanstalt für Landwirtschaft und Ernährung* is responsible for controls at the national level regarding the import and export of foods. At the *Land* level, responsibility lies with the federal states, which implement controls. For this purpose, federal states have installed checkpoints. In North Rhine Westphalia, for example, they are located in Cologne and Recklinghausen. The regulatory bodies, in contrast, carry out their control duties on the production level, the retail and wholesale level, and the export level. These controls are selective and take place in accordance with a risk analysis. Practically, food inspectors rely on tools to help them measure whether food products comply with size regulations, among other things. Figure 3.1 portrays such a measuring tool, in this case for onions.

24. https://www.laves.niedersachsen.de/lebensmittel/marktueberwachung/obst_und_gemuese/gueteeigenschaften/obst-und-gemuese---qualitaetskriterien-73854.html

25. Furthermore, several national associations, such as the German farmers' association, voiced criticisms of repeal. However, not even this broad support could save the cucumber standard: in 2009 the directive was repealed. Its legacy, however, continues in constant references to the cucumber standard as a case in point of EU bureaucracy 'gone mad'. (In the Brexit context, the equivalent is the so-called 'bendy banana directive' fabricated by former UK Prime Minister Boris Johnson while he was working as a journalist.) Still, the grounding of the standard in real-world requirements was also attested to in the course of its undoing. In fact, the standard is still applied today by many supermarket chains, including Aldi and Lidl in Germany.

26. NGOs such as the German *Querfeldein* or the Polish *Zachranjidlo* have criticized the—now voluntary—standard in the context of the food waste debate. They argue that the standard leads to a situation in which cucumbers not meeting the standard are left rotting in the fields because they cannot be sold. In general, though, the cucumber norm clearly shows that the uncertainty absorption that comes with standardization endows standards with longevity and persistence, even in the face of staunch political criticism.

CHAPTER 4

1. Stark and Marres say that 'our approach to testing cast a broad net' (2020b: 424). This means that what they are referring to is partly what is here called evaluation, and they also use the term 'evaluation' as almost synonymous with the notion of testing. Testing is in some cases an activity that occurs prior to evaluations. Testing is less 'clear-cut, and more open to unknown and unclear properties of whatever is 'tested'' (Marres, personal conversation, 4 December 2020).

2. Evaluations can be used by those who make decisions as a way, potentially also an excuse, to avoid taking full responsibility for the decision, because they 'only' follow the outcome of an evaluation that gives them reason to act in a certain way.

3. Evaluations can of course themselves be evaluated, but that is not the focus of the discussion. The question of whether a specific evaluation has reliability

and validity is of great practical interest. Objective evaluations—evaluations using institutionalized scales at least on the ratio scale—by definition produce reliability. The narrow usage of the notion of evaluation means that we check what is to be evaluated against clearly defined measures. More sociologically interesting, perhaps, is to find out how evaluation is done and what it does when there is a lack of decided rules against which to evaluate.

4. When did the first evaluation or valuation occur? An important qualitative step was taken with the introduction of formal evaluations, in other words, evaluations carried out to solve practical problems. In the United States they became institutionalized in 1965 when the Elementary and Secondary Education Act was passed, out of which evaluation became a federal mandate (House 1993). However, in various forms the phenomenon of evaluation has existed for thousands of years, including, for example, in marriage selection (Padgett and Ansell 1993).

   If one is willing to accept a broad conceptualization of evaluation, it is possible to study the term and the frequency of its use. To account for this, I have conducted an analysis of the use of the term 'evaluation' in large text corpuses. The analysis, searching Google Books by using the Ngram Viewer program, reports the relative frequency of evaluation. The term seems to have peaked in the 1980s, though this is merely an indication of the trends of the frequency of words in English.

   The abovementioned analysis captures all meanings of the term 'evaluation'. Many of these meanings are very far from the way I use it here, however.

5. There are international conferences and national evaluation societies. Even the United Nations has a division on evaluation, the United Nations Evaluation Group. http://www.unevaluation.org/about

   This group standardized the conduct of evaluators among its 43 members, consisting of other UNH organs.

6. 2015 International Year of Evaluation | UN-Habitat (unhabitat.org). This declaration, for what is known, was not successful in terms of impact. At the publication of this book it is hard to find even documents about it, the quotes are from 2019.

7. The US standard when the study was conducted did not recognise the presence of chalazae—the two membranous twisted strings by which the yolk is bound to the ends of the shell—though it was mentioned by the housewives included in the study. But even though this was mentioned, it did not affect their rating of eggs (Noles and Roush 1962: 24).

8. The scores used in the ratings of evaluations—for example, so-called indicators—may be numbered and thus be presented with an objective connotation. But in one sense they are objective only once they have been constructed. Plenty of indexes of various types are produced, including for example:

   > Control of Corruption and Rule of Law Indicators, under the imprimatur of the World Bank; the Millennium Development Goals indicators, under UN auspices; the Corruption Perceptions Index created by Transparency International; the Human Development Index (HDI), produced by the United Nations Development Programme (UNDP); the Trafficking in Persons indicators produced by the U.S. State Department; and various indicators produced by consultancies specialized in advising investors on

political risks. The Office of the United Nations High Commissioner for Human Rights has developed indicators for several core human rights. (Davis, Kingsbury, and Merry 2012: 72)

These indicators are meant to be essentially a function of raw data, to avoid interpretative work. An indicator can be defined as:

a named collection of rank-ordered data that purports to represent the past or projected performance of different units. The data are generated through a process that simplifies raw data about a complex social phenomenon. The data, in this simplified and processed form, are capable of being used to compare particular units of analysis (such as countries, institutions, or corporations), synchronically or over time, and to evaluate their performance by reference to one or more standards. (Davis, Kingsbury, and Merry 2012: 73–74)

This is an example of how some states of the world, in this case raw data— which of course do not come ready made but are constructed by decisions and procedures—are put together to generate yet other states of the world. These are called indicators and used for evaluations.

9. For this to be the case beauty must have become institutionalized.
10. More mundane, and less significant examples of how evaluations are used in society exist. One may, for example, evaluate a collector of model trains due to the number of different engines the person has. It is enough to know the number of trains in the collection, to position the model train enthusiast's collection in relation to other collections; no personal judgement need be given. In the evaluation process, actors' identities—'who they are'—do not affect the evaluation. What matters is what they do or what they have. In this case, it is consequently relatively easy to adjudicate and rate actors according to this institutionalized 'scale of value'. Once a standard is in place, the actors, deeds, or things evaluated—in short, the social things evaluated—are a function of this scale (value).
11. Evaluations categorize actors, and endow them with rank positions directly, or values enabling rank positions. There are consequences for events, organizations, and persons that are evaluated. The results of an evaluation may praise, or name and shame the evaluand. Evaluations thus have direct consequences for those being evaluated. Human beings and organizations may gain identities as a result.

PART II

1. Indisputable here means that a person who, for example, claimed that Sweden won the football world championship in 1958 would, in fact, be mad. Indeed, the championship did take place in Sweden, and Sweden reached the final, but lost 5:2 against Brazil. There are numerous reports, and close to 50,000 eyewitnesses saw the game, so it is, in practice, indisputable.
2. For valuation, not only do people's views matter; who they are matters, too. More precisely, who they are is conceptualized in terms of identity—each of them has more or less status. This condition is common also in the art world (Beckert and Rössel 2004; Bourdieu 1993; Menger 1999; Plattner 1996; Velthuis 2005), among critics (Bourdieu 1996), and in the markets in these spheres, as well as, generally speaking, in situations characterized by aesthetic values

(Podolny 2005:192; Warde 2002) and where there are goods that have been called 'singularities' by Lucien Karpik (2010b).

In markets, for example, the relationship between those who perform something and their audience 'constitute[s] one of the bases for evaluating the producers and their products' (Bourdieu 1993: 46; cf. Goffman 1971). The audience, which may be composed of ideal-typical consumers (cf. White 1981), by acknowledging the actors who take part and what they do, endows them, or indirectly endows their deeds, with status (Smith Spence 1974). In this way, a rank order of actors making up the social structure emerges. Audiences thereby fulfil a 'function' similar to the standard, although they cannot do this with a single act or decision because they are not one actor. But an audience, too, provides valuations and an ordering of alternatives that reduces uncertainty concerning what is 'good' and 'bad' (for example, 'in fashion', 'out of fashion', and so on). The important difference from a standard is that what the audience will say about a 'performance' cannot be known in advance.

CHAPTER 5

1. See Aspers (2008) for an early formulation of this concept.
2. Though today, many uncertainties are even turned into risks on which one can bet (e.g., elections), the uncertainty to which I refer does not have to be commensurable and be measured in terms of money.
3. As defined by the journal *Valuation Studies* (http://valuationstudies.liu.se/).
4. There have also been discussions of values and value conflicts. Lamont discusses the existence of matrices of evaluation, and studies above all practices of evaluation and valuation (2012; 2009), and, as has already been discussed, commensuration (Espeland and Stevens 1998; Fourcade and Healy 2007). Vatin introduces the notion of valorization, referring to the manner in which the worth of something increases in processes; he also points out that evaluation and what he calls valorization are intertwined in reality (2013: 32).

   Much work has been done on the variety of specific values (e.g., Boltanski and Thévenot 2006; Pareto 1935), tools, and strategies involved in processes of valuation and evaluation (cf. Aspers and Beckert 2011a; Beckert and Musselin 2013; Karpik 2010b; Stark 2009). Values in markets have also been discussed (e.g., Alexius and Tamm Hallström 2014). There is a literature on uncertainty reduction by means of attempts to affect and control outcomes (see Beckert 2016 for discussion of this literature). If we look at empirical cases, most forms of valuation imply a combination or commensuration of different values and the exclusion of other values, that is, values that are not part of the process. Many studies in this field take up uncertainty reduction from the perspective of the individual actor who tries to reduce their uncertainty.

   Lucien Karpik (2010) addresses the problem of uncertainty concerning which individual product is good; he thus addresses what non-homogenous offers are of high or low quality. What Karpik presents for assessing quality are called 'judgement devices'. The word 'device' is rooted in 'division'—division between qualities, or in more general terms, different values. This is exactly what these devices enable. They are devices for separating what is good in markets from what is not good, and make it easier for actors to make informed choices; they are also 'guideposts for individual and collective action' (Karpik 2010a: 44). Judgement devices reduce the quality uncertainty of products in markets.

5. Edvind Sandström conducted the empirical work, primarily fieldwork at performance art festivals in Sweden, France, and China between 2011 and 2012. Information from 10 festivals and 40 days observing the practice of performance art makes up the bulk of the empirical material. The primary material is field notes based on observations and informal conversations with artists, curators, support personnel, and members of audiences. Performances and scenes have been documented with camera and video recordings. The sample consists of over 130 artists from over 30 countries. From 2012, a specific collective of artists from Sweden via France to China was followed. This collective is a stable set of artists who travel to similar festivals and meet on a regular basis.

   To learn more about the practice of performance art, and reach a closer understanding of artists' meaning constructs, 'silent' observations were primarily used. Although some interviews were conducted, the focus was on investigating how actors themselves value each other when interacting. By observing artists' performances, peers' utterances and experiences before, during, and after performances could be noted as they unfolded. To be discrete, a cell phone instead of a notebook was used to write down notes such as utterances and other noteworthy observations. By using the cell phone it was possible to video-record performance artworks, which in turn captured ongoing discussions between artists perceiving their peers. Participating in artists' talks and lectures in which they discussed their experience of performing in the given context, and more general conversations of the meaning of performance art, added to the knowledge of the field.

   Additionally, secondary material in the form of literature on performance art, artist and festival homepages, interviews, and critical writings on performance was included in the analysis. It was also possible to look at artist talks posted on YouTube and notes from past panel discussions on performance art. In addition, archived documents in databases generated by artists themselves, such as *Asian Art Archive* (AAA) in Hong Kong and *The Archive for Performance, Performance Art, Performing Arts, Action and Intermedia Arts* (ASA) in Germany were examined. The material generated by Sandström serves two ends. The first is to give a thorough background and knowledge of the field as such; the second is to give detailed information about values and valuation practices in the field of contemporary performance art. The empirical data was analysed in the software program N-Vivo through thematic coding guided by theoretical concepts, but open to the field's unique logic and findings. It made it possible to analyse field notes, interview transcripts, photos, and video recordings in a productive way.

6. There may be over 400 festivals in Europe alone (2012). But festivals exist also in Asia, spearheaded by artists in South Korea, Japan, and China. Although some festivals, especially in the United States, have entrance fees, the great majority can be attended free of charge. Thus, these performance art festivals have not emulated the marketization of larger events such as music festivals or performing arts festivals.

7. While the festivals are small-scale productions, they need funding and are generally sponsored by local art institutions, galleries, and local companies. In general, artists are provided with accommodation and travel expenses, but they are seldom paid for their contribution. Few artists make their living from performance alone, and they are in general active in other artistic projects. Quite a few teach art at colleges or universities.

8. Depending on how one defines performance art, artists, critics, and art historians have offered multiple narratives, thus researching its emergence from different sources. For example, the medium has been traced back to the Italian Renaissance, promoted by Alberti, Leonardo, and Bernini (Felice 1984).

9. Performance art has been referred to as the 'presentation of taboos' (Howell 1999: 103are st).

10. Both those who see the market as the solution and, perhaps more surprisingly, many of those who are more critical of markets (Boyer 1990, 2005; Streeck 2005) refer explicitly or implicitly to mutual adjustment. The 'spontaneous (order)' (Hayek 1973: 39–52) or 'self-regulation', which are two other terms for mutual adjustment in markets, mean that 'all productions for sale on the market and incomes derive from such sales . . . [and that] [n]othing must be allowed to inhibit the formation of markets' (Polanyi 2001: 72). Sombart (1927, VilII: 530) calls this a 'natural' (*natürlich*) process. Accordingly, markets are 'spontaneous orders' (cosmos) that evolve out of 'chaos', as opposed to planned orders based on design (taxis) (Hayek 1973: 35–54). The actors involved need not have a conception of the market, which underlines that it is an 'unintended consequence'. Similar ideas can be found in neoclassical economics and institutional economics.

    Neoclassical economists (Bal and Goyla 1994; Smith Spence 1974) have discussed market-fashioning viewing actors as those who are like egos or monads, each being self-interested with a set of given preferences and whose activities result, in a natural way, in a market, often with price as the sole means of competition.

    The notion of mutual adjustment is essential in evolutionary economics (Nelson and Winter 1982: 9–10), while at the same time seeing institutions (rules) as the conceptual cornerstone of their explanations of how markets develop (Hodgson 1996: 175–179). They argue that the market rules and institutions are a consequence of humans' impulse to survive (Greif 2006: 126; cf. Hannan et al. 2003: 309; Hodgson 1996: 170–186).

11. *Temperament* in Greek medicine.

12. Attempts have been made to investigate whether it is possible to use predictors to reduce the uncertainty in film production. De Vany and Walls (1999: 286) say:

    > [W]e find that much conventional Hollywood wisdom is not valid. By making strategic choices in booking screens, budgeting, and hiring producers, directors and actors with marquee value, a studio can position a movie to improve its chances of success. But, after a movie opens, the audience decides its fate. The exchange of information among a large number of individuals interacting personally unleashes a dynamic that is complex and unpredictable. Even a carefully managed and expensive marketing program cannot direct the information cascade; it is a complex stochastic process that can go anywhere. We conclude that the studio model of risk management lacks a foundation in theory or evidence. Revenue forecasts have zero precision, which is just a formal way of saying that 'anything can happen'.

    They find, however, that some actors correlate with financially successful films.

13. However, Hayek (1973) acknowledges both the role of the state and attempts by economic actors to organize their efforts. For Hayek, organized market-making may indeed occur, and he finds this acceptable as long as the state is not in the

driving seat of the organization. By this inclusion of organization of markets, he broadens the notion of mutual adjustment to the extent that it is almost an all-inclusive concept.

14. Many activities termed 'evaluation' lack objective scales. In practice, polls may serve this purpose, as attempts made by firms or other organizations to find out what their customers or users think about them. These convaluations, hence, have adjustment effectively only on one side. That is, for each evaluation only one side gives voice to what they think. If there is a series of evaluations, one can speak of a mutual adjustment, but the convaluation still generates a set of particular states of the world, which, so to speak, replace one another when polls and new political proposals interplay. This is an example of how the term *evaluation* is used in a quite different way from the kind discussed in Chapter 4, namely an objectively existing scale for generating principles of states of the world. It is here more or less ongoing 'check' of the current opinion.

15. It is not a tax in terms of money, because the state does not gain from it.

16. The control, however, is highly complicated because it involves ways of measuring the amount of CO_2 actually emitted (Rosenström 2014).

17. It is logical that if a specific tie fashion were institutionalized, one could no longer speak of fashion, because fashion requires change (Aspers and Godart 2013).

CHAPTER 6

1. In addition to the fact that forms for decisions do not involve mutual adjustment, as was discussed in Chapter 5, to produce the attempts, there are two differences between Chapter 5 and Chapter 6. The first difference follows from the difference between mutual adjustment and decisions for others, and implies that convaluations produce unintentional outcomes, whereas decisions for others are intentional. The second difference between these chapters is that a convaluation is a form that can both emerge out of mutual adjustment or be organized, whereas a form of decision is always organized.

2. https://fashionchecker.org/

3. Thus, actors may be affected by what others do; they may be 'pulled in' to be evaluated, valued, and this may happen even against their will. This is typical of NGOs setting up 'labels' that can be used to evaluate firms and activities (Aspers 2006a). No matter how, evaluations can affect actors' existential uncertainty. However, evaluations and the results of evaluations will lead to reactions from those evaluated (Bomark 2016; Espeland and Sauder 2007; Furst 2017). As a result of the evaluations, not only do actors gain identities, but reactions are triggered from those being evaluated, as shown by Espeland and Sauders (2007) in their study of law schools. The effects of evaluation are very important for individual actors, and there may be many different interpretations of states of the world. An evaluation is more likely to be considered fair by those evaluated if it is objective, and if they can decide to take part or not. In cases in which actors are evaluated despite being against it, and when there are no clear rules, it is less likely to be legitimate in the eyes of those evaluated.

4. https://www.oscars.org/sites/oscars/files/93aa_rules.pdf

5. https://www.oscars.org/about/join-academy

6. For an example see H&M Design Award (https://hm.com).

7. It was already clear to Austin that a performative sentence is not to be judged as being either 'true' or 'false' (Austin 1986: 1–11). By going back to Austin, one

avoids the problem of expanding the use of performativity to mean a whole range of quite different things (Mäki 2013), and it is possible to focus on the fact that the statement made is to take certain action.

8. At a certain point, the number of different prizes awarded can be commensurated into 'number of prizes' or the amount of prize money they have made. This is a quantification of prizes, meaning that there is one scale according to which they can be measured.

CHAPTER 7

1. Corrupt judges can make their decisions also against existing rules. And in contemporary military conflicts, it is the international audience, not least the UN Security Council, which decides on outcomes. But with the strong external parties making decisions, we can no longer speak of a strong or 'pure' form.

2. While in boxing sometimes—for example, if there was no knockout, and if the call of the judge was a close shot—a rematch, a chance to take revenge for a loss, may be scheduled. When a defending champion, such as Floyd Patterson, lost to an opponent (in his case Ingemar Johansson) and then won the rematch, both matches together become a state of the world. Hence, a series may be the unit. This can, for example, be the case in the NHL, which is organized so that the playoff runs over seven matches.

3. In even more violent games, such as Mixed Martial Arts, this is even more distinct, because draws are less frequent.

4. Elias points out that war and fighting were normal life among knights in the Middle Ages, but this violent way of interaction gradually gave way to more civilized interactions (1969: 263–301).

5. Economics and biologists too use the term *tournament*. Tournaments have been used primarily to account for disproportional wage differences in hierarchies: the higher pay for those with higher rank can be seen as a reward for winning several 'competitions' to get promoted (Rosen 1981). This economic usage of the term, as well as the usage by biologists, is above all metaphorical. In biology the notion 'contest' is often used (Fitzpatrick et al. 2012), but not in a clear-cut way.

6. For example, if boxer A won against B at a certain point in time, and B around the same time won against C, it does not follow that A would win against C.

7. Holmgång refers to a physical fight taking place between two men on a tiny island, typically with no trees. The one who could force the other from the 'holme' won, or put differently, was 'right' and the looser, if he survived, was 'wrong'.

8. Simmel (1923) seems to view war games as nothing but games for the fun of it, which means that he missed many important dimensions.

9. 'The NHL Draft Lottery is a weighted system to determine the order of selection for the first 14 picks of the 2015 NHL Draft. Teams finishing with the fewest points during the regular season possess the greatest chance of winning the right to the first pick in the NHL Draft. Fourteen balls numbered 1 to 14, are placed in a lottery machine. The machine expels four balls, forming a series of numbers. The four-digit series resulting from the expulsion of the balls is matched against a probability chart that divides the possible combinations among the 14 participating clubs'. http://www.nhl.com/ice/m_page. htm?id=68856

10. http://www.nhl.com/ice/page.htm?id=26394

11. https://en.wikipedia.org/wiki/Naim_S%C3%BCleymano%C4%9Flu

12. At the Olympics and other diving competitions, seven judges score, out of which the highest and lowest scores are eliminated, from 0 (failed) to 10 (perfect). The remaining five are added, and this score is multiplied by 0.6. Finally, this score is multiplied by the points that represent the specific dive's degree of difficulty. The scoring by the judges is by no means 'random', but it is supposed to follow conventions of what is a 'good' dive. But the idea of scoring is not recommended to be an objective scale. It is even recommended that 'when judging, it is important to use the [scoring] scale [from 0–10 with detailed information on how to judge] as a 'flexible' scale to compare divers in a particular contest, rather than a straight scale to apply across all diving competitions' https://cdn.revolu tionise.com.au/site/phexkt28.pdf: 9. It follows that there can be no world record in diving.

13. The cocks are extensions of male social life, not only of male genitals, but the term cock denotes also 'hero', 'warrior', 'champion', 'lady killer' (Geertz 1973: 418). Moreover, other forms of interfaces of conflicts are compared with cockfighting, such as 'court trials, wars, political contests, inheritance disputes, and street arguments' (Geertz 1973: 418). According to the anthropological analysis of Geertz, cockfighting is a form of magical ritual, and the winner of a fight, takes 'the carcass of the loser—often torn limb by limb by its enraged owner—home to eat, he does so with a mixture of social embarrassment, moral satisfaction, aesthetic disgust, and cannibal joy', whereas the loser goes home and commits a kind of metaphysical (and social) suicide' (Geertz 1973: 421). What Geertz describes is not completely different from the combat by trial, though instead of hiring someone to fight in one's place, cocks are fighting.

    Cockfighting is organized, and there is an umpire making the calls, though the result often is clear—one cock dies from the blows from the other cock's razor-sharp spurs that are attached to their feet. Geertz says that many cockfights are organized mainly for the sake of betting. These fights, however, are of lesser importance. The important fights are fights for status. In these fights too, betting is central, though the betting is not primarily made for the sake of winning money, but to gain and establish status. The odds for the fights are quite even, and Geertz assumes that, in the long run, it evens out. The game is a means to 'lay one's public self, allusively and metaphorically, through the medium of one's cock, on the line' (Geertz 1973: 434). So it is not money, but 'the migration of the Balinese status hierarchy into the body of the cockfight' (Geertz 1973: 436) that makes it so important. It is a social affair, and the states of the world—in terms of the status of the members of this society—is confirmed and distributed in these fights. It is a 'hierarchy of pride,' of the society that is both on display and created in the cockfights, and Geertz says that without these fights, 'the Balinese would have a much less certain understanding' (Geertz 1973: 447) of their social life, and the logic and principles of the social status of their society. It is an activity that helps the Balinese to interpret their lives. Hence, it is here that the social structure reduces uncertainty because it is ordered, meaning that: 'a state of affairs in which a multiplicity of elements of various kinds are so related to each other that we may learn from our acquaintance with some spatial or temporal part of the whole to form expectations concerning the rest' (Hayek 1973: 36).

CHAPTER 8

1. An entrepreneur may prefer 'the uncertain chance of differentiation [of the products] to that of the certain half of the gain of which he could be sure if his and the other's offers are exactly alike' (Simmel 1955: 75).

2. There is thus a significant difference between the ratio of a lottery and the real world. A lottery, say with 100 tickets with only one win, yields a chance of winning of 1 per cent. This is a clear odds ratio, with no human contingencies as discussed above.

REFERENCES

Abend, Gabriel. 2018. 'Outline of a Sociology of Decisionism.' *The British Journal of Sociology* 69 (2):237–264. https://doi.org/10.1111/1468-4446.12320.

Abercrombie, Nicholas, Stephen Hill, and Bryan Turner. 2006. *Dictionary of Sociology, 5th edition*. London: Penguin.

Adams, James. 2012. 'Causes and Electoral Consequences of Party Policy Shifts in Multiparty Elections: Theoretical Results and Empirical Evidence.' *Annual Review of Political Science* 15 (1):401–419. https://doi.org/10.1146/annurev-poli sci-031710-101450.

Ahrne, Göran, and Nils Brunsson. 2005. 'Organizations and Meta-Organizations.' *Scandinavian Journal of Management* 21:429–449.

Ahrne, Göran, and Nils Brunsson. 2008. *Meta-Organizations*. Cheltenham: EdwardElgar.

Ahrne, Göran, and Nils Brunsson. 2011. 'Organization Outside Organizations: The Significance of Partial Organization.' *Organization* 18 (1):83–104.

Ahrne, Göran, and Nils Brunsson. 2019. 'Organization Unbound.' In *Organization Outside Organizations: The Abundance of Partial Organization in Social Life*, edited by Göran Ahrne and Nils Brunsson, 3–36. Cambridge: Cambridge University Press.

Ahrne, Göran, Patrik Aspers, and Nils Brunsson. 2015. 'The Organization of Markets.' *Organization* 36 (1):7–27.

Ahrne, Göran. 1994. *Social Organizations. Interaction Inside, Outside and Between Organizations*. London: Sage.

Akerlof, George. 1970. 'The Market for 'Lemons': Quality Uncertainty and the Market Mechanism.' *Quarterly Journal of Economics* 84 (3):488–500.

Alaszewski, Andy. 2015. 'Anthropology and Risk: Insights into Uncertainty, Danger and Blame from Other Cultures – A Review Essay.' *Health, Risk & Society* 17 (3–4):205–225.

Alexius, Susanna, and Christina Tamm Hallström, eds. 2014. *Configuring Value Conflicts in Markets*. Cheltenham, UK: Edward Elgar.

Alpers, Isabel. 2019. 'Managing the "Unknowns" Exploring the Nature of Uncertainty and its Effects on Strategic Decisions.' Dissertation, School of Management, Economics, Law, Social Sciences, and International Affairs, University of St Gallen.

Alvarez, Sharon A., and Jay B. Barney. 2005. "How Do Entrepreneurs Organize Firms Under Conditions of Uncertainty?' *Journal of Management* 31 (5):776–793. https://doi.org/10.1177/0149206305279486.

Alvarez, Sharon, Allan Afuah, and Cristina Gibson. 2018. 'Editors' Comments: Should Management Theories Take Uncertainty Seriously?' *Academy of Management Review* 43 (2):169–172. https://doi.org/10.5465/amr.2018.0050.

Amsden, Alice. 2001. *The Rise of the Rest: Challenges to the West from Late-Industrializing Economies*. Oxford: Oxford University Press.

Arendt, Hannah. 1988 [1958]. *The Human Condition*. Chicago: University of Chicago Press.

Arora-Jonsson, Stefan, Nils Brunsson, and Raimund Hasse. 2020. 'Where Does Competition Come From? The Role of Organization.' *Organization Theory* 1 (1):2631787719889977. https://doi.org/10.1177/2631787719889977.

Arrow, Kenneth. 1974. *The Limits of Organization*. New York: W.W. Norton & Company.

Arrow, Kenneth. 1983. *General Equilibrium. Collected Papers of Kenneth J. Arrow (Vol.2)*. Cambridge, MA: The Belknap Press of Harvard University Press.

Arrow, Kenneth. 1984. *Collected Papers of Kenneth Arrow: The Economics of Information (Vol. 4)*. Cambridge, MA: Harvard University Press.

Arrow, Kenneth. 1984. *Individual Choice under Certainty and Uncertainty. Collected Papers of Kenneth J. Arrow (Vol. 3)*. Cambridge, MA: Harvard University Press.

Aspers, Patrik, and Frédéric Godart. 2013. 'Sociology of Fashion: Order and Change.' *Annual Review of Sociology* 39:171–192.

Aspers, Patrik, and Jens Beckert. 2011a. 'Introduction.' In *The Worth of Goods*, edited by Jensh Beckert and Patrik Aspers, 1–39. Oxford: Oxford University Press.

Aspers, Patrik, and Jens Beckert, eds. 2011b. *The Worth of Goods*. Oxford: Oxford University Press.

Aspers, Patrik, Petter Bengtsson, and Alexander Dobeson. 2020. 'Market Fashioning.' *Theory and Society* 49:417–438.

Aspers, Patrik. 2001. 'A Market in Vogue, Fashion Photography in Sweden.' *European Societies* 3 (1):1–22.

Aspers, Patrik. 2006. 'Contextual Knowledge.' *Current Sociology* 54 (5):745–763.

Aspers, Patrik. 2006a. 'Ethics in Global Garment Market Chains.' In *The Moralization of the Markets*, edited by Nico Stehr, Christoph Henning, and Bernd Weiler, 287–307. London: Transaction Press.

Aspers, Patrik. 2006b [2001]. *Markets in Fashion: A Phenomenological Approach*. London: Routledge.

Aspers, Patrik. 2008. *Convaluations*. Stockholm: Department of Sociology, Working Paper Series.

Aspers, Patrik. 2009. 'Knowledge and Value in Markets.' *Theory and Society* 38:111–131.

Aspers, Patrik. 2010. *Orderly Fashion: A Sociology of Markets*. Princeton, NJ: Princeton University Press.

Aspers, Patrik. 2011. *Markets*. Cambridge: Polity Press.

Aspers, Patrik. 2013. 'Quality and Temporality in Timber Markets.' In *Constructing Quality: The Classification of Goods in Markets*, edited by Jens Beckert and Christine Musselin, 58–76. Oxford: Oxford University Press.

Aspers, Patrik. 2015. 'Phenomenological Identity Theory in Economic Sociology.' In *Re-Imagining Economic Sociology*, edited by Patrik Aspers and Nigel Dodd, 252–274. Oxford: Oxford University Press.

Austin, John L. 1986 [1972]. *How to Do Things with Words?* Oxford: University Press.

Azarian, Reza. 2016. 'Uncertainty as a Common Ground for a Dialogue Between Economics and Sociology.' *International Review of Sociology* 26 (2):262–275.

Baird, Davis. 2004. *Thing Knowledge: A Philosophy of Scientific Instruments*. Berkeley: University of California Press.

Bal, Venkatesh, and Sanjeev Goyla. 1994. 'The Birth of a New Market.' *Economic Journal* 104 (423):282–290.

Bang, Peter Fibiger. 2008. *The Roman Bazaar: A Comparative Study of Trade and Markets in a Tributary Empire*. Cambridge: Cambridge University Press.

Banks, Quentin. 1963. 'Grade Standards and Product Identification Labels Influence the Demand for Eggs and Other Farm Products.' *Journal of Farm Economics* 45(5):1365–1369.

Barbalet, Jack. 2001. *Emotion, Social Theory, and Social Structure, A Macrosociological Approach*. Cambridge: Cambridge University Press.

Barty-King, Hugh. 1977. *Baltic Exchange: The History of a Unique Market*. London: Hutchinson.

Bauman, Zymunt. 2006. *Liquid Fear*. Cambridge: Polity.

Beck, Ulrich. 1999. *World Risk Society*. Cambridge: Polity Press.

Becker, Howard. 1982. *Art Worlds*. Berkeley: University of California Press.

Beckert, Jens, and Christine Musselin, eds. 2013. *Constructing Quality: The Classification of Goods in Markets*. Oxford: Oxford University Press.

Beckert, Jens, and Jörg Rössel. 2004. 'Reputation als Mechanismus der Reduktion von Ungewissheit am Kunstmarkt.' *Kölner Zeitschrift für Soziologie und Sozialpsychologie* 56 (1):32–50.

Beckert, Jens, and Richard Bronk. 2018. 'An Introduction to Uncertain Futures.' In *Uncertain Futures: Imaginaries, Narratives, and Calculation in the Economy*, edited by Jens Beckert and Richard Bronk, 1–36. Oxford: Oxford University Press.

Beckert, Jens. 1996. 'What is Sociological About Economic Sociology? Uncertainty and the Embeddedness of Economic Action.' *Theory and Society* 25:803–840.

Beckert, Jens. 2016. *Imagined Futures: Fictional Expectations and Capitalist Dynamics*. Cambridge, MA: Harvard University Press.

Beckert, Jens. 2021. 'The Firm as an Engine of Imagination: Organizational Prospection and the Making of Economic Futures.' *Organization Theory* 2 (2):26317877211005773. https://doi.org/10.1177/26317877211005773.

Berger, Charles. 1986. 'Uncertain Outcome Values in Predicted Relationships: Uncertainty Reduction Theory Then and Now.' *Human Communication Research* 13 (1):34–38. https://doi.org/10.1111/j.1468-2958.1986.tb00093.x.

Berger, Peter, and Thomas Luckmann. 1991 [1966]. *The Social Construction of Reality: A Treatise in the Sociology of Knowledge*. London: Penguin Books.

Berghaus, Günter. 2005. *Avant-Garde Performance: Live Events and Electronic Technologies*. New York: Palgrave Macmillan.

Bernstein, Lisa. 1992. 'Opting out of the Legal System: Extralegal Contractual Relations in the Diamond Industry.' *Journal of Legal Studies* 21 (1):115–157.

Berthoin Antal, Ariane, Michael Hutter, and David Stark. 2105. *Moments of Valuation: Exploring Sites of Dissonance*. Oxford: Oxford University Press.

Besedovsky, Natalia. 2018. 'Uncertain Meanings of Risk: Calculative Practices and Risk Conceptions in Credit Rating Agencies.' In *Uncertain Futures: Imaginariers, Narratives, and Calculations in the Economy*, edited by Jens Beckert and Richard Bronk, 236–256. Oxford: Oxford University Press.

Blank, Gran. 2007. *Critics, Ratings, and Society: The Sociology of Reviews*. Lanham: Rowman and Littlefield.

Boas, Franz. 1884–1885. *The Central Eskimo*. Washington: Bureau of Ethnology.

Boeckelmann, Lukas, and Stormy-Ammika Mildner. 2011. 'Unsicherheit, Ungewissheit, Risiko: Die aktuelle wissenschaftlicheDiskussion über die Bestimmungen von Risiken.' *Stiftung Wissenschaft und Politik: SWP Zeitschriftenschau* 2 (September):1–8.

Boettke, Peter J. 2002. 'Information and Knowledge: Austrian Economics in Search of its Uniqueness.' *Review of Austrian Economics* 15 (4):263–274. https://doi.org/10.1023/A:1021190719156.

Boltanski, Luc, and Laurent Thévenot. 2006 [1991]. *On Justification, Economies of Worth*. Princeton, NJ: Princeton University Press.

Bomark, Niklas. 2016. *Drawing Lines in the Sand: Organizational Responses to Evaluations in a Swedish University*. Uppsala: Uppsala University.

Bonatti, Luigi. 1984. *Uncertainty: Studies in Philosophy, Economics, and Socio-Political Theory*. Amsterdam: Verlag B.R. Grüner.

Bonss, W. 1995. *Vom Risiko: Unsicherheit und Ungewissheit in der Moderne*: Hamburger Edition.

Bonss, Wolfgang. 1991. 'Unsicherheit und Gesellschaft — Argumente für eine soziologische Risikoforschung.' *Soziale Welt* 42 (2):258–277.

Bonss, Wolfgang. 1996. 'Die Ruckkehr der Unsicherheit. Zur gesellschaftstheoretischen edeutung des Risikobegriffs.' In *Risikoforschung zwischen Disziplinarität und Interdisziplinarität*, edited by Gerhard Banse, 165–184. Berlin: Sigma.

Bordalo, Pedro, Nicoala Gennaioli, and Andrei Shleifer. 2016. 'Competition for Attention.' *Review of Economic Studies* 83:481–513.

Borman, C., W. Franzen, and L. Oeing-Hanhoff. 1971. 'Form und Materia.' In *Historisches Wörterbuch der Philosophie*, edited by Joachim Ritter, 978–1027. Darmstadt: Wissenschaftliche Buchgesellschaft.

Bourdieu, Pierre, and Loic Wacquant. 2002 [1992]. *An Invitation to Reflexive Sociology*. Cambridge: Polity Press.

Bourdieu, Pierre. 1984 [1979]. *Distinctions: A Social Critique of the Judgement of Taste*. Cambridge, MA: Harvard University Press.

Bourdieu, Pierre. 1993. *The Fields of Cultural Production, Essays on Art and Literature*. Oxford: Polity Press.

Bourdieu, Pierre. 1996 [1992]. *The Rules of Art, Genesis and Structure of the Literary Field*. Stanford: Stanford University Press.

Bourdieu, Pierre. 2001 [1983]. 'The Forms of Social Capital.' In *The Sociology of Economic Life*, edited by Mark Granovetter and Richard Swedberg, 96–111. Boulder: Westview Press.

Bowker, Geoffrey, and Susan Leigh Star. 2000. *Sorting Things Out: Classification and Its Consequences*. Cambridge: MIT Press.

Boyer, Robert. 1990. *The Regulation School: A Critical Introduction*. New York: Columbia University Press.

Boyer, Robert. 2005. *How and Why Capitalism Differ*. Cologne: Max Planck Institute for the Study of Societies, Discussion Paper 05/4.

Braudel, Fernand. 1992a. *Civilization and Capitalism 15th-18th Century, Volume II, The Wheels of Commerce*. Berkeley: University of California Press. Original edition, 1975.

Braudel, Fernand. 1992b. *Civilization and Capitalism, 15th-18th Century, Volume I, The Structure of Everyday Life*. Berkeley: University of California Press. Original edition, 1979.

Braudel, Fernand. 1992c. *Civilization and Capitalism, 15th-18th Century, Volume III, The Perspective of the World*. Berkeley: University of California Press. Original edition, 1979.

Brosziewski, Achim. 2014. 'Unsicherheit als Grundkonzept der Organizationssoziologie.' In *Organization und Unsicherheit*, edited by Maja Apelt and Konstanze Senge, 17–33. Wiesbaden: Springer.

Brown, C. A. 1933. 'Future Trading in Butter and Eggs.' *Journal of Farm Economics* 15 (4):670–675.

Brunnermeier, Markus, Harold James, and Jean-Pierre Landau. 2016. Princeton, NJ: Princeton University Press.

Brunsson, Nils, Bengt Jacobsson, and Associates. 2000. *A World of Standards*. Oxford: Oxford University Press.

Brunsson, Nils. 2007. *The Consequences of Decision-Making*. Oxford: Oxford University Press.

Bühler, Martin. 2019. *Von Netzwerken zu Märkten: Die Entstehung eines globalen Getreidemarktes* Frankfurt am Main: Campus Verlag AG.

Bumke, Joachim. 1986. *Höfische Kultur: Literatur und Gesellschaft im hohen Mittelalter*. 2 Vols. München: Deutscher Taschenbuchverlag.

Burt, Ronald S. 1988. 'The Stability of American Markets.' *American Journal of Sociology* 94 (2):356–395.

Burton-Jeangros, Claudine, Samuele Cavalli, Solène Gouilhers, and Raphaël Hammer. 2013. 'Between Tolerable Uncertainty and Unacceptable Risks: How Health Professionals and Pregnant Women Think about the Probabilities Generated by Prenatal Screening.' *Health, Risk & Society* 15 (2):144–161. https://doi.org/10.1080/13698575.2013.771737.

Busch, Lawrence. 2011. *Standards: Recipes for Reality*. Cambridge, MA: MIT Press.

Bylund, Per L. 2021. 'Introduction to the special issue on the Centenary of Frank H. Knight's Risk, Uncertainty, and Profit.' *Journal of Institutional Economics* 17:1–5. https://doi.org/ 10.1017/S1744137421000564.

Callon, Michel, ed. 1990. *The Laws of the Market*. Oxford: Blackwell Publishers

Campbell, John L. and Lindberg, Leon N. 1990. 'Property Rights and the Organization of Economic Activity by the State.' *American Sociological Review* 55 (5):634–647.

Carlson, Marvin. 1996. *Performance: A Critical Introduction*. New York: Routledge.

Carruthers, Bruce. 2005. 'The Sociology of Money and Credit.' In *Handbook of Economic Sociology*, edited by Neil Smelser and Richard Swedberg, 355–378. Princeton, NJ: Princeton University Press and Russell Sage.

Carruthers, Bruce. 2013. 'From Uncertainty Toward Risk: The Case of Credit Ratings.' *Socio-Economic Review* 11 (3):525–551.

Chamberlin, Edward. 1933. *The Theory of Monopolistic Competition*. Cambridge, MA: Harvard University Press.

Chandler, Alfred. 1962. *Strategy and Structure. Chapters in the History of the Industrial Enterprise*. Cambridge, MA: MIT Press.

Childess, Clayton. 2017. *Under the Cover: The Creation, Production, and Reception of a Novel*. Princeton, NJ: Princeton University Press.

Chong, Philippa. 2020. *Inside the Critics' Circle: Book Reviewing in Uncertain Times*. Princeton, NJ: Princeton University Press.

Christin, Angèle. 2020. 'The Ethnographer and the Algorithm: Beyond the Black Box.' *Theory and Society* 49 (5):897–918. https://doi.org/10.1007/s11 186-020-09411-3.

Ciklamini, Marlene C. 1963. 'The Old Icelandic Duel.' *Scandinavian Studies* 35 (3):175–194.

Coase, R. H. 1937. 'The Nature of the Firm.' *Economica* 4 (16):386–405.

Coase, R. H. 1988. *The Firm, The Market, and The Law.* Chicago: University of Chicago Press.

Collier, Stephen J., Rebecca Elliott, and Turo-Kimmo Lehtonen. 2021. 'Climate Change and Insurance.' *Economy and Society* 50 (2):158–172. https://doi.org/10.1080/03085147.2021.1903771.

Cooley, Charles Horton. 1894. 'Personal Competition: Its Place in the Social Order and Effect Upon Individuals; With Some Considerations on Success.' *Economic Studies* 4 (2):163–226.

Correll, Shelley J., Cecilia L. Ridgeway, Ezra W. Zuckerman, Sharon Jank, Sara Jordan-Bloch, and Sandra Nakagawa. 2017. 'It's the Conventional Thought That Counts: How Third-Order Inference Produces Status Advantage.' *American Sociological Review* 82 (2):297–327. https://doi.org/10.1177/0003122417691503.

Corte, Ugo. 2022. *Dangerous Fun: The Social Life of Big Wave Surfers.* Chicago: Chicago University Press.

Courtney, Hugh, Jane Kirkland, and Patrick Viguerie. 1997. 'Strategy Under Uncertainty.' *Harvard Business Review* 75 (6):67–79.

Crowston, Clare Haru. 2013. *Credit, Fashion, Sex: Economies of Regard in Old Regime France.* Durham: Duke University Press.

Czada, Roland, and Uwe Schimank. 2000. 'Institutionendynamik und politische Institutionengestaltung: Die zwei Gesichter sozialer Ordnungsbildung.' In *Gesellschaftliche Komplexität und kollektive Handlungsfähigkeit*, edited by Raymund Werle and Uwe Schimank, 23–44. Frankfurt am Main: Campus.

Dahler-Larsen, Peter. 2011. *The Evaluation Society.* Stanford: Stanford University Press.

Dahrendorf, Ralf. 1968. *Essays in the Theory of Society.* Stanford: Stanford University Press.

Dahrendorf, Ralf. 1985. *Law and Order.* London: Stevens and Sons.

Daipha, Phaedra. 2015. *Masters of Uncertainty: Weather Forecasters and the Quest for Ground Truth.* Chicago: University of Chicago Press.

Dana, Rose-Anne, and Frank Riedel. 2013. 'Intertemporal Equilibria with Knightian Uncertainty.' *Journal of Economic Theory* 148 (4):1582–1605.

Darr, Asaf. 2003. 'Gifting Practices and Interorganizational Relations: Constructing Obligation Networks in the Electronics Sector.' *Sociological Forum* 18 (1):31–51.

Darr, Asaf. 2006. *Selling Technology: The Changing Shape of Sales in an Information Economy.* Ithaca: Cornell University Press.

Daston, Lorraine, and Peter Galison. 2007. *Objectivity.* New York: Zone Books.

Davidson, Donald. 2004. *Problems of Rationality.* Oxford: Oxford University Press.

Davis, Kevin, Benedict Kingsbury, and Sally Merry. 2012. 'Indicators as a Technology of Global Governance.' *Law and Society Review* 46 (1):71–104.

De Vany, Arthur, and W. David Walls. 1999. 'Uncertainty in the Movie Industry: Does Star Power Reduce the Terror of the Box Office?' *Journal of Cultural Economics* 23 (4):285–318. https://doi.org/10.1023/A:1007608125988.

Dequech, David. 2003. 'Uncertainty and Economic Sociology.' *American Journal of Economics and Sociology* 62 (3):509–532.

Dewan, Torun, and Rafael Hortala-Vallve. 2017. 'Electoral Competition, Control and Learning.' *British Journal of Political Science* 49 (3):923–939. https://doi.org/10.1017/S0007123416000764.

Dewey, John. 1929. *The Quest for Certainty*. New York: J. Little and Ives Co.

Diaz-Bone, Rainer, and Robert Salais. 2011. 'Economics of Convention and the History of Economies. Towards a Transdisciplinary Approach in Economic History.' *Historical Social Research / Historische Sozialforschung* 36 (4 (138)):7–39.

Diaz-Bone, Rainer. 2012. 'Elaborating the Conceptual Difference between Conventions and Institutions.' *Historical Social Research* 37 (4):64–75.

Diaz-Bone, Rainer. 2015. *Die 'Economie des conventions': Grundlagen und Entwicklung der neun französischen Wirtschaftssoziologie*. Wiesbaden: Springer VS.

DiMaggio, Paul J., and Walter W. Powell. 1983. 'The Iron Cage Revisited: Institutional Isomorphism and Collective Rationality in Organizational Fields.' *American Sociological Review* 48 (2):147–160. https://doi.org/10.2307/2095101.

Djelic, Marie-Laure, and Sigrid Quack. 2007. 'Overcoming Path Dependency: Path Generation.' *Theory and Society* 36 (2):161–186.

Dobeson, Alexander. 2016. 'Scopic valuations: How Digital Tracking Technologies Shape Economic Value.' *Economy and Society* 45:454–478.

Dodd, Nigel. 2005. 'Reinventing Monies in Europe.' *Economy and Society* 34 (4):558–583.

Döllinger, Dominik. 2021. *From Custom to Code: A Sociological Interpretation of the Making of Association Football*. Uppsala: Uppsala University.

Donald, MacKenzie, and Millo Yuval. 2003. 'Constructing a Market, Performing Theory: The Historical Sociology of a Financial Derivatives Exchange.' *American Journal of Sociology* 109 (1):107–145. https://doi.org/10.1086/374404.

Douglas, Mary, and Aaron Wildawsky. 1982. *Risk and Culture: An Essay on the Selection of Technical and Environmental Dangers*. Berkeley: University of California Press.

Douglas, Mary. 1986. *How Institutions Think*. Syracuse: Syracuse University Press.

Douglas, Mary. 1992. *Risk and Blame: Essays in Cultural Theory*. London: Routledge.

Downey, Kirk, and John Slocum. 1975. 'Uncertainty: Measures, Research and Sources of Variation.' *Administrative Science Quarterly* 18:562–577.

Durkheim, Émile. 1984 [1895]. *The Division of Labour in Society*. London: Macmillan. Original edition, 1893.

Durkheim, Émile. 1982 [1901]. *The Rules of Sociological Method*. New York: The Free Press.

Eberle, Thomas. 1984. *Sinnkonstitution in Alltag und Wissenschaft. Der Beitrag der Phänomenologie an die Methodologie der Sozialwissenschaften*. Bern: Verlag Paul Haupt.

Edlund, Peter, Pallas, Josef, and Wedlin, Linda. 2019. 'Prizes and the Organization of Status.' In *Organization outside Organizations: The Abudance of Partial Organization in Social Life*, edited by Göran Ahrne and Nils Brunsson, 62–83. Cambridge: Cambridge University Press.

Eisenstadt, Shmuel. 1968. 'Social Institutions.' In *International Encyclopedia of the Social Sciences*, edited by David L. Sills, 23–36. London: The Macmillan Company.

Elias, Norbert. 1956. 'Problems of Involvement and Detachment.' *British Journal of Sociology* 7 (3):226–252.

Elias, Norbert. 1969. *Über den Prozess der Zivilisation: Soziogenetische und Psychogentische Untersuchungen, Erster Band*. Bern and Munich: Francke Verlag.

Elias, Norbert. 1989. *Studien über dir Deutschen: Machtkämpfe und Habitusentwicklung im 19- und 20. Jahrhundert*. Frankfurt am Main: Suhrkamp.

Elias, Norbert. 1994 [1939]. *The Civilization Process: Sociogenetic Process and Physchogenetic Investigations*. Oxford: Blackwell.

Elster, Jon 1989. *Nuts and Bolts for the Social Science*. Cambridge: Cambridge University Press.

Emmenegger, Patrick. 2021. 'Agency in Historical Institutionalism: Coalitional Work in the Creation, Maintenance, and Change of Institutions.' *Theory and Society* 50 (4):607–626. https://doi.org/10.1007/s11186-021-09433-5.

English, James. 2005. *The Economy of Prestige: Prizes, Awards, and the Circulation of Cultural Value*. Cambridge, MA: Harvard University Press.

Entwistle, Joanne, and Agnes Rocamora. 2006. 'The Field of Fashion Materialized: A Study of London Fashion Week.' *Sociology* 40 (4):735–751.

Espeland, Wendy, and Michael Sauder. 2007. 'Rankings and Reactivity: How Public Measures Recreate Social Worlds.' *American Journal of Sociology* 113 (1):1–40.

Espeland, Wendy, and Mitschell Stevens. 1998. 'Commensuration as a Social Process.' *Annual Review of Sociology* 24:313–43.

Espeland, Wendy. 2020. 'Formalized Evaluation: The Work that Rankings Do.' In *The Performance Complex: Competition and Competitions in Social Life*, edited by David Stark, 99–122. Oxford: Oxford University Press.

Esping-Andersen, Gösta. 1990. *The Three Worlds of Welfare Capitalism*. Cambridge: Polity Press.

Esposito, Elena, and David Stark. 2020. 'What's Observed in a Rating: Rankings as Orientation in the Face of Uncertainty.' In *The Performance Complex: Competition and Competitions in Social Life*, edited by David Stark, 123–143. Oxford: Oxford University Press.

Esposito, Elena. 2013. 'The Structures of Uncertainty: Performativity and Unpredictability in Economic Operations.' *Economy and Society* 42 (1):102–129. https://doi.org/10.1080/03085147.2012.687908.

Evera, Van. 1999. *Causes of War: Power and the Roots of Conflict*. Nornell, NY: Cornell University Press.

Faulkner, Robert. 1983. *Music on Demand. Composers and Careers in the Hollywood Film Industry*. New Brunswick: Transaction Books.

Favereau, Olivier, Olivier Biencourt, and Francois Eymard-Duvernay. 2002. 'Where Do Markets Come From? From (Quality) Conventions!' In *Conventions and Structures in Economic Organization: Markets, Networks and Hierarchies*, edited by Olivier Favereau and Emmanuel Lazega, 213–252. Cheltenham: Edward Elgar.

Felice, Attanasio. 1984. 'Renaissance Performance: Notes on Prototypical Artistic Actions in the Age of the Platonic Princes.' In *The Art of Performance, A Critical Anthology*, edited by Gregory Battcock and Robert Nickas, 142–156. New York: E. P. Dutton.

Fey, Mark, and Kristopher W. Ramsay. 2011. "Uncertainty and Incentives in Crisis Bargaining: Game-Free Analysis of International Conflict.' *American Journal of Political Science* 55 (1):149–169.

Fiddle, Seymour (ed.). 1980. *Uncertainty: Behavioral and Social Dimensions*. New York: Praeger.

Fine, Gary Alan. 2007. *Authors of the Storm: Meteorologists and the Culture of Prediction*. Chicago: University of Chicago Press.

Finnis, John. 2002. 'Natural Law: The Classic Tradition.' In *The Oxford Handbook of Jurisprudence and the Philosophy of Law*, edited by Jules Coleman and Scott Shapiro (online resource). Oxford: Oxford University Press.

Fitzpatrick, John, Maria Almbro, Alejandro Gonzalez-Voyer, Niclas Kolm, and Leigh Simmons. 2012. 'Male Contest Competitions and the Coevolution of Weaponry and Testes in Pinnipeds.' *Evolution: International Journal of Organic Evolution* 66 (11):3595–3604.

Fligstein, Neil, and Doug McAdam. 2012. *A Theory of Fields*. Oxford: Oxford University Press.

Fligstein, Neil. 1990. *The Transformation of Corporate Control*. Cambridge: Harvard University Press.

Fligstein, Neil. 2001. *The Architecture of Markets: An Economic Sociology for the Twenty-First Century Capitalist Societies*. Princeton, NJ: Princeton University Press.

Flynn, J., P. Slovic, and C. K. Mertz. 1994. 'Gender, Race, and Perception of Environmental Health Risks.' *Risk Analysis* 14 (6):1101–1109.

Foucault, Michel. 1989. *The Archaeology of Knowledge*. London: Routledge.

Foucault, Michel. 2019. *Penal Theories and Institutions: Lectures at the Collège de France 1971–1972*. New York: Picador.

Fourcade, Marion, and Fleur Johns. 2020. 'Loops, Ladders and Links: The Recursivity of Social and Machine Learning.' *Theory and Society* 49 (5):803–832. https://doi.org/10.1007/s11186-020-09409-x.

Fourcade, Marion, and Kieran Healy. 2007. 'Moral Views of Market Society.' *Annual Review of Sociology* 33:285–311.

Fourcade, Marion. 2016. 'Ordinalization: Lewis A. Coser Memorial Award for Theoretical Agenda Setting 2014.' *Sociological Theory* 34 (3):175–195. https://doi.org/10.1177/0735275116665876.

Franssen, Thomas, and Giselinde Kuipers. 2013. 'Coping with Uncertainty, Abundance and Strife: Decision-making Processes of Dutch Acquisition Editors in the Global Market for Translations.' *Poetics* 41:48–74.

Friedman, Jeffrey A., and Richard Zeckhauser. 2012. 'Assessing Uncertainty in Intelligence.' *Intelligence and National Security* 27 (6):824–847.

Frisell Ellburg, Ann 2008. *Ett fåfängt arbete, möten med modeller i den svenska modeindustrin*. Stockholm: Makadam.

Furst, Henrik. 2017. *Selected or Rejected? Assessing Aspiring* Writers' Attempts to Achieve Publication. Uppsala: Uppsala University.

Furst, Henrik. 2018. 'Aspiring Writers and Appraisal Devices under Market Uncertainty.' *Acta Sociologica* 61 (4):389–401.

Gadamer, Hans Georg. 1988 [1959]. 'On the Circle of Understanding.' In *Hermeneutics Versus Science, Three German Views: Wolfgang Stegmüller, Hans Georg Gadamer, Ernst Konrad Specht*, edited by J Connolly and T Keutner, 68–78. Notre Dame: University of Notre Dame.

Gadamer, Hans Georg. 1990 [1960]. *Wahrheit und Methode, Grundzüge einer philosophischen Hermeneutik, Band 1, Hermeneutik*. Tübingen: J. C. B. Mohr.

Gandhi, Jennifer, and Ellen Lust-Okar. 2009. 'Elections Under Authoritarianism.' *Annual Review of Political Science* 12 (1):403–422. https://doi.org/10.1146/annurev.polisci.11.060106.095434.

Garfinkel, Harold. 1967. *Studies in Ethnomethodology*. Englewood Cliffs, NJ: Prentice-Hall.

Garud, Raghu, Cynthia Hardy, and Steve Maguire. 2007. 'Institutional Entrepreneurship as Embedded Agency: An Introduction to the Special Issue.' *Organization Studies* 28:957–969.

Garud, Raghu, Sanjay Jain, and Arun Kumaraswamy. 2002. 'Institutional Entrepreneurship in the Sponsorship of Common Technological Standards: The Case of Sun Microsystems and Java.' *Academy of Management Journal* 45 (1):196–214.

Gaumnitz, E. W. 1933. 'An Indication of Seasonal Variation in Quality of Eggs on Terminal Markets.' *Journal of Farm Economics* 15 (3):573–574.

Geertz, Clifford. 1973. *The Interpretation of Cultures*. New York: Basic Books.

Geertz, Clifford. 1979. 'Suq: The Bazaar Economy in Sefrou.' In *Meaning and Order in Moroccan Society: Three Essays in Cultural Analysis*, edited by Clifford Geertz, Hildred Geertz, and Lawrence Rosen, 123–313. Cambridge: Cambridge University Press.

Gehlen, Arnold. 1986. *Moral and Hypermoral: Eine pluralistiche Ethik*. Wiesbaden: Aula-Verlag.

Giddens, Anthony. 1984. *The Constitution of Society, Outline of the Theory of Structuration*. Berkeley: University of California Press.

Godart, Frédéric C., and Ashley Mears. 2009. 'How Do Cultural Producers Make Creative Decisions? Lessons from the Catwalk.' *Social Forces* 88 (2):671–692.

Goffman, Erving. 1967. *Interaction Ritual: Essays on Face-to-Face Behavior*. New York: Pantheon.

Goffman, Erving. 1969. *Strategic Interaction*. Philadelphia: University of Pennsylvania.

Goffman, Erving. 1971 [1959]. *The Presentation of Self in Everyday Life*. London: Penguin Books.

Goffman, Erving. 1972. *Relations in Public*. New York: Harper & Row.

Goffman, Erving. 1974. *Frame Analysis, An Essay on the Organization of Experience*. Cambridge: Harvard University Press.

Goldberg, RoseLee. 2011 [1979]. *Performance Art: From Futurism to Present*. London: Thames & Hudson.

Gourevitch, Peter, David Lake, and Janice Stein. 2012. *The Credibility of Transnational NGOs*. Cambridge: Cambridge University Press.

Granovetter, Mark. 2017. *Society and Economy: Framework and Principles*. The Belknap Press of Harvard University Press: Harvard University Press.

Greenhut, M. L. C. 1975. 'A Theoretical Mapping from Perfect Competition to Imperfect Competition.' *Southern Economic Journal* 42 (2):177–192.

Greif, Avner. 2006. *Institutions and the Path to the Modern Economy: Lessons from Medieval Trade*. Cambridge: Cambridge University Press.

Greif, Avner. 2006. *Institutions and the Path to the Modern Economy: Lessons from Medieval Trade*. Cambridge: Cambridge University Press.

Greif, Avner. 2014. 'Do Institutions Evolve?' *Journal of Bioeconomics* 16 (1):53–60. https://doi.org/10.1007/s10818-013-9173-5.

Greif, Avner. 2015. 'How Did Markets Evolve?' In *Institutions, Innovation, and Industrialization: Essays in Economic History and Development*, edited by Avner Greif, Lynn Kiesling, and John Nye, 72–96. Princeton, NJ: Princeton University Press.

Grindley. 1995. *Standards Strategy and Policy: Cases and Stories*. Oxford: Oxford University Press.

Gronow, Antti. 2011. *From Habits to Social Structures: Pragmatism and Contemporary Social Theory*. Frankfurt am Main: Peter Lang.

Gudeman, Stephen. 2009. 'Necessity and Contingency.' In *Market and Society: The Great Transformation Today*, edited by Chris Hann and Keith Hart, 17–37. Cambridge: Cambridge University Press.

Guseva, Alya, and Akos Rona-Tas. 2001. 'Uncertainty, Risk and Trust: Russian and American Credit Card Markets Compared.' *American Sociological Review* 66 (5):623–646.

Habermas, Jürgen. 1962. *Strukturwandel der Öffentlichkeit: Untersuchungen zu einer Kategorie der bürgerlsichen Gesellschaft*. Darmstadt: Luchterhand.

Habermas, Jürgen. 1973 [1971]. *Theory and Practice*. Boston: Beacon Press.

Habermas, Jürgen. 1981. *Theorie des Kommunikatives Handelns: Band 2, Zur Kritik der funktionalistischen Vernuft*. Frankfurt: Suhrkamp.

Habermas, Jürgen. 1987. *Theory of Communicative Action, Volume Two, The Critique of Functionalist Reason*. Cambridge: Polity Press.

Habermas, Jürgen. 1998. *On the Pragmatics of Communication*. Cambridge, MA: MIT Press.

Hacking, Ian. 1990. *The Taming of Chance*. Cambridge: Cambridge University Press.

Hadziabdic, Sinisa, and Sebastian Kohl. 2022. 'Private Spanner in Public Works? The Corrosive Effects of Private Insurance on Public Life.' *British Journal of Sociology* 73 (4):799–821. https://doi.org/10.1111/1468-4446.12961.

Hall, Peter A., and Rosemary C. R. Taylor. 1996. 'Political Science and the Three New Institutionalisms.' MPIfG discussion paper., Köln.

Hamilton, Walton. 1932. Institution. In *Encyclopedia of the Social Sciences*, edited by Edwin Seligman and Alvin Johnson, 141–147. New York: MacMillan.

Hannan, Michael, Glenn Carroll, and Laszlo Polos. 2003. 'The Organizational Niche.' *Sociological Theory* 21 (4):309–340.

Hansen, Casper Worm. 2013. 'Economic Growth and Individualism: The Role of Informal Institutions.' *Economics Letters* 118 (2):378–380.

Hardin, Russell. 2009. *How Do You Know? The Economics of Ordinary Knowledge*. Princeton, NJ: Princeton University Press.

Harris, Joseph. 1932. Elections. In *Encyclopedia of the Social Sciences*, edited by E Seligman, 450–456. New York: MacMillan.

Hasse, Raimund, and Georg Krücken. 1999. *Neo-Instituationalismus*. Bielefeld: Transcript.

Hasselström, Anna. 2003. *On and Off the Trading Floor: An Inquiry into the Everyday Fashioning of Financial Market Knowledge*. Stockholm: Department of Social Anthropology, Stockholm University.

Hayek, Friedrich A. 1973. *Law, Legislation and Liberty. Volume I. Rules and Order*. Chicago, IL: University of Chicago Press.

Hayek, Friedrich von. 1945. 'The Use of Knowledge in Society.' *American Economic Review* 35 (4):519–530.

Hayek, Friedrich von. 1976. *Law, Legislation and Liberty, A New Statement of the Liberal Principles of Justice and Political Economy, Volume 2, The Mirage of Social Justice*. Chicago: University of Chicago Press.

Heidegger, Martin. 1977. *Phänomenologische Interpretation von Kants Kritik der Reinen Vernuft, Gesamtausgabe, II Abteilung: Vorlesungen 1923–1944, Wintersemester 1927/28, Gesamtausgabe Band 25* Frankfurt am Main: Vittorio Klostermann.

Heidegger, Martin. 1979. *Prolegomena zur Geschichte des Zeitbegriffs, Gesamtausgabe, Abteilung II, Vorlesungen 1923–1944, Band 20*. Frankfurt am Main: Vittorio Klostermann.

Heidegger, Martin. 1994. *Einführung in die phänomenologische Forschung, Gesamtausgabe, II. Abteilung: Vorlesungen 1919–1944, Band 17*. Frankfurt am Main: Vittorio Klostermann.

Heidegger, Martin. 1997 [1957]. *Der Satz vom Grund, Gesamtausgabe, I Abteilung: Veröffentliche Schriften 1910–1976, Band 10*. Frankfurt am Main: Vittorio Klostermann.

Heidegger, Martin. 2001 [1927]. *Sein und Zeit*. Tübingen: Max Niemeyer Verlag.

Helmke, Gretchen, and Steven Levitsky, eds. 2006. *Informal Institutions and Democracy: Lessons from Latin America*. Baltimore: Johns Hopkins University Press.

Herranen, Olli. 2020. *Social Institutions and the Problem of Order: A Relational Approach to Neo-Institutionalism through Social System theory, Social Constructivism, and Critical Ideology Theory*. Tampere: Tampere University Dissertations.

Hertwig, Ralph, Timothy J. Pleskac, and Thorsten Pachur. 2019. *Taming Uncertainty*: The MIT Press.

Hodgson, Geofrrey. 1988. *Economics and Institution: A Manifesto for a Modern Institutional Economics*. Cambridge: Polity Press.

Hodgson, Geofrrey. 1996. *Economics and Evolution: Bringing Life Back into Economics*. Ann Arbor: University of Michigan Press.

Hofstede, Geert. 1983. 'The Cultural Relativity of Organisational Practices and Theories.' *Journal of International Business Studies* 14:75–89.

House, Ernest. 1993. *Professional Evaluation: Social Impact and Political Consequences*. Newbury Park: Sage.

Howell, Anthony. 1999. *The Analysis of Performance Art: A Guide to Its Theory and Practice*. London: Routledge.

Hsu, Greta, Michael T. Hannan, and Özgecan Koçak. 2009. 'Multiple Category Memberships in Markets: An Integrative Theory and Two Empirical Tests.' *American Sociological Review* 74 (1):150–169.

Hume, David. 1826. *An Inquiry Concerning the Human Understanding*. Edinburgh: Black and Tait.

Humphreys, Ashlee, and Gregory S. Carpenter. 2018. 'Status Games: Market Driving through Social Influence in the U.S. Wine Industry.' *Journal of Marketing* 82 (5):141–159. https://doi.org/10.1509/jm.16.0179.

Husserl, Edmund. 1970. *The Crisis of European Sciences and Transcendental Phenomenology*. Evanston: Northwestern University Press.

Husserl, Edmund. 1989. *Ideas Pertaining to a Pure Phenomenology and to a Phenomenological Philosophy. Book II: Studies in the Phenomenology of Constitution*. Dordrecht: Kluwer.

Husserl, Edmund. 1992. *Die Krisis der europäischen Wissenschaften und die transzendentale Phänomenologie*. Hamburg: Felix Meiner Verlag.

Husserl, Edmund. 2008. *Die Lebenswelt. Auslegungen der vorgegebenen Welt und ihrer Konstitution. Texte aus dem Nachlass (1916–1937): Husserliana LXXXII*. Edited by Rochus Sowa. Dordrecht: Springer.

Hutter, Michael. 2011. 'Infitinite Surprises: On the Stabilization of Value in the Creative Industries.' In *The Worth of Goods: Valuation and Pricing in the Economy*, edited by Jens Beckert and Patrik Aspers, 201–222. Oxford: Oxford University Press.

Ibert, Oliver, Gregory Jackson, Tobias Theel, and Lukas Vogelgsang. 2021. 'Organizing Uncertainty as an Asset in Creative Collaboration: A Comparison of the Music and Pharmaceutical Industries.' In *Organizing Creativity in the Innovation Journey*, edited by Elke Schuessler, Patrick Cohendet and Silviya Svejenova, 115–136. Emerald Publishing.

Iversen, Clara, and Ann-Carita Evaldsson. 2020. 'Respecifying Uncertainty in Pupil Health Team Collaboration: The Morality of Interpreting Pupils' School Problems.' *Qualitative Research in Psychology* 17 (3):430–449. https://doi.org/10.1080/14780887.2020.1725948.

Jacob, Jaqueline, Richard Miles, and Ben Mather. 2002. *Egg Quality*. Florida: University of Florida.

James, William. 1955 [1907]. *Pragmatism. And Four Essays From 'The Meaning of Truth'*. New York: Meridian Books.

Janssen, Wilhelm, Joachim Krause, Otto Kimminich, and Ernst Nagel. 1987. Krieg. In *Staatslexikon: Recht, Wirtschaft, Gesellschaft*. Freiburg: Verlag Herder.

Jevons, Stanley. 1871. *The Theory of Political Economy*. New York: Kelley (reprint).

Joas, Hans, and Wolfgang Knöbel. 2004. *Sozialtheori: Zwanzig einführende Vorelesungen*. Frankfurt am Main: Suhrkamp.

Kahneman, Daniel, and Amos Tversky. 1979. 'Prospect Theory: An Analysis under Risk.' *Econometrica* 47 (2):263–291.

Kahneman, Daniel, and Amos Tversky. 1982. 'Variants of Uncertainty.' *Cognition* 11 (2):143–157. https://doi.org/10.1016/0010-0277(82)90023-3.

Kampourakis, Kostas, and Kevin McCain. 2020. *Uncertainty: How It Makes Science Advance*. Oxford: Oxford University Press.

Kant, Immanuel. 1964 [1783]. 'Beantwortung der Frage: Was ist Aufklärung?' In *Kant Werke*, 53–61. Darmstadt: Wischenschafliche Buchgesellschaft.

Kant, Immanuel. 1957. *Kritik der Urteilskraft und Schriften zur Naturphilospohie*. Wiesbaden: Insel Verlag.

Karpik, Lucien. 2010. *Valuing the Unique: The Economics of Singularities*. Princeton, NJ: Princeton University Press.

Kay, John, and Mervyn King. 2020. *Radical Uncertainty: Decision-Making Beyond the Numbers*. New York: W. W. Norton.

Kennedy, Mark. 2005. 'Behind the One-Way Mirror: Refraction in the Construction of Product Market Categories.' *Poetics* 33:201–226.

Keynes, John Maynard. 1973 [1936]. *The General Theory of Employment, Interest and Money*. London: Macmillan.

Kirzner, Israel. 1960. *The Economic Point of View*. Kansas City: William Volker Foundation.

Knight, Frank. 1921. *Risk, Uncertainty and Profit*. Boston: Houghton Mifflin Company

Kohl, Sebastian. 2017. *Homeownership, Renting and Society: Historical and Comparative Perspectives*. London: Routledge.

Komarova, Nataliya. 2017. 'Ups and Downs of Art Commerce: Narratives of "Crisis" in the Contemporary Art Markets of Russia and India." *Theory and Society* 46:319–352. https://doi.org/10.1007/s11186-017-9295-1.

Komporozos-Athanasiou, Aris. 2022. *Speculative Communities: Living with Uncertainty in a Financialized World*. Chicago: University of Chicago Press.

Krasniqi, Besnik, and Sameeksha Desai. 2016. 'Institutional Drivers of High-growth Firms: Country-level Evidence from 26 Transition Economies.' *Small Business Economics* 47 (4):1075–1094.

Kreiner, Kristian. 2020. 'Pick the Winner, So You Can Then Choose the Reasons.' In *The Performance Complex: Competition and Competitions in Social Life*, edited by David Stark, 31–54. Oxford: Oxford University Press.

Kuhn, Thomas. 1962. *The Structure of Scientific Revolutions*. Chicago: University of Chicago Press.

Lamont, Michele. 2009. *How Professors Think: Inside the Curious World of Academic Judgment*. Cambridge, MA: Harvard University Press.

Lamont, Michèle. 2012. 'Toward a Comparative Sociology of Valuation and Evaluation.' *Annual Review of Sociology* 38:201–221.

Latour, Bruno. 1999. *Pandora's Hope: Essays on the Reality of Science Studies*. Cambridge, MA: Harvard University Press.

Lauth, Hans-Joachim. 2000. 'Informal Institutions and Democracy.' *Democratization* 7 (4):21–50.

Lawrence, Thomas, Roy Suddaby, and Bernard Leca. 2011. 'Institutional Work: Refocusing Institutional Studies of Organization.' *Journal of Management Inquiry* 20 (1):52–58. https://doi.org/10.1177/1056492610387222.

Lee, Jooyoung. 2009. 'Battlin' on the Corner: Techniques for Sustaining Play.' *Social Problems* 56 (3):578–598.

Lehtonen, Turo-Kimmo, and Ine Van Hoyweghen. 2014. 'Editorial: Insurance and the Economization of Uncertainty.' *Journal of Cultural Economy* 7 (4):532–54. https://doi.org/10.1080/17530350.2013.875929.

Lehtonen, Turo-Kimmo. 2017. 'Objectifying Climate Change: Weather-Related Catastrophes as Risks and Opportunities for Reinsurance.' *Political Theory* 45 (1):32–51. https://doi.org/10.1177/0090591716680684.

Leung, Wanda, Bram Noble, Jill Gunn, and Jochen A. G. Jaeger. 2015. 'A Review of Uncertainty Research in Impact Assessment.' *Environmental Impact Assessment Review* 50:116–123. https://doi.org/10.1016/j.eiar.2014.09.005.

Levi Martin, John. 2009. *Social Structures*. Princeton, NJ: Princeton University Press.

Levi Martin, John. 2011. *The Explanation of Social Action*. Oxford: Oxford University Press.

Lewandowska, Kamila, and Zofia Smolarska. 2020. 'Artistic quality and consensus decision-making: On reviewing panels in the performing arts.' *International Journal of Media & Cultural Politics* 16:159–174. https://doi.org/10.1386/macp_00022_1.

Lindblom, Charles. 2001. *The Market System: What It Is, How It Works, and What to Make of It*. New Haven: Yale University Press.

Lipshitz, Raanan, and Orna Strauss. 1997. 'Coping with Uncertainty: A Naturalistic Decision-Making Analysis.' *Organizational Behavior and Human Decision Processes* 69 (2):149–163. https://doi.org/10.1006/obhd.1997.2679.

Luce, Duncan, and Howard Raiffa. 1957. *Games and Decisions: Introduction and Critical Analysis*. New York: John Wiley and Sons.

Luhmann, Niklas. 1987. *Soziale Systeme: Grundriss einer allgemeinen Theori*. Frankfurt am Main: Suhrkamp.

Luhmann, Niklas. 1988. *Die Wirtschaft der Gesellschaft*. Frankfurt am Main: Suhrkamp.

Luhmann, Niklas. 1991. *Soziologische Aufklärung 1: Aufsätze zur Theorie sozialer Systeme*. Opladen: Westdeutscher Verlag.

Luhmann, Niklas. 1995 [1984]. *Social Systems*. Stanford: Stanford University Press.

Luhmann, Niklas. 1997. *Die Gesellschaft der Gesellschaft*. Frankfurt: Surhkamp.

Luhmann, Niklas. 2000. *Organisation und Entscheidung*. Opladen: Westdeutscher Verlag.

Luhmann, Niklas. 2001. *Legitimation durch Verfahren*. Frankfurt am Main: Suhrkamp.

MacGormick, Lisa. 2020. 'Classic Music competitions as Complex Performances.' In *The Performance Complex: Competition and Competitions in Social Life*, edited by David Stark, 78–95. Oxford: Oxford University Press.

MacKenzie, Donald. 2009. *Material Market: How Economic Agents are Constructed*. Oxford: Oxford University Press.

Maguire, Steve, Cynthia Hardy, and Lawrence. Thomas. 2004. 'Institutional Entrepreneurship in Emerging Fields: HIV/AIDS Treatment Advocacy in Canada.' *Academy of Management Journal* 47 (5):657–679.

Mäki, Uskali. 2013. 'Performativity: Saving Austin from MacKenzie.' In *Recent Progress in Philosophy of Science: Perspectives and Foundational Problems*, edited by Vassilios Karakostas and Dennis Dieks, 443–453. Dordrecht: Springer.

Malinowski, Bronislaw. 1922. *Argonauts of the Western Pacific: An Account of Native Enterprise and Adventure in the Archipelagos of Melanesian New Guinea*. London: Routledge.

Mandeville, Bernard. 1924 [1732]. *The Fable of the Bees, or Private Vices, Publick Benefits*. Reprint, T. F. B. Kaye (ed.). Oxford: Oxford University Press.

Mann, Michael. 2018. 'Have Wars and Violence Declined?' *Theory and Society* 47 (1):37–60. https://doi.org/10.1007/s11186-018-9305-y.

Mantzavinos, C. 2016. *Explanatory Pluralism*. Cambridge: Cambridge University Press.

Mantzavinos, Chrysostomos. 2001. *Individuals, Institutions and Markets*. Cambridge: Cambridge University Press.

March, James, and Herbert Simon. 1958. *Organizations*. Cambridge, MA: Blackwell.

March, James. 1994. *A Primer on Decision Making: How Decisions Happen*. New York: Free Press.

Marres, Noortje, and David Stark. 2020a. 'Preface to a Special Issue on the Sociology of Testing.' *British Journal of Sociology* 71 (3):420–422. https://doi.org/10.1111/1468-4446.12757.

Marres, Noortje, and David Stark. 2020b. 'Put to the Test: For a New Sociology of Testing.' *The British Journal of Sociology* 71 (3):423–443. https://doi.org/10.1111/1468-4446.12746.

Marris, Peter. 1996. *The Politics of Uncertainty: Attachment in Private and Public Life*. London: Routledge.

Marshall, Alfred. 1920. *Industry and Trade: A Study of Industrial Technique and Business Organization; of Their Influences on the Conditions of Various Classes and Nations*. London: Macmillan.

Mauss, Marcel. 2002 [1950]. *The Gift: The Form and Reason for Exchange in Archaic Societies*. London: Routledge.

Mead, Margaret. 1937. 'The Manus of the Admiralty Islands.' In *Cooperation and Competition among Primitive People*, edited by Margaret Mead, 210–239. Boston: Beacon Press.

Mears, Ashley, and William Finlay. 2005. 'Not Just a Paper Doll: How Models Manage Bodily Capital and Why They Perform Emotional Labor.' *Journal of Contemporary Ethnography* 34 (3):317–343.

Mears, Ashley. 2011. 'Pricing Looks: Circuits of Value in Fashion Modeling Markets.' In *The Worth of Goods: Valuation and Pricing in the Economy*, edited by Jens Beckert and Patrik Aspers, 155–177. Oxford: Oxford University Press.

Menger, Pierre-Michel. 1999. 'Artistic Labor Markets and Careers.' *Annual Review of Sociology* 25:541–574.

Menger, Pierre-Michel. 2014 [2009]. *The Economics of Creativity: Art and Achievement und Uncertainty*. Cambridge, MA: Harvard University Press.

Mennicken, Andrea, and Wendy Nelson Espeland. 2019. 'What's New with Numbers? Sociological Approaches to the Study of Quantification.' *Annual Review of Sociology* 45 (1):223–245. https://doi.org/10.1146/annurev-soc-073117-041343.

Merton, Robert. 1957. *Social Theory and Social Structure*. Glencoe: The Free Press.

Merton, Robert, and Harriet Zuckermann. 1971. 'Institutionalized Patterns of Evaluation in Science.' In *Robert K. Merton: The Sociology of Science, Theoretical and Empirical Investigations*, edited by Norman Storer, 460–496. Chicago: University of Chicago Press.

Meyer, J. W., and B. Rowan. 1977. 'Institutionalized Organizations—Formal Structure as Myth and Ceremony.' *American Journal of Sociology* 83 (2):340–363.

Milliken, Frances J. 1987. 'Three Types of Perceived Uncertainty about the Environment: State, Effect, and Response Uncertainty.' *Academy of Management Review* 12 (1):133–143. https://doi.org/10.2307/257999.

Mirsky, Jeanette. 1937. 'The Eskimo of Greenland.' In *Cooperation and Competition among Primitive People*, edited by Margeret Mead, 51–86. Boston: Beacon Press.

Mische, Ann, and Harrison White. 1998. 'Between Conversation and Situation: Public Switching Dynamics across Network Domains.' *Social Research* 65 (3):695–724.

Miyazaki, Hirokazu, and Richard Swedberg, eds. 2017. *The Economy of Hope.* Philadelphia: University of Pennsylvania Press.

Möllering, Guido, and Gordon Müller-Seitz. 2018. 'Direction, not Destination: Institutional Work Practices in the Face of Field-level Uncertainty.' *European Management Journal* 36 (1):28–37. https://doi.org/10.1016/j.emj.2017.10.004.

Möllering, Guido. 2006. *Trust: Reason, Routine, Reflexivity.* Oxford: Elsevier.

Montesquieu, Charles de Secondat. 2001 [1748]. *The Spirit of Laws.* Kitchener: Batoche Books.

Müller, Walter. 2015. 'Von der angewandten Sozialforschung zur Sozialforschung der Verwendung.' In *Nachhaltige Evaluation? Auftragsforschung zwischen Praxis und Wissenschaft*, edited by Vera Hennefeld, Wolfgang Meyer and Stefan Silvestrini, 15–40. Münster: Waxmann.

Münch, Richard. 1982. *Theories des Handelns: Zur Rekonstruktion der Beiträge von Talcott Parsons, Emile Durkheim und Max Weber.* Frankfurt am Main: Suhrkamp.

Murmann, Johan Peter. 2003. *Knowledge and Competitive Advantage: The Coevolution of Firms, Technology and National Institutions.* Cambridge: Cambridge University Press.

Nästesjö, Jonatan. 2020. 'Navigating Uncertainty: Early Career Academics and Practices of Appraisal Devices.' *Minerva* (Online publication).

Nee, Victor. 1998. 'Sources of New Institutionalism.' In *The New Institutionalism in Sociology*, edited by Mary Brinton and Victor Nee, 1–16. New York: Russel Sage Foundation.

Nelson, Randy, Michael Donihue, D. M. Waldman, and C. Wheaton. 2001. 'What's an Oscar Worth.' *Economic Inquiry* 39:1–6. https://doi.org/10.1111/j.1465-7295.2001.tb00046.x.

Nelson, Richard R., and Sidney G. Winter. 1982. *An Evolutionary Theory of Economic Change.* London: The Belknap Press of Harvard University Press.

Nietzsche, Friedrich. 1911. *Der Wille zur Macht. Band XV-XVI in Nachgelassene Werke.* Leipzig: Alfred Kröner Verlag.

Nietzsche, Friedrich. 1994 [1887]. *On the Genealogy of Morals.* Translated by Carol Diethe. Cambridge: Cambridge University Press.

Noles, R. K., and J. R. Roush. 1962. 'Consumers' Egg Preferences and Their Relationship to United States Quality Standards.' *Illinois Agricultural Economics* 2 (1):21–26.

North, Douglass C. 1984. 'Transaction Costs, Institutions, and Economic History.' *Zeitschrift für die gesamte Staatswissenschaft / Journal of Institutional and Theoretical Economics* 140 (1):7–17.

North, Douglass. 1990. *Institutions, Institutional Change and Economic Performance.* Cambridge: Cambridge University Press.

North, Douglass. 1991. 'Institutions.' *Journal of Economic Perspectives* 5 (1):97–112.
Nowotny, Helga. 2016. *The Cunning of Uncertainty*. Hoboken, NJ: Wiley and Son.
Nozick, Robert. 1974. *Anarchy, State, and Utopia*. New York: Basic Books.
O'Malley, Pat. 2004. *Risk, Uncertainty and Government*. London: Routledge.
O'Malley, Pat. 2008. 'Governmentality and Risk.' In *Social Theories of Risk and Uncertainty: An Introduction*, edited by Jens Zinn, 52–75. Oxford: Blackwell.
Olofsson, Tobias. 2020. *Mining Futures, Predictions and Uncertainty in Swedish Mineral Explorations*. Uppsala: Uppsala University.
Olson, Mancur. 1971 [1965]. *The Logic of Collective Action, Public Goods and the Theory of Groups*. Cambridge: Harvard University Press.
Oosten, Jarich and Frédéric Laugrand. 2002. 'Qaujimajatuqangit and Social Problems in Modern Inuit Society. An Elders Workshop on Angakkuuniq.' *Études/Inuit/Studies* 26 (1):17–44.
Øygarden, Geir Angell. 2000. *Den brukne neses estetikk. En bok om boksning*. Uppsala: Uppsala University.
Padgett, John F., and Walter W. Powell. 2012. *The Emergence of Organization and Markets*. Princeton, NJ: Princeton University Press.
Padgett, John, and Christopher Ansell. 1993. 'Robust Action and the Rise of the Medici, 1400–1434.' *American Journal of Sociology* 98 (6):1259–1319.
Pareto, Vilfredo. 1935 [1915–1916]. *Mind and Society, A Treatise on General Sociology*. New York: Dover Publications.
Parson, Talcott, and Edward Shils. 1951. *Toward a General Theory of Action*. Cambridge, MA: Harvard University Press.
Parson, Talcott. 1980. 'Health, Uncertainty, and the Actio Situation.' In *Uncertainty: Behavioral and Social Dimensions*, edited by Seymour Fiddle, 145–162. New York: Praeger.
Parsons, Talcott, and Neil Smelser. 1956. *Economy and Society*. Glencoe, IL: Free Press.
Parsons, Talcott. 1977. *Social Systems and the Evolution of Action Theory*. New York: Free Press.
Pentzlin, Kurt. 1959. 'Standardisierung.' In *Handwörterbuch der Sozialwissenschaften*, edited by E et.al. Beckerath, 16–21. Stuttgart: Gustav Fischer.
Perrow, Charles. 2005. *Organizing America. Wealth, Power, and the Origins of Corporate Capitalism*. Princeton, NJ: Princeton University Press.
Phelan, Peggy. 1993. *Unmarked: The Politics of Performance*. New York: Routledge.
Plattner, Stuart. 1996. *High Art Down Home. An Economic Ethnography of a Local Art Market*. Chicago: University of Chicago Press.
Podolny, Joel, and Greta Hsu. 2003. 'Quality, Exchange, and Knightian Uncertainty.' *Research in Sociology of Organizations* 20:77–103.
Podolny, Joel. 1993. 'A Status-based Model of Market Competition.' *American Journal of Sociology* 98 (4):829–872.
Podolny, Joel. 2005. *Status Signals: A Sociological Study of Market Competition*. Princeton, NJ: Princeton University Press.
Polanyi, Karl. 2001 [1944]. *The Great Transformation. The Political and Economic Origins of Our Time*. Boston: Beacon.
Popper, Karl. 1963. *Conjectures and Refutations: The Growth of Scientific Knowledge*. London: Routledge and Kegan Paul.
Popper, Karl. 1966. *The Open Society and its Enemies. Volume II, The High Tide of Prophecy: Hegel, Marx and the Aftermath*. London: Routledge and Kegan Paul.
Popper, Karl. 1972. *Objective Knowledge*. Oxford: Oxford University Press.

Powell, Walter and Rerup, Claus. 2017. 'Opening the Black Box: The Microfoundations of Institutions.' In *The Sage Handbook of Organizational Institutionalism 2nd. ed.*, edited by et al. Royston Greenwood, 311–337. London: Sage.

Power, Michael. 1997. *The Audit Society, Rituals of Verification.* Oxford: Oxford University Press.

Power, Michael. 2007. *Organized Uncertainty: Designing a World of Risk Management.* Oxford: Oxford University Press.

Priddat, Birger. 1996. 'Risiko, Ungewissheit und Neues: Epistemologische Probleme ökonomischer Entscheidungsbildung.' In *Risikoforschung zwischen Disziplinarität und Interdisziplinarität: von der Illusion der Sicherheit zum Umgang mit Unsicherheit*, edited by Gerhard Banse, 105–124. Berlin: Sigma.

Putnam, Robert. 1993. *Making Democracy Work: Civic Traditions in Modern Italy.* Princeton, NJ: Princeton University Press.

Quack, Sigrid, and Marie-Laure Djelic. 2005. 'Adaption, Recombination, and Reinforcement. The Story of Antitrust and Competition Law in Germany and Europe.' In *Beyond Continuity. Institutional Change in Advanced Political Economies*, edited by Wolfgang Streeck, 255–281. Oxford: Oxford University Press.

Quine, Willard, and J. S. Ullian. 1970. *The Web of Belief.* New York: Random House.

Ramsay, Kristopher W. 2017. 'Information, Uncertainty, and War.' *Annual Review of Political Science* 20 (1):505–527. https://doi.org/10.1146/annurev-polisci-051 215-022729.

Rapp, Jenny K., Richard A. Bernardi, and Susan M. Bosco. 2010. 'Examining the Use of Hofstede's Uncertainty Avoidance Construct in International Research: A 25-year Review.' *International Business Research* 4 (1):3–15.

Rawls, John. 1971. *A Theory of Justice.* Oxford: Oxford University Press.

Reckwitz, Andreas. 2017. *Die Gesellschaft der Singularitäten: Zum Strukturwandel der Moderne.* Frankfurt: Suhrkamp.

Reddy, Sanjay G. 1996. 'Claims to Expert Knowledge and the Subversion of Democracy: The Triumph of Risk over Uncertainty.' *Economy and Society* 25 (2):222–254. https://doi.org/10.1080/03085149600000011.

Reinstein, David A., and Christopher M. Snyder. 2005. 'The Influence of Expert Reviews on Consumer Demand for Experience Goods: A Case Study of Movie Critics.' *Journal of Industrial Economics* 53 (1):27–51. https://doi.org/10.1111/ j.0022-1821.2005.00244.x.

Reiter, Herwig. 2010. 'Context, Experience, Expectation, and Action—Towards an Empirically Grounded, General Model for Analyzing Biographical Uncertainty.' *Forum: Qualitative Social Research Sozialforschung* 11 (1 (2)):1–20.

Rilinger, Georg. 2022. 'Conceptual Limits of Performativity: Assessing the Feasibility of Market Design Blueprints.' *Socio-Economic Review* 21 (2):885–908. https:// doi.org/10.1093/ser/mwac017.

Ringel, Leopold, and Tobias Werron. 2020. 'Where Do Rankings Come From? A Historical-Sociological Perspective on the History of Modern Rankings.' In *Practices of Comparing. Towards a New Understanding of a Fundamental Human Practice*, edited by Epple A and Grave J Erhart W, 37–170. Bielefeld: Bielefeld University Press.

Ringel, Leopold, Wendy Espeland, Michael Sauder, and Thomas Werron, eds. 2021. *Worlds of Rankings (Research in the Sociology of Organizations).* Bingley: Emerald.

Robinson, Joan. 1933. *The Economics of Imperfect Competition.* London: Macmillan and Co., Limited.

Rorty, Richard. 2009. *Philosophy and the Mirror of Nature*. Princeton, NJ: Princeton University Press.

Rosen, Sherwin. 1981. 'The Economics of Superstars.' *The American Economic Review* 71 (5):845–858.

Rosenström, Martin. 2014. *Att skapa en marknad: marknad och politisk styrning i symbios?* Doctoral dissertation; Stockholm: Stockholm School of Economics.

Roumbanis, Lambros. 2017. 'Academic Judgments under Uncertainty: A Study of Collective Anchoring Effects in Swedish Research Council Panel Groups.' *Social Studies of Science* 47 (1):95–116.

Rouse, Joseph. 2003. 'Power/Knowledge.' In *The Cambridge Companion to Foucault*, edited by Gary Gutting, 95–122. Cambridge: Cambridge University Press.

Sandström, Edvin. 2018. *The Convaluation of Performance Art: A Study of Peer Recognition Among Performance Artists*. Uppsala: Uppsala University Department of Sociology.

Scalia, Antonin C. 1989. 'The Rule of Law as a Law of Rules.' *University of Chicago Law Review* 56 (4):1175–1188.

Schelsky, Helmut. 1980. *Die Soziologen und das Recht: Abhandlungen und Vorträge zur Soziologie von Recht Institution und Planung*. Opladen: Westdeutscher Verlag.

Schmidt, Susanne, and Raymund Werle. 1998. *Coordinating Technology: Studies in the International Standardization of Telecommunications*. Cambridge, MA: MIT Press.

Schülein, Johann. 1987. *Theorie der Institution: Eine dogmengeschichtliche und konzeptionelle Analyse*. Opladen: Westdeutscher Verlag.

Schumpeter, Joseph. 2000 [1911]. 'Entrepreneurship as Innovation.' In *Entrepreneurship, The Social Science View*, edited by Richard Swedberg, 51–75. Oxford: Oxford University Press.

Schütz, Alfred. 1964. *Collected Papers II, Studies in Social Theory*. The Hague: Nijhoff.

Schütz, Alfred. 1971. *Das Problem der Relevanz*. Frankfurt am Main: Suhrkamp.

Schütz, Alfred. 1975 [1966]. *Collected Papers III: Studies in Phenomenological Philosophy*. The Hague: Nijhoff.

Schutz, Alfred. 1976 [1932]. *The Phenomenology of the Social World*. London: Heineman Educational Books.

Schütz, Alfred. 1982. *Life Forms and Meaning Structure* London: Routledge and Kegan Paul.

Schütz, Alfred. 2003. *Theorie der Lebenswelt 1: Die Pragmatische Schichtung*. Konstanz: UVK Verlagsgesellschaft mbH.

Schütz, Alfred. 1962. *Collected Papers I, the Problem of Social Reality*. The Hague: Nijhoff.

Schütz, Alfred, and Thomas Luckmann. 1989 [1983]. *The Structures of the Life-world, Volume II*. Evanston: Northwestern University Press.

Scott, W.R. 1995. *Institutions and Organizations*. London: Sage.

Searle, John 2005. 'What Is an Institution?' *Journal of Institutional Economics* 1 (1):1–22.

Searle, John. 1995. *The Construction of Social Reality*. New York: Free Press.

Searle, John. 2008a. 'Language and Social Ontology.' *Theory and Society* 37 (5):443–459.

Searle, John. 2008b. *Philosophy in a New Century: Selected Essays*. Cambridge: Cambridge University Press.

See, Herni. 1968 [1928]. *Modern Capitalism: Its Origin and Evolution*. New York: Augustus M. Kelley.

Sennet, Richard. 1977. *The Fall of Public Man*. New York: Vintage Books.

Simmel, Georg. 1923. *Soziologie, Untersuchungen über die Formen der Vergesellschaftung*. München und Leipzig: Duncker und Humblot.

Simmel, Georg. 1955. *Conflict & The Web of Group-Affiliations*. New York: Free Press. Original edition, 1922.

Simon, Grand. 2016. *Routines, Strategies, and Management: Engaging for the Recurrent Creation 'At the Edge'*. Cheltenham: Edward Elgar.

Smith Spence, Thomas. 1974. 'Aestheticism and Social Structure: Style and Social Network in the Dandy Life.' *American Sociological Review* 39:725–743.

Smith, Charles. 1989. *Auctions, the Social Construction of Value*. Berkeley: University of California.

Smith, Charles. 2011. 'Coping with Contingencies in Equity Optio Markets: The "Rationality" of Pricing.' In *The Worth of Goods: Valuation and Pricing in the Economy*, edited by Jens Beckert and Patrik Aspers, 272–296. Oxford: Oxford University Press.

Smith-Birket, Kaj. 1948 [1927]. *Die Eskimos*. Translated by Hans-Georg Bandi. Zurich: Orell Fussli Verlag.

Sniazhko, Sniazhana. 2019. 'Uncertainty in decision-making: A review of the international business literature.' *Cogent Business & Management* 6 (1):1650692. https://doi.org/10.1080/23311975.2019.1650692.

Sombart, Werner. 1927. *Das Wirtschaftsleben im Zeitalter des Hochkapitalismus*, 2 Volumes. München and Leipzig: Verlag von Duncker und Humblot.

Spence, Michael. 2002. 'Signaling in Retrospect and the Informational Structure of Markets.' *The American Economic Review* 92 (3):434–459.

Stark, David. 2009. *The Sense of Dissonance: Accounts of Worth in Economic Life*. Princeton, NJ: Princeton University Press.

Stark, David. 2020. *The Performance Complex: Competition and Competitions in Social Life*. Oxford: Oxford University Press.

Stiles, Kristine. 1996. *Theories and Documents of Contemporary Art. A Sourcebook of Artists' Writings*. Berkeley and Los Angeles: University of California Press.

Stiles, Kristine. 1998. 'Uncorrupted Joy: International Art Actions.' In *Out of Actions: Between Performance and the Object, 1949–1979*, edited by R. Ferguson. New York: Thames and Hudson, Inc.

Streeck, Wolfgang, and Katherine Thelen, eds. 2005. *Beyond Continuity: Institutional Change in Advanced Political Economies*. Oxford: Oxford University Press.

Streeck, Wolfgang. 2005. 'The Sociology of Labor Markets and Trade Unions.' In *The Handbook of Economic Sociology. Second Edition*, edited by Neil Smelser and Richard Swedberg, 254–283. Princeton, NJ: Princeton University Press.

Swedberg, Richard. 2003. 'The Case for an Economic Sociology of Law.' *Theory and Society* 32 (1):1–37.

Thévenot, Laurent. 2015. 'Certifying the World.' In *Re-Imagining Economic Sociology*, edited by Patrik Aspers and Nigel Dodd, 195–223. Oxford: Oxford University Press.

Thévenot, Laurent. 2016. 'From Social Coding to Economics of Convention: A Thirty-Year Perspective on the Analysis of Qualification and Quantification Investments.' *Historical Social Research / Historische Sozialforschung* 41 (2):96–117.

Thornton, Patricia H. and Ocasio, William. 1999. 'Institutional Logics and the Historical Contingency of Power in Organizations: Executive Succession in the Higher Education Publishing Industry, 1958–1990.' *The American Journal of Sociology* 105 (3):801–843.

Thornton, Patricia, and William Ocasio. 2008. 'Institutional Logics.' In *Handbook of Organizational Institutionalism*, edited by Royston Greenwood, Christine Oliver, Roy Suddaby, and Kerstin Sahlin-Andersson, 99–129. Thousand Oaks: Sage.

Tocqueville, Alexis de. 1969 [1835]. *Democracy in America*. New York: Harper and Row.

Tosi, Henry, Ramon Aldag, and Ronald Storey. 1973. 'On the Measurement of the Environment: An Assessment of the Lawrence and Lorsch Environmental Uncertainty Subscale.' *Administrative Science Quarterly* 18 (1):27–36. https://doi.org/10.2307/2391925.

Tversky, Amos, and Daniel Kahneman. 1974. 'Judgement and Uncertainty: Heuristics and Biases.' *Science* 185 (4157):1124–1131.

Uzzi, Brian. 1997. 'Social Structure in Interfirm Networks: The Paradox of Embeddedness.' *Administrative Science Quarterly* 42:35–67.

Van Creveld, Martin. 2013. *Wargames: From Gladiators to Gigabytes*. Cambridge: Cambridge University Press.

Vatin, François. 2013. 'Valuation as Evaluating and Valorizing.' *Valuation Studies* 1 (1):31–50.

Vedung, Evert. 2010. 'Four Waves of Evaluation.' *Evaluation* 16 (3):263–277.

Vedung, Evert. 2015. 'Six Uses of Evaluation.' In *Nachhaltige Evaluation? Auftragsforschung zwischen Praxis und Wissenschaft*, edited by Vera Hennefeld, Wolfgang Meyer, and Stefan Silvestrini, 187–210. Münster: Waxman.

Velthuis, Olav, and Niels Van Doorn. 2020. 'Weathering Winner-Take-All: How Rankings Constitute Competition on Webcam Sex Platforms, and What Performers Can Do About it.' In *The Performance Complexity: Competition and Competitions in Social Life*, edited by David Stark, 163–183. Oxford: Oxford University Press.

Velthuis, Olav. 2005. *Talking Prices: Symbolic Meanings of Prices on the Market for Contemporary Art*. Princeton, NJ: Princeton University Press.

Wakker, Peter. 2010. *Prospect Theory: For Risk and Ambiguity*. Cambridge: Cambridge University Press.

Warde, Alan. 1994. 'Consumption, Identity formation and Uncertainty.' *Sociology* 25 (4):878–898.

Warde, Alan. 2002. 'Production, Consumption and 'Cultural Economy'.' In *Cultural Economy, Cultural Analysis and Commercial Life*, edited by Paul Du Gay and Michael Pryke, 185–200. London: Sage.

Weber, Max. 1968 [1904–1905]. *The Protestant Ethic and the Spirit of Capitalism*. London: Unwin University Books.

Weber, Max. 1922. 'Wirtschaft und Gesellschaft.' In *Grundriss der Sozialökonomik*, edited by M. Weber *III Abteilung*. Tübingen: Verlag von J. C. B. Mohr.

Weber, Max. 1946. *From Max Weber: Essays in Sociology*, edited by H. Gerth and C. Wright Mills. London: Routledge.

Weber, Max. 1978 [1921–1922]. *Economy and Society: An Outline of Interpretive Sociology*. Translated by Guenther Roth and Claus Wittich (ed.), 2 volumes. Berkeley: University of California Press.

Weber, Max. 1985 [1922]. *Gesammelte Aufsätze zur Wissenschaftslehre*. Edited by Johannes Winckelmann. Tübingen: J. C. B. Mohr.

White, Harrison, Frédéric Godart, and Victro Corona. 2007. 'Mobilizing Identities: Uncertainty and Control in Strategy.' *Theory, Culture and Society* 25 (7–8):181–202.

White, Harrison. 1970. *Chains of Opportunity, System Models of Mobility in Organizations*. Cambridge, MA: Harvard University Press.

White, Harrison. 1981. 'Where Do Markets Co.me From?' *American Journal of Sociology* 87 (3):517–547.

White, Harrison. 1992. *Identity and Control: A Structural Theory of Social Action*. Princeton, NJ: Princeton University Press.

White, Harrison. 2002. *Markets from Networks, Socioeconomic Models of Production*. Princeton, NJ: Princeton University Press.

White, Harrison. 2008. *Identity and Control: How Social Formations Emerge*. Princeton, NJ: Princeton University Press.

Williamson, Oliver. 1975. *Markets and Hierarchies: Analysis and Antitrust Implication*. New York: Free Press.

Williamson, Oliver. 1981. 'The Economics of Organization: The Transaction Cost Approach.' *American Journal of Sociology* 87 (3):548–577.

Williamson, Oliver. 1985. *The Economic Institutions of Capitalism: Firms, Market, Relational Contracting*. New York: Free Press.

Williamson, Oliver. 2000. 'The New Institutional Economics: Taking Stock, Looking Ahead.' *Journal of Economic Literature* 38:595–613.

Wittgenstein, Ludwig. 2009. *Philosophical Investigations*. Oxford: Blackwell.

Wohlmb-Sahr, Monika. 1993. *Biographische Unsicherheit. Formen weiblicher Identität in der,, reflexiven Moderne': das Beispiel der Zeitarbeiterinnen*. Opladen: Leske and Budrich.

Wood, J. G. 1871. *The Uncivilized Races of Men in All Countries of the World*. 2 Vols. Hartford: J. B. Burrr.

Wood, J. G. 1980 [1870]. *Customs and Manners of the Uncivilized Races of Men*. London: Routledge.

Zeckhauser, Richard. 2014. 'New Frontiers Beyond Risk and Uncertainty: Ignorance, Group Decision, and Unanticipated Themes.' In *Handbook of the Economics of Risk and Uncertainty*, edited by Mark Machina and W. Kip Viscusi, xvii–xxix. Amsterdam: Elsevier.

Zellweger, Dr. Thomas Markus, and Professor Todd R. Zenger. 2023. 'Entrepreneurs as Scientists: A Pragmatist Approach to Producing Value out of Uncertainty.' *Academy of Management Review* 48 (3):379–408.

Zerbib, Oliver. 2022. 'Place Your Bets, All Bets Are Off! Film Festivals as Devices for the Construction and Management of Uncertainty for Distributors and Arthouse Cinemas.' In *Trade Shows in the 21st Century: The Role of Events in Structuring Careers and Professions*, edited by Anne-Sophie Béliard and Sidonie Naulin, 122–138. Cheltenham: Edward Elgar.

Zinn, Jens, ed. 2008. *Social Theories of Risk and Uncertainty: An Introduction*. Oxford: Blackwell.

Zuckerman, Ezra W. 1999. 'The Categorical Imperative: Securities Analysts and the Illegitimacy Discount.' *The American Journal of Sociology* 104 (5):1398–1438.

Zuckerman, Ezra W. 2012. 'Construction, Concentration, and (Dis)Continuities in Social Valuations.' *Annual Review of Sociology* 38:223–245.

Zuckerman, Ezra W., Tai-Young Kim, Kalinda Ukanwa, and James von Rittmann. 2003. 'Robust Identities or Nonentities? Typecasting in the Feature-Film Labor Market.' *American Journal of Sociology* 108 (5):1018–1074.

INDEX

For the benefit of digital users, indexed terms that span two pages (e.g., 52–53) may, on occasion, appear on only one of those pages.

'Tables, figures, and boxes are indicated by an italic *t*, *f*, and *b* following the para ID.'

Bolded entries are definitions of key terms.

acclamation, 84
Ahrne, Göran, 1, 17–18, 30, 48, 49, 61, 62, 106
algorithm, 11, 17–18, 76–77, 110
ambiguity, 6, 90–91, 94, 106, 152
Arendt, Hannah, 3–4, 14, 21, 41, 162
Arrow, Kenneth, 5–6, 7, 18, 112
audience, 81–82, 84, 88, 94, 103–4, 110–12, 114, 115–16, 118, 128, 132, 136–37, 153–54
award. *See* prize

Beck, Ulrich, 3–4, 5, 10–11
Becker, Howard, 93, 94, 97, 112, 118
Beckert, Jens, 14–15, 17, 19–20, 21–22, 51–52, 90–91, 129, 130–31
being. *See* human being
Berger, Peter, 36, 37–38, 41, 43, 91–92
betting, 7–8, 136–37, 141–42, 157, 189n.13
body, 33, 97–98, 145–46
Boltanski, Luc, 40, 50–51, 78, 115–16
Bonss, Wolfgang, 1–2, 6, 9–10, 38
Braudel, Fernand, 28, 59–60
Brunsson, Nils, Ahrne, Göran, 17–18, 30, 48, 49, 58–60, 61, 62, 73, 106

calculation, 7–8, 17–18, 37, 44–45, 51–52, 57, 59–60, 61, 77, 78, 169n.12

Callon, Michel, 5, 73–74, 130
certainty, vii, 3, 8, 9, 10–14, 15, 21–22, 27, 39–43, 46–47, 49, 60, 75, 87, 105, 121, 129, 131, 138–39, 151–52, 158. *See also* uncertainty reduction
change, 30, 37
    formal institutions, 48
    informal institutions, 39–40, 48
Coase, Ronald, 20, 29–30
commensuration, 7, 58–59, 78, 80, 119–20, 124, 152
competition, 53–55, 75, 95, 100, 104–5, 111–12, 115–16, 117, 124–27, 128, 132, 135, 141–44, 156
    direct, 136
    imperfect, 100–1
    indirect, 125
    for women, 31–32, 33
complexity, 2, 11, 12–13, 17, 42–43, 48–49, 123, 129–30, 152, 154, 161–62
contingency, 14–15
    double, contingency, 14–15, 45
consensus, 21, 106, 111–12
contest, 97, 135–36, 141–46
convaluation, 88
coping. *See* uncertainty reduction
creativity, 4, 7, 15, 119–20, 155–56
culture, 48, 50–51, 88–89, 97, 104–5, 106–7, 113–14, 135–36, 144–46

danger, 1–2, 161–62
decision, decision for others. *See* decision
    making; organization
decision making, 2, 4–8, 17, 18–19, 21,
    40, 48, 49, 50, 52, 54–55, 58–60,
    70, 129, 154, 157–58
Dewey, John, 8, 9–10, 159
Djelic, Marie-Laure, 34–35, 54–55
Douglas, Mary, 4–5, 9, 12, 16, 30, 31, 43
duel, 139–41
Durkheim, Emile, 52, 65–66

election, 109*t*
Elias, Norbert, 31, 34–35, 138, 149
emotion, 1, 4, 16, 84, 136–37, 156
Espeland, Wendy, 7–8, 58–59, 73, 78–
    69, 123, 126–27, 128
Esposito, Elena, 15
ethics. *See* moral
evaluation, 73
existential, 1–2, 4–5, 50–51, 120–21, 122,
    135, 141–42, 146, 151, 152, 156,
    158–59, 160–61

fact, 3, 11, 13–14, 35, 50–51, 58–59,
    81, 82–83, 115, 126, 152, 153–
    54, 161–62
fear, 4–5, 9–10, 37
Fligstein, Neil, 53–54, 56–57, 58–
    59, 88–89
forecasting, 19–20
forgiving, 162
form, 83
forms of decisions for others, 113
Furst, Henrik, 17, 89, 121, 122
future, vii, 1, 5–6, 7–8, 9–10, 13–14, 18–
    20, 41, 49, 82, 109, 115, 119–20,
    129–31, 156, 157, 158

Gadamer, Hans Georg, 16, 31, 78
Garfinkel, Harold, 11, 38–39
Geertz, Clifford, 21, 146
Goffman, Erving, 6, 14–15, 36
Grief, Avner, 27, 29, 31–32
grown order. *See* mutual adjustment

Habermas, Jürgen, 3–4, 12
Hayek, Friedrich von, 91–92, 148–49,
    169n.12, 186n.10
Heidegger, 14, 37–38, 40, 41, 43, 158

Holmgång, 140
horizon of relevance, 5–6, 155
human being, 4–5, 14, 34, 35, 39,
    43, 151
Husserl, Edmund, 14, 35

illegality, 17–18, 51, 54
individual, 1, 2, 7, 10, 14, 17–21, 31–33,
    37–38, 49–50, 70, 90, 91–92, 111,
    113, 130, 146, 149, 151, 152–53,
    158–59, 160–61
information, 3–4, 10, 14, 15, 17–19, 20,
    21, 82–83, 91, 128
institution, 27
    dissapearing (fading away) 40, 148
    formal, 27, 47
    informal, 35–36
institutionalisation, 37–38, 88
insurance, 7, 18, 35, 48–49
interpretation, 10, 11, 16, 78, 111,
    116, 122–23

Kahneman, Daniel, 18–19, 44
Karpik, Lucien, 5, 17, 58–59, 90–
    91, 123
Knight, Frank, vii, 5, 6, 12, 14, 48–49,
    58–59, 77, 101–2,
    155–56
knowledge, vii, 1–4, 5–6, 7, 8, 9–13,
    16–18, 21, 25, 33–34, 35, 36, 41,
    74, 139–40, 148, 151–52, 153,
    154, 159–61
    codified, 59–61
    distribution of, 2, 21
    institutionalized, 43
    private, 128, 154
    public, 82
    scientific, 11–13, 111, 152
    stock of, 160–61
Kula ring, 17

law, 2–3, 10, 11, 27, 28, 33–35, 46–47,
    51–53, 65–66, 104, 107, 114–15,
    136–37, 153
    antitrust law, 53–57
Lehtonen, Turo-Kimmo, 7–9
liberal, 160
life-world, 14, 35–37
Luckmann, Thomas, 1, 36, 37–38, 41,
    43, 91–92

Luhmann, Niklas, 5, 12–13, 14–15, 20, 41–42, 48–49, 52, 58–59, 92, 104, 156

March, James, 5–6, 18, 20, 48–49
market, 10, 14, 17, 21, 50, 53–54, 55–56, 87–88, 90–91, 106–8, 112, 164*f*
  exchange market, 106–9, 109*t*
  fixed role, 165
  future market, 73–74
  labour market, 75, 165
  producer market, 100–3, 109*t*, 129, 132, 149
  standard market, 58–59, 61
  status market, 96, 110
  switch role, 165
marketplace, 14, 21, 50, 53–54, 92–93, 106, 108
Marshall, Alfred, 53–54, 58–61, 101
Menger, Pierre-Michel, 15, 16, 90, 92, 156
moral (Ethics) 36, 50, 61, 73, 74, 82, 113, 146
mutual adjustment, 35–36, 37–38, 43–44, 51, 61, 64, 66–67, 90, 91–102, 103, 104–5, 106, 109*t*, 110, 111, 115–16, 146–47, 148–49

narrative, 19–20, 126–27, 131
network, 2, 17
norm, 3, 10, 11, 27–28, 29, 50–51, 115–16, 144–45
North, Douglas, 6, 27, 29–30, 41, 46, 48
Nowotny, Helga, 4–5, 6, 9, 11–12, 149, 154–55

opinion polls, 105–6
order, vii, 2, 25, 39–40, 44–45, 46–47, 52, 75, 96, 100, 102, 103, 128–29, 136, 149, 152
  decided, 66–67, 115–16, 149–50
  grown, 43–44, 91–92, 148–49 (*see also* status)
organization, 1, 7–8, 17–18, 20, 35, 37–38, 47, 48–50, 57, 88–89, 103–7, 109*t*, 118–19, 146–47
  meta organization, 61
  partial organization, 106, 147–48

Parson, Talcott, 14–15, 70
phenomenology, 30, 159

Podolny, Joel, 5, 101–3, 129, 149
Popper, Karl, 159–60
power, 3, 21–22, 49, 50–51, 122–23, 139, 159–60
Power, Michael, 7–8, 72, 77, 78
practice, 1–2, 34, 35, 37–38, 41–42, 51, 53–54, 65–66, 78–79, 90, 99, 102, 115–16, 125–26, 143–44, 159, 160, 162
prediction, 9–10, 12–13, 14, 19–20, 105, 129–31
price, 10, 14, 21, 59–60, 75, 83, 91, 100, 106, 108, 109
prize, 82–83, 114, 115, 124–27
probability, 5–6, 7, 14–15
profit, 10, 15, 52, 53–54, 155–56
promise, 162
public, vii, 2–4, 10, 11, 16, 18, 19–20, 21–22, 34, 35–36, 37–38, 47–53, 70, 82–83, 88, 111–12, 113, 118–19, 123, 130–31, 140, 159–62
  care of, 159–60
  prices, 58–59, 100
  standard, 60–61 (*see also* standard)

Quack, Sigrid, 34–35, 54–55
quantification, 7–8, 57–58, 152

ranking, 127–29
rating, 122–24
religion, 9–10, 11, 161–62
responsibility, 160–61
responsibility, private, 160–61
review, 120–22
risk, vii, 5, 6, 8, 9–11, 35, 46–47, 48–49, 51–52, 77–78, 90–91, 98–99, 157
  transformation of uncertainty, 7–8, 58–59, 77–78, 124

sanctions, 39
Schütz, Alfred, 1, 3, 5–6, 16, 35, 36, 38, 41, 155
Searle, John, 41
sect, 161–62
social capital, 42–43
sport, 138, 142–44, 148, 156–57
standard, 57–65
standardization, 60–61
Stark, David, 68, 90, 122–23, 128, 129, 132

state of the world, 3, 12, 148–
50, 153–54
principles of states of the world, 25
status, 82–83, 93, 96, 99–100, 101–3,
110, 121–22, 124, 139–41, 163
surprise, 15, 143, 156

Thèvenot, Laurent, 40, 50–51,
78, 115–16
tournament, 138
transaction cost, 20
trust, 40–41, 44, 97, 99, 124, 162
truth, 3–4, 44, 135–36, 159–62
scientific, 88, 111, 154
Tversky, Amos, 18–19, 44

uncertainty, 5–6
reduction of, 4, 12–13 (see also
certainty)
private means of, 10, 17–19
public means of, 10, 21, 28
subjectivity, 12–13

understanding, 16
unintended consequences, 11, 19–20, 29,
66–67, 87, 91–92, 96, 102, 110,
148–49, 154–55

valuation, 90
value, 3, 10, 11, 161–62
violence, 31, 139–41, 142, 147
virtue, 2, 33–34, 37–38, 42–43, 66–67,
149, 154, 160, 162

war, 135, 136, 138–40
Weber, Max, 9–10, 19–20, 36, 47, 48,
51–52, 65–66, 73, 74, 131,
136, 161–62
White, Harrison, 5, 17, 19, 65–66, 84,
88, 90–91, 100, 101–2, 103, 104–
5, 119, 129, 132
Williamson, Oliver, 5, 29–30, 32–33

Zuckerman, Ezra, 57, 84, 90, 113–14,
119–20, 129